Decompiling Android

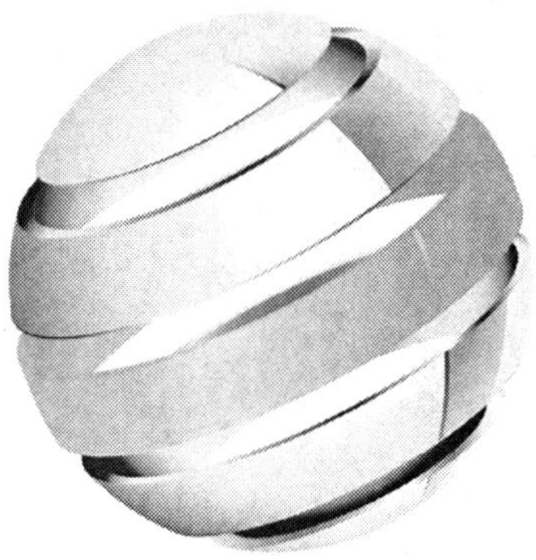

Godfrey Nolan

Apress®

Decompiling Android

ISBN-13 (pbk): 978-1-4302-4248-2

ISBN-13 (electronic): 978-1-4302-4249-9

President and Publisher: Paul Manning
Lead Editor: James Markham
Technical Reviewer: Martin Larochelle
Editorial Board: Steve Anglin, Ewan Buckingham, Gary Cornell, Louise Corrigan, Morgan Ertel, Jonathan Gennick, Jonathan Hassell, Robert Hutchinson, Michelle Lowman, James Markham, Matthew Moodie, Jeff Olson, Jeffrey Pepper, Douglas Pundick, Ben Renow-Clarke, Dominic Shakeshaft, Gwenan Spearing, Matt Wade, Tom Welsh
Coordinating Editor: Corbin Collins
Copy Editor: Tiffany Taylor
Compositor: Bytheway Publishing Services
Indexer: SPi Global
Artist: SPi Global
Cover Designer: Anna Ishchenko

Distributed to the book trade worldwide by Springer Science+Business Media New York, 233 Spring Street, 6th Floor, New York, NY 10013. Phone 1-800-SPRINGER, fax (201) 348-4505, e-mail orders-ny@springer-sbm.com, or visit www.springeronline.com.

For information on translations, please e-mail rights@apress.com, or visit www.apress.com.

Apress and friends of ED books may be purchased in bulk for academic, corporate, or promotional use. eBook versions and licenses are also available for most titles. For more information, reference our Special Bulk Sales–eBook Licensing web page at www.apress.com/bulk-sales.

Any source code or other supplementary materials referenced by the author in this text is available to readers at www.apress.com. For detailed information about how to locate your book's source code, go to www.apress.com/source-code.

For Nancy, who was there when I wrote my first published article, gave my first talk at a conference, and wrote my first book, and is still here for my second. Here's to the next one.

–Godfrey Nolan

Contents at a Glance

Contents

About the Author

Godfrey Nolan is the founder and president of RIIS LLC in Southfield, MI. He has over 20 years of experience running software development teams. Originally from Dublin, Ireland, he has a degree in mechanical engineering from University College Dublin and a masters in computer science from the University of the West of England. He is also the author of *Decompiling Java*, published by Apress in 2004.

About the Technical Reviewer

Martin Larochelle has more than 10 years of experience in software development in project leader and architect roles. Currently, Martin works at Macadamian as a solutions architect, planning and supporting projects. His current focus is on mobile app development for Android and other platforms. Martin's background is in C++ and VoIP development on soft clients, hard phones, and SIP servers.

Acknowledgments

Thanks to my technical reviewer, Martin Larochelle, for all the suggestions and support. Book writing can be like pulling teeth, so it's always easier when the reviewer comments are logical and nudge the author in the right direction. I still have some teeth left—no hair, but some teeth.

Thanks to the Apress staff: Corbin Collins and James Markham for all the help and Steve Anglin for helping me get the book accepted in the first place. I hope your other authors aren't as difficult to work with as I.

Thanks to Rory and Dayna, my son and daughter, for making me laugh as much as you do. Thanks to Nancy, my wife, for putting up with the endless hours spent writing when I should have been spending them with you.

Thanks to all the staff at RIIS who had to put up with my book deadlines more than most.

Preface

Decompiling Java was originally published in 2004 and, for a number of reasons, became more of an esoteric book for people interested in decompilation rather than anything approaching a general programming audience.

When I began writing the book way back in 1998, there were lots of applets on websites, and the thought that someone could download your hard work and reverse-engineer it into Java source code was a frightening thought for many. But applets went the same way as dial-up, and I suspect that many readers of this book have never seen an applet on a web page.

After the book came out, I realized that the only way someone could decompile your Java class files was to first hack into your web server and download them from there. If they'd accomplished that, you had far more to worry about than people decompiling your code.

With some notable exceptions—applications such as Corel's Java for Office that ran as a desktop application, and other Swing applications—for a decade or more Java code primarily lived on the server. Little or nothing was on the client browser, and zero access to class files meant zero problems with decompilation. But by an odd twist of fate, this has all changed with the Android platform: your Android apps live on your mobile device and can be easily downloaded and reverse-engineered by someone with very limited programming knowledge.

An Android app is downloaded to your device as an APK file that includes all the images and resources along with the code, which is stored in a single `classes.dex` file. This is a very different format from the Java class file and is designed to run on the Android Dalvik virtual machine (DVM). But it can be easily transformed back into Java class files and decompiled back into the original source.

Decompilation is the process that transforms machine-readable code into a human-readable format. When an executable or a Java class file or a DLL is decompiled, you don't quite get the original format; instead, you get a type of pseudo source code, which is often incomplete and almost always without the comments. But, often, it's more than enough to understand the original code.

Decompiling Android addresses an unmet need in the programming community. For some reason, the ability to decompile Android APKs has been largely ignored, even though it's relatively easy for anyone with the appropriate mindset to decompile an APK back into Java code. This book redresses the balance by looking at what tools and tricks of the trade are currently being employed by people who are trying to recover source code and those who are trying to protect it using, for example, obfuscation.

This book is for those who want to learn Android programming by decompilation, those who simply want to learn how to decompile Android apps into source code, those who want to protect their Android code, and, finally, those who want to get a better understanding of `.dex` bytecodes and the DVM by building a `.dex` decompiler.

This book takes your understanding of decompilers and obfuscators to the next level by

- Exploring Java bytecodes and opcodes in an approachable but detailed manner
- Examining the structure of DEX files and opcodes and explaining how it differs from the Java class file
- Using examples to show you how to decompile an Android APK file
- Giving simple strategies to show you how to protect your code
- Showing you what it takes to build your own decompiler and obfuscator

Decompiling Android isn't a normal Android programming book. In fact, it's the complete opposite of a standard textbook where the author teaches you how to translate ideas and concepts into code. You're interested in turning the partially compiled Android opcodes back into source code so you can see what the original programmer was thinking. I don't cover the language structure in depth, except where it relates to opcodes and the DVM. All emphasis is on low-level virtual machine design rather than on the language syntax.

The first part of this book unravels the APK format and shows you how your Java code is stored in the DEX file and subsequently executed by the DVM. You also look at the theory and practice of decompilation and obfuscation. I present some of the decompiler's tricks of the trade and explain how to unravel the most awkward APK. You learn about the different ways people try to protect their source code; when appropriate, I expose any flaws or underlying problems with the techniques so you're suitably informed before you use any source code protection tools.

The second part of this book primarily focuses on how to write your own Android decompiler and obfuscator. You build an extendable Android bytecode decompiler. Although the Java virtual machine (JVM) design is fixed, the language isn't. Many of the early decompilers couldn't handle Java constructs that appeared in the JDK 1.1, such as inner classes. So if new constructs appear in `classes.dex`, you'll be equipped to handle them.

Chapter 1

Laying the Groundwork

To begin, in this chapter I introduce you to the problem with decompilers and why virtual machines and the Android platform in particular are at such risk. You learn about the history of decompilers; it may surprise you that they've been around almost as long as computers. And because this can be such an emotive topic, I take some time to discuss the legal and moral issues behind decompilation. Finally, you're introduced to some of options open to you if you want to protect your code.

Compilers and Decompilers

Computer languages were developed because most normal people can't work in machine code or its nearest equivalent, Assembler. Fortunately, people realized pretty early in the development of computing technology that humans weren't cut out to program in machine code. Computer languages such as Fortran, COBOL, C, VB, and, more recently, Java and C# were developed to allow us to put our ideas in a human-friendly format that can then be converted into a format a computer chip can understand.

At its most basic, it's the compiler's job to translate this textual representation or source code into a series of 0s and 1s or machine code that the computer can interpret as actions or steps you want it to perform. It does this using a series of pattern-matching rules. A lexical analyzer tokenizes the source code—and any mistakes or words that aren't in the compiler's lexicon are rejected. These tokens are then passed to the language parser, which matches one or more tokens to a series of rules and translates the tokens into intermediate code (VB.NET, C#, Pascal, or Java) or sometimes straight into machine code (Objective-C, C++, or Fortran). Any source code that doesn't match a compiler's rules is rejected, and the compilation fails.

Now you know what a compiler does, but I've only scratched the surface. Compiler technology has always been a specialized and sometimes complicated area of computing. Modern advances mean things are going to get even more complicated, especially in the virtual machine domain. In part, this drive comes from Java and .NET. Just in time (JIT) compilers have tried to close the gap between Java and C++ execution times by optimizing the execution of Java bytecode. This seems like an impossible task, because Java bytecode is, after all, interpreted, whereas C++ is compiled. But JIT compiler technology is making significant advances and also making Java compilers and virtual machines much more complicated beasts.

Most compilers do a lot of preprocessing and post-processing. The preprocessor readies the source code for the lexical analysis by stripping out all unnecessary information, such as the programmer's comments, and adding any standard or included header files or packages. A typical post-processor stage is code optimization, where the compiler parses or scans the code, reorders it, and removes any redundancies to increase the efficiency and speed of your code.

Decompilers (no big surprise here) translate the machine code or intermediate code back into source code. In other words, the whole compiling process is reversed. Machine code is tokenized in some way and parsed or translated back into source code. This transformation rarely results in the original source code, though, because information is lost in the preprocessing and post-processing stages.

Consider an analogy with human languages: decompiling an Android package file (APK) back into Java source is like translating German (`classes.dex`) into French (Java class file) and then into English (Java source). Along they way, bits of information are lost in translation. Java source code is designed for humans and not computers, and often some steps are redundant or can be performed more quickly in a slightly different order. Because of these lost elements, few (if any) decompilations result in the original source.

A number of decompilers are currently available, but they aren't well publicized. Decompilers or disassemblers are available for Clipper (Valkyrie), FoxPro (ReFox and Defox), Pascal, C (dcc, decomp, Hex-Rays), Objective-C (Hex-Rays), Ada, and, of course, Java. Even the Newton, loved by *Doonesbury* aficionados everywhere, isn't safe. Not surprisingly, decompilers are much more common for interpreted languages such as VB, Pascal, and Java because of the larger amounts of information being passed around.

Virtual Machine Decompilers

There have been several notable attempts to decompile machine code. Cristina Cifuentes' dcc and more recently the Hex-Ray's IDA decompiler are just a couple of examples. However, at the machine-code level, the data and instructions are comingled, and it's a much more difficult (but not impossible) task to recover the original code.

In a virtual machine, the code has simply passed through a preprocessor, and the decompiler's job is to reverse the preprocessing stages of compilation. This makes interpreted code much, much easier to decompile. Sure, there are no comments and, worse still, there is no specification, but then again there are no R&D costs.

Why Java with Android?

Before I talk about "Why Android?" I first need to ask, "Why Java?" That's not to say all Android apps are written in Java—I cover HTML5 apps too. But Java and Android are joined at the hip, so I can't really discuss one without the other.

The original Java virtual machine (JVM) was designed to be run on a TV cable set-top box. As such, it's a very small-stack machine that pushes and pops its instructions on and off a stack using a limited instruction set. This makes the instructions very easy to understand with relatively little practice. Because compilation is now a two-stage process, the JVM also requires the compiler to pass a lot of information, such as variable and method names, that wouldn't otherwise be available. These names can be almost as helpful as comments when you're trying to understand decompiled source code.

The current design of the JVM is independent of the Java Development Kit (JDK). In other words, the language and libraries may change, but the JVM and the opcodes are fixed. This means that if Java is prone to decompilation now, it's always likely to be prone to decompilation. In many cases, as you'll see, decompiling a Java class is as easy as running a simple DOS or UNIX command.

In the future, the JVM may very well be changed to stop decompilation, but this would break any backward compatibility and all current Java code would have to be recompiled. And although this has happened before in the Microsoft world with different versions of VB, many companies other than Oracle have developed virtual machines.

What makes this situation even more interesting is that companies that want to Java-enable their operating system or browser usually create their own JVMs.

Oracle is only responsible for the JVM specification. This situation has progressed so far that any fundamental changes to the JVM specification would have to be backward compatible. Modifying the JVM to prevent decompilation would require significant surgery and would in all probability break this backward compatibility, thus ensuring that Java classes will decompile for the foreseeable future.

There are no such compatibility restrictions on the JDK, and more functionality is added with each release. And although the first crop of decompilers, such as Mocha, dramatically failed when inner classes were introduced in the JDK 1.1, the current favorite JD-GUI is more than capable of handling inner classes or later additions to the Java language, such as generics.

You learn a lot more about why Java is at risk from decompilation in the next chapter, but for the moment here are seven reasons why Java is vulnerable:

- For portability, Java code is partially compiled and then interpreted by the JVM.
- Java's compiled classes contain a lot of symbolic information for the JVM.
- Due to backward-compatibility issues, the JVM's design isn't likely to change.
- There are few instructions or opcodes in the JVM.
- The JVM is a simple stack machine.
- Standard applications have no real protection against decompilation.
- Java applications are automatically compiled into smaller modular classes.

Let's begin with a simple class-file example, shown in Listing 1-1.

Listing 1-1. *Simple Java Source Code Example*

```
public class Casting {
 public static void main(String args[]){
 for(char c=0; c < 128; c++) {
     System.out.println("ascii " + (int)c + " character "+ c);
 }
 }
}
```

Listing 1-2 shows the output for the class file in Listing 1-1 using javap, Java's class-file disassembler that ships with the JDK. You can decompile Java so easily because—as you see later in the book—the JVM is a simple stack machine with no registers and a limited number of high-level instructions or opcodes.

Listing 1-2. *Javap Output*

```
Compiled from Casting.java
public synchronized class Casting extends java.lang.Object
 /* ACC_SUPER bit set */
{
 public static void main(java.lang.String[]);
/* Stack=4, Locals=2, Args_size=1 */
 public Casting();
/* Stack=1, Locals=1, Args_size=1 */
}

Method void main(java.lang.String[])
 0 iconst_0
 1 istore_1
 2 goto 41
 5 getstatic #12 <Field java.io.PrintStream out>
 8 new #6 <Class java.lang.StringBuffer>
 11 dup
 12 ldc #2 <String "ascii ">
 14 invokespecial #9 <Method java.lang.StringBuffer(java.lang.String)>
 17 iload_1
 18 invokevirtual #10 <Method java.lang.StringBuffer append(char)>
 21 ldc #1 <String " character ">
 23 invokevirtual #11 <Method java.lang.StringBuffer append(java.lang.String)>
 26 iload_1
 27 invokevirtual #10 <Method java.lang.StringBuffer append(char)>
 30 invokevirtual #14 <Method java.lang.String toString()>
 33 invokevirtual #13 <Method void println(java.lang.String)>
 36 iload_1
 37 iconst_1
 38 iadd
 39 i2c
 40 istore_1
 41 iload_1
 42 sipush 128
 45 if_icmplt 5
 48 return

Method Casting()
 0 aload_0
 1 invokespecial #8 <Method java.lang.Object()>
 4 return<
```

It should be obvious that a class file contains a lot of the source-code information. My aim in this book is to show you how to take this information and reverse-engineer it into source code. I'll also show you what steps you can take to protect the information.

Why Android?

Until now, with the exception of applets and Java Swing apps, Java code has typically been server side with little or no code running on the client. This changed with the introduction of Google's Android operating system. Android apps, whether they're written in Java or HTML5/CSS, are client-side applications in the form of APKs. These APKs are then executed on the Dalvik virtual machine (DVM).

The DVM differs from the JVM in a number of ways. First, it's a register-based machine, unlike the stack-based JVM. And instead of multiple class files bundled into a jar file, the DVM uses a single Dalvik executable (DEX) file with a different structure and opcodes. On the surface, it would appear to be much harder to decompile an APK. However, someone has already done all the hard work for you: a tool called dex2jar allows you to convert the DEX file back into a jar file, which then can be decompiled back into Java source.

Because the APKs live on the phone, they can be easily downloaded to a PC or Mac and then decompiled. You can use lots of different tools and techniques to gain access to an APK, and there are many decompilers, which I cover later in the book. But the easiest way to get at the source is to copy the APK onto the phone's SD card using any of the file-manager tools available in the marketplace, such as ASTRO File Manager. Once the SD card is plugged into your PC or Mac, it can then be decompiled using dex2jar followed by your favorite decompiler, such as JD-GUI.

Google has made it very easy to add ProGuard to your builds, but obfuscation doesn't happen by default. For the moment (until this issue achieves a higher profile), the code is unlikely to have been protected using obfuscation, so there's a good chance the code can be completely decompiled back into source. ProGuard is also not 100% effective as an obfuscation tool, as you see in Chapter 4 and 7.

Many Android apps talk to backend systems via web services. They look for items in a database, or complete a purchase, or add data to a payroll system, or upload documents to a file server. The usernames and passwords that allow the app to connect to these backend systems are often hard-coded in the Android app. So, if you haven't protected your code and you leave the keys to your backend system in your app, you're running the risk of someone compromising your database and gaining access to systems that they should not be accessing.

It's less likely, but entirely possible, that someone has access to the source and can recompile the app to get it to talk to a different backend system, and use it as a means of harvesting usernames and passwords. This information can then be used at a later stage to gain access to private data using the real Android app.

This book explains how to hide your information from these prying eyes and raise the bar so it takes a lot more than basic knowledge to find the keys to your backend servers or locate the credit-card information stored on your phone.

It's also very important to protect your Android app before releasing it into the marketplace. Several web sites and forums share APKs, so even if you protect your app by releasing an updated version, the original unprotected APK may still be out there on phones and forums. Your web-service APIs must also be updated at the same time, forcing users to update their app and leading to a bad user experience and potential loss of customers.

In Chapter 4, you learn more about why Android is at risk from decompilation, but for the moment here is a list of reasons why Android apps are vulnerable:

- There are multiple easy ways to gain access to Android APKs.
- It's simple to translate an APK to a Java jar file for subsequent decompilation.
- As yet, almost nobody is using obfuscation or any form of protection.
- Once the APK is released, it's very hard to remove access.
- One-click decompilation is possible, using tools such as apktool.
- APKs are shared on hacker forums.

Listing 1-3 shows the dexdump output of the `Casting.java` file from Listing 1-1 after it has been converted to the DEX format. As you can see, it's similar information but in a new format. Chapter 3 looks at the differences in greater detail.

Listing 1-3. *Dexdump Output*

```
Class #0            -
 Class descriptor : 'LCasting;'
 Access flags   : 0x0001 (PUBLIC)
 Superclass     : 'Ljava/lang/Object;'
 Interfaces     -
 Static fields -
 Instance fields -
 Direct methods -
 #0           : (in LCasting;)
  name       : '<init>'
  type       : '()V'
  access     : 0x10001 (PUBLIC CONSTRUCTOR)
  code       -
  registers : 1
  ins       : 1
  outs      : 1
  insns size : 4 16-bit code units
  catches    : (none)
  positions :
    0x0000 line=1
  locals     :
    0x0000 - 0x0004 reg=0 this LCasting;
 #1           : (in LCasting;)
  name       : 'main'
  type       : '([Ljava/lang/String;)V'
  access     : 0x0009 (PUBLIC STATIC)
  code       -
  registers : 5
  ins       : 1
  outs      : 2
  insns size : 44 16-bit code units
  catches    : (none)
  positions :
    0x0000 line=3
    0x0005 line=4
    0x0027 line=3
    0x002b line=6
  locals     :
 Virtual methods -
 source_file_idx : 3 (Casting.java)
```

History of Decompilers

Very little has been written about the history of decompilers, which is surprising because for almost every compiler, there has been a decompiler. Let's take a moment to talk about their history so you can see how and why decompilers were created so quickly for the JVM and, to a lesser extent, the DVM.

Since before the dawn of the humble PC—scratch that, since before the dawn of COBOL, decompilers have been around in one form or another. You can go all the way back to ALGOL to find the earliest example of a decompiler. Joel Donnelly and Herman Englander wrote D-Neliac at the U.S. Navy Electronic Labs (NEL) laboratories as early as 1960. Its primary function was to convert non-Neliac compiled programs into Neliac-compatible binaries. (Neliac was an ALGOL-type language and stands for Navy Electronics Laboratory International ALGOL Compiler.)

Over the years there have been other decompilers for COBOL, Ada, Fortran, and many other esoteric as well as mainstream languages running on IBM mainframes, PDP-11s, and UNIVACs, among others. Probably the main reason for these early developments was to translate software or convert binaries to run on different hardware.

More recently, reverse-engineering to circumvent the Y2K problem became the acceptable face of decompilation—converting legacy code to get around Y2K often required disassembly or full decompilation. But reverse engineering is a huge growth area and didn't disappear after the turn of the millennium. Problems caused by the Dow Jones hitting the 10,000 mark and the introduction of the Euro have caused financial programs to fall over.

Reverse-engineering techniques are also used to analyze old code, which typically has thousands of incremental changes, in order to remove redundancies and convert these legacy systems into much more efficient animals.

At a much more basic level, hexadecimal dumps of PC machine code give programmers extra insight into how something was achieved and have been used to break artificial restrictions placed on software. For example, magazine CDs containing time-bombed or restricted copies of games and other utilities were often patched to change demonstration copies into full versions of the software; this was often accomplished with primitive disassemblers such as the DOS's debug program.

Anyone well versed in Assembler can learn to quickly spot patterns in code and bypass the appropriate source-code fragments. Pirate software is a huge problem for the software industry, and disassembling the code is just one technique employed by professional and amateur bootleggers. Hence the downfall of many an arcane copy-protection technique. But these are primitive tools and techniques, and it would probably be quicker to write the code from scratch rather than to re-create the source code from Assembler.

For many years, traditional software companies have also been involved in reverse-engineering software. New techniques are studied and copied all over the world by the competition using reverse-engineering and decompilation tools. Generally, these are in-house decompilers that aren't for public consumption.

It's likely that the first real Java decompiler was written in IBM and not by Hanpeter van Vliet, author of Mocha. Daniel Ford's white paper "Jive: A Java Decompiler" (May 1996) appears in IBM Research's search engines; this beats Mocha, which wasn't announced until the following July.

Academic decompilers such as dcc are available in the public domain. Commercial decompilers such as Hex-Ray's IDA have also begun to appear. Fortunately for the likes of Microsoft, decompiling Office using dcc or Hex-Rays would create so much code that it's about as user friendly as debug or a hexadecimal dump. Most modern commercial software's source code is so huge that it becomes unintelligible without the design documents and lots of source-code comments. Let's face it: many people's C++ code is hard enough to read six months after they wrote it. How easy would it be for someone else to decipher without help C code that came from compiled C++ code?

Reviewing Interpreted Languages More Closely: Visual Basic

Let's look at VB as an example of an earlier version of interpreted language. Early versions of VB were interpreted by its runtime module `vbrun.dll` in a fashion somewhat similar to Java and the JVM. Like a Java class file, the source code for a VB program is bundled within the binary. Bizarrely, VB3 retains more information than Java—even the programmer comments are included.

The original versions of VB generated an intermediate pseudocode called *p-code*, which was in Pascal and originated in the P-System (`www.threedee.com/jcm/psystem/`). And before you say anything, yes, Pascal and all its derivatives are just as vulnerable to decompilation—that includes early versions of Microsoft's C compiler, so nobody feels left out. The p-codes aren't dissimilar to bytecodes and are essentially VB opcodes that are interpreted by `vbrun.dll` at run time. If you've ever wondered why you needed to include `vbrun300.dll` with VB executables, now you know. You have to include `vbrun.dll` so it can interpret the p-code and execute your program.

Doctor H. P. Diettrich, who is from Germany, is the author of the eponymously titled DoDi—perhaps the most famous VB decompiler. At one time, VB had a culture of decompilers and obfuscators (or protection tools, as they're called in VB). But as VB moved to compiled rather than interpreted code, the number of decompilers decreased dramatically. DoDi provides VBGuard for free on his site, and programs such as Decompiler Defeater, Protect, Overwrite, Shield, and VBShield are available from other sources. But they too all but disappeared with VB5 and VB6.

That was of course before .NET, which has come full circle: VB is once again interpreted. Not surprisingly, many decompilers and obfuscators are again appearing in the .NET world, such as the ILSpy and Reflector decompilers as well as Demeanor and Dotfuscator obfuscators.

Hanpeter van Vliet and Mocha

Oddly enough for a technical subject, this book also has a very human element. Hanpeter van Vliet wrote the first public-domain decompiler, Mocha, while recovering from a cancer operation in the Netherlands in 1996. He also wrote an obfuscator called Crema that attempted to protect an applet's source code. If Mocha was the UZI machine gun, then Crema was the bulletproof jacket. In a now-classic Internet marketing strategy, Mocha was free, whereas there was a small charge for Crema.

The beta version of Mocha caused a huge controversy when it was first made available on Hanpeter's web site, especially after it was featured in a CNET article. Because of the controversy, Hanpeter took the very honorable step of removing Mocha from his web site. He then allowed visitor's to his site to vote about whether Mocha should once again be made available. The vote was ten to one in favor of Mocha, and soon after it reappeared on Hanpeter's web site.

However, Mocha never made it out of Beta. And while doing some research for a Web Techniques article on this subject, I learned from his wife, Ingrid, that Hanpeter's throat cancer finally got him and he died at the age of 34 on New Year's Eve 1996.

The source code for both Crema and Mocha were sold to Borland shortly before Hanpeter's death, with all proceeds going to Ingrid. Some early versions of JBuilder shipped with an obfuscator, which was probably Crema. It attempted to protect Java code from decompilation by replacing ASCII variable names with control characters.

I talk more about the host of other Java decompilers and obfuscators later in the book.

Legal Issues to Consider When Decompiling

Before you start building your own decompiler, let's take this opportunity to consider the legal implications of decompiling someone else's code for your own enjoyment or benefit. Just because Java has taken decompiling technology out of some very serious propeller-head territory and into more mainstream computing doesn't make it any less likely that you or your company will be sued. It may make it more fun, but you really should be careful.

As a small set of ground rules, try the following:

- Don't decompile an APK, recompile it, and then pass it off as your own.
- Don't even think of trying to sell a recompiled APK to any third parties.
- Try not to decompile an APK or application that comes with a license agreement that expressly forbids decompiling or reverse-engineering the code.
- Don't decompile an APK to remove any protection mechanisms and then recompile it for your own personal use.

Protection Laws

Over the past few years, big business has tilted the law firmly in its favor when it comes to decompiling software. Companies can use a number of legal mechanisms to stop you from decompiling their software; you would have little or no legal defense if you ever had to appear in a court of law because a company discovered that you had decompiled its programs. Patent law, copyright law, anti-reverse-engineering clauses in shrinkwrap licenses, as well as a number of laws such as the Digital Millennium Copyright Act (DMCA) may all be used against you. Different laws may apply in different countries or states: for example, the "no reverse engineering clause" software license is a null and void clause in the European Union (EU). But the basic concepts are the same: decompile a program for the purpose of cloning the code into another competitive product, and you're probably breaking the law.The secret is that you shouldn't be standing, kneeling, or pressing down very hard on the legitimate rights (the copyright) of the original author. That's not to say it's *never* ok to decompile. There are certain limited conditions under which the law favors decompilation or reverse engineering through a concept known as *fair use*. From almost the dawn of time, and certainly from the beginning of the Industrial Age, many of humankind's greatest inventions have come from individuals who created something special while Standing on the Shoulders of Giants. For example, the invention of the steam train and the light bulb were relatively modest incremental steps in technology. The underlying concepts were provided by other people, and it was up to someone like George Stephenson or Thomas Edison to create the final object. (You can see an excellent example of Stephenson's debt to many other inventors such as James Watt at `www.usgennet.org/usa/topic/steam/Early/Time.html`). This is one of the reasons patents appeared: to allow people to build on other creations while still giving the original inventors some compensation for their initial ideas for period of, say, 20 years.

Patents

In the software arena, trade secrets are typically protected by copyright law and increasingly through patents. Patents can protect certain elements of a program, but it's highly unlikely that a complete program will be protected by a patent or series of patents. Software companies want to protect their investment, so they typically turn to copyright law or software licenses to prevent people from essentially stealing their research and development efforts.

Copyright

But copyright law isn't rock solid, because otherwise there would be no inducement to patent an idea, and the patent office would quickly go out of business. Copyright protection doesn't extend to interfaces of computer programs, and a developer can use the fair-use defense if they can prove that they have decompiled the program to see how they can interoperate with any unpublished *application programming interfaces (APIs)* in a program.

Directive on the Legal Protection of Computer Programs

If you're living in the EU, then you more than likely come under the Directive on the Legal Protection of Computer Programs. This directive states that you can decompile programs under certain restrictive circumstances: for example, when you're trying to understand the functional requirements to create a compatible interface to your own program. To put it another way, you can decompile if you need access to the internal calls of a third-party program and the authors refuse to divulge the APIs at any price. But you can only use this information to create an interface to your own program, not to create a competitive product. You also can't reverse-engineer any areas that have been protected in any way.

For many years, Microsoft's applications had allegedly gained unfair advantage from underlying unpublished APIs calls to Windows 3.1 and Windows 95 that are orders of magnitude quicker than the published APIs. The Electronic Frontier Foundation (EFF) came up with a useful road-map analogy to help explain this situation. Say you're travelling from Detroit to New York, but your map doesn't show any interstate routes; sure, you'll eventually get there by traveling on the back roads, but the trip would be a lot shorter if you had a map complete with interstates. If these conditions were true, the EU directive would be grounds for disassembling Windows 2000 or Microsoft Office, but you'd better hire a good lawyer before you try it.

Reverse Engineering

Precedents allow legal decompilation in the United States, too. The most famous case to date is Sega v. Accolade (`http://digital-law-online.info/cases/24PQ2D1561.htm`). In 1992, Accolade won a case against Sega; the ruling said that Accolade's unauthorized disassembly of the Sega object code wasn't copyright infringement. Accolade reverse-engineered Sega's binaries into an intermediate code that allowed Accolade to extract a software key to enable Accolade's games to interact with Sega Genesis video consoles. Obviously, Sega wasn't going to give Accolade access to its APIs or, in this case, the code to unlock the Sega game platform. The court ruled in favor of Accolade, judging that the reverse engineering constituted fair-use. But before you think this gives you carte blanche to decompile code, you might like to know that Atari v. Nintendo (`http://digital-law-online.info/cases/24PQ2D1015.htm`) went against Atari under very similar circumstances.

The Legal Big Picture

In conclusion—you can tell this is the legal section—both the court cases in the United States and the EU directive stress that under certain circumstances, reverse engineering *can* be used to understand interoperability and create a program interface. It *can't* be used to create a copy and sell it as a competitive product. Most Java decompilation doesn't fall into the interoperability category. It's far more likely that the decompiler wants to pirate the code or, at best, understand the underlying ideas and techniques behind the software.

It isn't clear whether reverse-engineering to discover how an APK was written would constitute fair use. The US Copyright Act of 1976 excludes "any idea, procedure, process, system, method of operation, concept, principle or discovery, regardless of the form in which it is described," which sounds like the beginning of a defense and is one of the reasons why more and more software patents are being issued. Decompilation to pirate or illegally sell the software can't be defended.

But from a developer's point of view, the situation looks bleak. The only protection—a user license—is about as useful as the laws against copying MP3s. It won't physically stop anyone from making illegal copies and doesn't act as a real deterrent for the home user. No legal recourse will protect your code from a hacker, and it sometimes seems that the people trying to create today's secure systems must feel like they're Standing on the Shoulder of Morons. You only have to look at the investigation into eBook-protection schemes (`http://slashdot.org/article.pl?sid=01/07/17/130226`) and the DeCSS fiasco (`http://cyber.law.harvard.edu/openlaw/DVD/resources.html`) to see how paper-thin a lot of so-called secure systems really are.

Moral Issues

Decompiling is an excellent way to learn Android development and how the DVM works. If you come across a technique that you haven't seen before, you can quickly decompile it to see how it was accomplished. Decompiling helps people climb up the Android learning curve by seeing other people's programming techniques. The ability to decompile APKs can make the difference between basic Android understanding and in-depth knowledge. True, there are plenty of open source examples out there to follow, but it helps even more if you can pick your own examples and modify them to suit your needs.

But no book on decompiling would be complete if it didn't discuss the morality issues behind what amounts to stealing someone else's code. Due to the circumstances, Android apps come complete with the source code: forced open source, if you wish.

The author, the publisher, the author's agent, and the author's agent's mother would like to state that we *are not* advocating that readers of this book decompile programs for anything other than educational purposes. The purpose of this book is to show you how to decompile source code, but we aren't encouraging anyone to decompile other programmers' code and then try to use it, sell it, or repackage it as if it was your own code. Please don't reverse-engineer any code that has a licensing agreement stating that you shouldn't decompile the code. It isn't fair, and you'll only get yourself in trouble. (Besides, you can never be sure that the decompiler-generated code is 100% accurate. You could be in for a nasty surprise if you intend to use decompilation as the basis for your own products.) Having said that, thousands of APKs are available that, when decompiled, will help you understand good and bad Android programming techniques.

To a certain extent, I'm pleading the "Don't shoot the messenger" defense. I'm not the first to spot this flaw in Java, and I certainly won't be the last person to write about the subject. My reasons for writing this book are, like the early days of the Internet, fundamentally altruistic. In other words, I found a cool trick, and I want to tell everyone about it.

Protecting Yourself

Pirated software is a big headache for many software companies and big business for others. At the very least, software pirates can use decompilers to remove licensing restrictions; but imagine the consequences if the technology was available to decompile Office 2010, recompile it, and sell it as a new competitive product. To a certain extent, that could easily have happened when Corel released the Beta version of its Office for Java.

Is there anything you can do to protect your code? Yes:

- *License agreements:* License agreements don't offer any real protection from a programmer who wants to decompile your code.
- *Protection schemes in your code:* Spreading protection schemes throughout your code (such as checking whether the phone is rooted) is useless because the schemes can be commented out of the decompiled code.
- *Code fingerprinting:* This is defined as spurious code that is used to mark or fingerprint source code to prove ownership. It can be used in conjunction with license agreements, but it's only really useful in a court of law. Better decompilation tools can profile the code and remove any spurious code.
- *Obfuscation:* Obfuscation replaces the method names and variable names in a class file with weird and wonderful names. This can be an excellent deterrent, but the source code is often still visible, depending on your choice of obfuscator.
- *Intellectual Property Rights (IPR) protection schemes:* These schemes, such as the Android Market digital rights management (DRM), are usually busted within hours or days and typically don't offer much protection.

- *Server-side code:* The safest protection for APKs is to hide all the interesting code on the web server and only use the APK as a thin front-end GUI. This has the downside that you may still need to hide an API key somewhere to gain access to the web server.
- *Native code:* The Android Native Development Kit (NDK) allows you to hide password information in C++ files that can be disassembled but not decompiled and that still run on top of the DVM. Done correctly, this technique can add a significant layer of protection. It can also be used with digital-signature checking to ensure that no one has hijacked your carefully hidden information in another APK.
- *Encryption:* Encryption can also be used in conjunction with the NDK to provide an additional layer of protection from disassembly, or as a way of passing public and private key information to any backend web server.

The first four of these options only act as deterrents (some obfuscators are better than others), and the remaining four are effective but have other implications. I look at all of them in more detail later in the book.

Summary

Decompilation is one of the best learning tools for new Android programmers. What better way to find out how to write an Android app than by taking an example off your phone and decompiling it into source code? Decompilation is also a necessary tool when a mobile software house goes belly up and the only way to fix its code is to decompile it yourself. But decompilation is also a menace if you're trying to protect the investment of countless hours of design and development.

The aim of this book is to create dialogue about decompilation and source-code protection—to separate fact from fiction and show how easy it is to decompile an Android app and what measures you can take to protect your code. Some may say that decompilation isn't an issue and that a developer can always be trained to read a competitor's Assembler. But once you allow easy access to the Android app files, anyone can download dex2jar or JD-GUI, and decompilation becomes orders of magnitude easier. Don't believe it? Then read on and decide for yourself.

Chapter 2

Ghost in the Machine

If you're trying to understand just how good an obfuscator or decompiler really is, then it helps to be able to see what's going on inside a DEX file and the corresponding Java class file. Otherwise you're relying on the word of a third-party vendor or, at best, a knowledgeable reviewer. For most people, that's not good enough when you're trying to protect mission-critical code. At the very least, you should be able to talk intelligently about the area of decompilation and ask the obvious questions to understand what's happening.

> *"Pay no attention to the man behind the curtain."*
>
> *The Wizard of Oz*

At this moment there are all sorts of noises coming from Google saying that there isn't anything to worry about when it comes to decompiling Android code. Hasn't everyone been doing it for years at the assembly level? Similar noises were made when Java was in its infancy.

In this chapter, you pull apart a Java class file; and in the next chapter, you pull apart the DEX file format. This will lay the foundation for the following chapters on obfuscation theory and help you during the design of your decompiler. In order to get to that stage, you need to understand bytecodes, opcodes, and class files and how they relate to the Dalvik virtual machine (DVM) and the Java virtual machine (JVM).

There are several very good books on the market about the JVM. The best is Bill Venners' *Inside the Java 2 Virtual Machine* (McGraw-Hill, 2000). Some of the book's chapters are available online at `www.artima.com/insidejvm/ed2/`. If you can't find the book, then check out Venners' equally excellent "Under the Hood" articles on JavaWorld.com. This series of articles was the original material that he later expanded into the book. Sun's *Java Virtual Machine Specification,* 2nd edition (Addison-Wesley, 1999), written by Tim Lindholm and Frank Yellin, is both comprehensive and very informative for would-be decompiler writers. But being a specification, it isn't what you would call a good read. This book is also available online at `http://java.sun.com/docs/books/vmspec`.

However, the focus here is very different from other JVM books. I'm approaching things from the opposite direction. My task is getting you from bytecode to source, whereas everyone else wants to know how source is translated into bytecode and ultimately executed. You're interested in how a DEX file can be converted to a class file and how the class file can be turned into source rather than how a class file is interpreted.

This chapter looks at how a class file can be disassembled into bytecodes and how these bytecodes can be turned into source. Of course, you need to know how each bytecode functions; but you're less interested in what happens to them when they're in the JVM, and the chapter's emphasis differs accordingly.

The JVM: An Exploitable Design

Java class files are designed for quick transmission across a network or via the Internet. As a result, they're compact and relatively simple to understand. For portability, a class file is only partially compiled into bytecode by javac, the Java compiler. This is then interpreted and executed by a JVM, usually on a different machine or operating system.

The JVM's class-file interface is strictly defined by the *Java Virtual Machine Specification*. But how a JVM ultimately turns bytecode into machine code is left up to the developer. That really doesn't concern you, because once again your interest stops at the JVM. It may help if you think of class files as being analogous to object files in other languages such as C or C++, waiting to be linked and executed by the JVM, only with a lot more symbolic information.

There are many good reasons why a class file carries so much information. Many people view the Internet as a bit of a modern-day Wild West, where crooks are plotting to infect your hard disk with a virus or waiting to grab any credit-card details that might pass their way. As a result, the JVM was designed from the bottom up to protect web browsers from rogue applets. Through a series of checks, the JVM and the class loader make sure no malicious code can be uploaded onto a web page.

But all checks have to be performed lightning quick, to cut down on the download time, so it's not surprising that the original JVM designers opted for a simple stack machine with lots of information available for those crucial security checks. In fact, the design of the JVM is pretty secure even though some of the early browser implementations made a couple or three serious blunders. These days, it's unlikely that Java applets will run in any browsers, but the JVM design is still the same.

Unfortunately for developers, what keeps the code secure also makes it much easier to decompile. The JVM's restricted execution environment and uncomplicated architecture as well as the high-level nature of many of its instructions all conspire against the programmer and in favor of the decompiler.

At this point it's probably also worth mentioning the fragile superclass problem. Adding a new method in C++ means that all classes that reference that class need to be recompiled. Java gets around this by putting all the necessary symbolic information into the class file. The JVM then takes care of the linking and final name resolution, loading all the required classes—including any externally referenced fields and methods—on the fly. This delayed linking or dynamic loading, possibly more than anything else, is why Java is so much more prone to decompilation.

By the way, I ignore native methods in these discussions. *Native methods* of course are native C or C++ code that is incorporated into the application. Using them spoils Java application portability, but it's one surefire way of preventing a Java program from being decompiled.

Without further ado, let's take a brief look at the design of the JVM.

Simple Stack Machine

The JVM is in essence a simple stack machine, with a program register to take care of the program flow thrown in for good luck. The Java class loader takes the class and presents it to the JVM.

You can split the JVM into four separate, distinct parts:

- Heap
- Program counter (PC) registers
- Method area
- JVM stack

Every Java application or applet has its own heap and method area, and every thread has its own register or program counter and JVM stack. Each JVM stack is then further subdivided into stack frames, with each method having its own stack frame. That's a lot of information in one paragraph; Figure 2-1 illustrates in a simple diagram.

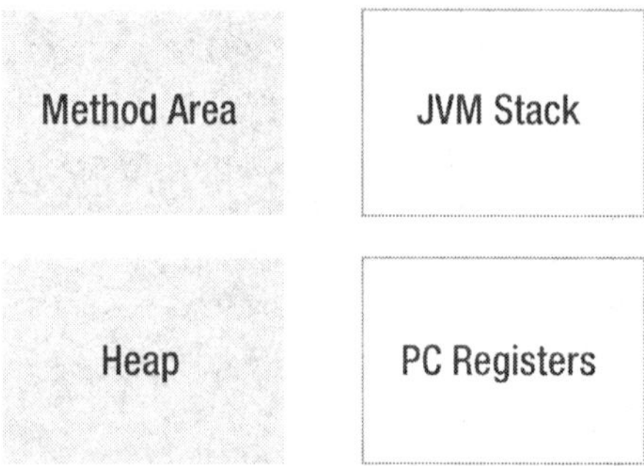

Figure 2-1. *The Java virtual machine*

The shaded sections in Figure 2-1 are shared across all threads, and the white sections are thread specific.

Heap

Let's deal with the heap first to get it out of the way, because it has little or no effect on the Java decompilation process.

Unlike C or C++ developers, Java programmers can't allocate and deallocate memory; it's taken care of by the JVM. The new operator allocates objects and memory on the heap, which are then automatically freed by the JVM garbage collector when an object is no longer being referenced by the program.

There are several good reasons for this; security dictates that pointers aren't used in Java so hackers can't break out of an application and into the operating system. No pointers means that something else—in this case, the JVM—has to take care of the allocating and freeing memory. Memory leaks should also become a thing of the past, or so the theory goes. Some applications written in C and C++ are notorious for leaking memory like a sieve because programmers don't pay attention to freeing up unwanted memory at the appropriate time—not that anybody reading this would be guilty of such a sin. Garbage collection should also make programmers more productive, with less time spent on debugging memory problems.

If you do want to know more about what's going on in your heap, try Oracle's Heap Analysis Tool (HAT). It uses the `hprof` file dumps or snapshots of the JVM heap that can be generated by Java 2 SDK version 1.2 and above. It was designed—get this—"to debug unnecessary object retention" (memory leaks to you and me). See, garbage-collection algorithms, such as reference-counting and mark-and-sweep techniques, aren't 100% accurate either. Class files can have threads that don't terminate properly, `ActionListeners` that fail to de-register, or static references to an object that hang around long after the object should have been garbage collected.

HAT has little or no impact on the decompilation process. I mention it only because it's something interesting to play with—or a crucial utility that helps debug your Java code, depending on your mindset or where your boss is standing.

This leaves three areas to focus on: program registers, the stack, and the method area.

Program Counter Registers

For simplicity's sake, the JVM uses very few registers: the program counter that controls the flow of the program, and three other registers in the stack. Having said that, every thread has its own program counter register that holds the address of the current instruction being executed on the stack. Sun chose to use a limited number of registers to cater to architectures that could support very few registers.

Method Area

If you skip to the "Inside a Class File" section, you see the class file broken down into its many constituents and exactly where the methods can be found. Within every method is its own code attribute, which contains the bytecodes for that particular method.

Although the class file contains information about where the program counter should point for every instruction, the class loader takes care of where the code is placed in the memory area before the code begins to execute.

As the program executes, the program counter keeps track of the current position of the program by moving to point to the next instruction. The bytecode in the method area goes through its assembler-like instructions, using the stack as a temporary storage area as it manipulates its variables, while the program steps through the complete bytecode for that method. A program's execution isn't necessarily linear within the method area; jumps and gotos are very common.

JVM Stack

The stack is no more than a storage area for temporary variables. All program execution and variable manipulation take place via pushing and popping the variables on and off a stack frame. Each thread has its very own JVM stack frame.

The JVM stack consists of three different sections for the local variables (vars), the execution environment (frame), and the operand stack (optop). The vars, frame, and optop registers point to each different area of the stack. The method is executed in its own environment, and the operand stack is used as the workspace for the bytecode instructions. The optop register points at the top of the operand stack.

As I said, the JVM is a very simple machine that pops and pushes temporary variables off and on the operand stack and keeps any local variables in the vars, while continuing to execute the method in the stack frame. The stack is sandwiched between the heap and the registers.

Because the stack is so simple, no complex objects can be stored there. These are farmed out to the heap.

Inside a Class File

To get an overall view of a class file, let's take another look at the `Casting.java` file from Chapter 1, shown here in Listing 2-1. Compile it using javac, and then make a hexadecimal dump of the binary class file, shown in Figure 2-2.

Listing 2-1. *`Casting.java`, Now with Fields!*

```
public class Casting {

 static final String ascStr = "ascii ";
 static final String chrStr = " character ";

 public static void main(String args[]){

 for(char c=0; c < 128; c++) {
  System.out.println(ascStr + (int)c + chrStr + c);
 }
 }
}
```

```
CA FE BA BE 00 00 00 33  00 35 0A 00 0D 00 1B 09
00 1C 00 1D 07 00 1E 0A  00 03 00 1B 08 00 1F 0A
00 03 00 20 0A 00 03 00  21 08 00 22 0A 00 03 00
23 0A 00 03 00 24 0A 00  25 00 26 07 00 27 07 00
28 01 00 06 61 73 63 53  74 72 01 00 12 4C 6A 61
76 61 2F 6C 61 6E 67 2F  53 74 72 69 6E 67 3B 01
00 0D 43 6F 6E 73 74 61  6E 74 56 61 6C 75 65 01
00 06 63 68 72 53 74 72  01 00 06 3C 69 6E 69 74
3E 01 00 03 28 29 56 01  00 04 43 6F 64 65 01 00
0F 4C 69 6E 65 4E 75 6D  62 65 72 54 61 62 6C 65
01 00 04 6D 61 69 6E 01  00 16 28 5B 4C 6A 61 76
61 2F 6C 61 6E 67 2F 53  74 72 69 6E 67 3B 29 56
01 00 0D 53 74 61 63 6B  4D 61 70 54 61 62 6C 65
01 00 0A 53 6F 75 72 63  65 46 69 6C 65 01 00 0C
43 61 73 74 69 6E 67 2E  6A 61 76 61 0C 00 12 00
13 07 00 29 0C 00 2A 00  2B 01 00 17 6A 61 76 61
2F 6C 61 6E 67 2F 53 74  72 69 6E 67 42 75 69 6C
64 65 72 01 00 07 61 73  63 69 69 20 20 0C 00 2C
00 2D 0C 00 2C 00 2E 01  00 0B 20 63 68 61 72 61
63 74 65 72 20 0C 00 2C  00 2F 0C 00 30 00 31 07
00 32 0C 00 33 00 34 01  00 07 43 61 73 74 69 6E
67 01 00 10 6A 61 76 61  2F 6C 61 6E 67 2F 4F 62
6A 65 63 74 01 00 10 6A  61 76 61 2F 6C 61 6E 67
2F 53 79 73 74 65 6D 01  00 03 6F 75 74 01 00 15
4C 6A 61 76 61 2F 69 6F  2F 50 72 69 6E 74 53 74
72 65 61 6D 3B 01 00 06  61 70 70 65 6E 64 01 00
2D 28 4C 6A 61 76 61 2F  6C 61 6E 67 2F 53 74 72
69 6E 67 3B 29 4C 6A 61  76 61 2F 6C 61 6E 67 2F
53 74 72 69 6E 67 42 75  69 6C 64 65 72 3B 01 00
1C 28 49 29 4C 6A 61 76  61 2F 6C 61 6E 67 2F 53
74 72 69 6E 67 42 75 69  6C 64 65 72 3B 01 00 1C
28 43 29 4C 6A 61 76 61  2F 6C 61 6E 67 2F 53 74
72 69 6E 67 42 75 69 6C  64 65 72 3B 01 00 08 74
6F 53 74 72 69 6E 67 01  00 14 28 29 4C 6A 61 76
61 2F 6C 61 6E 67 2F 53  74 72 69 6E 67 3B 01 00
13 6A 61 76 61 2F 69 6F  2F 50 72 69 6E 74 53 74
72 65 61 6D 01 00 07 70  72 69 6E 74 6C 6E 01 00
15 28 4C 6A 61 76 61 2F  6C 61 6E 67 2F 53 74 72
69 6E 67 3B 29 56 00 21  00 0C 00 0D 00 00 00 02
00 18 00 0E 00 0F 00 01  00 10 00 00 00 02 00 05
00 18 00 11 00 0F 00 01  00 10 00 00 00 02 00 08
00 02 00 01 00 12 00 13  00 01 00 14 00 00 00 1D
00 01 00 01 00 00 00 05  2A B7 00 01 B1 00 00 00
01 00 15 00 00 00 06 00  01 00 00 00 01 00 09 00
16 00 17 00 01 00 14 00  00 00 67 00 03 00 02 00
00 00 34 03 3C 1B 11 00  80 A2 00 2D B2 00 02 BB
00 03 59 B7 00 04 12 05  B6 00 06 1B B6 00 07 12
08 B6 00 06 1B B6 00 09  B6 00 0A B6 00 0B 1B 04
60 92 3C A7 FF D2 B1 00  00 00 02 00 15 00 00 00
12 00 04 00 00 00 08 00  09 00 09 00 2B 00 08 00
33 00 0B 00 18 00 00 00  09 00 02 FC 00 02 01 FA
00 30 00 01 00 19 00 00  00 02 00 1A
```

Figure 2-2. *Casting.class*

As you can see, Casting.class is small and compact, but it contains all the necessary information for the JVM to execute the `Casting.java` code.

To open the class file further, in this chapter you simulate the actions of a disassembler by breaking the class file into its different parts. And while we break down Casting.class we're also going to build a primitive disassembler called ClassToXML, which outputs the class file into an easy-to-read XML format. ClassToXML uses the Java Class File Library (jCFL) from `www.freeinternals.org` to do the heavy lifting and is available as a download from the book's page on Apress.com.

You can break the class file into the following constituent parts:

- Magic number
- Minor and major version numbers
- Constant-pool count
- Constant pool
- Access flags
- `this` class
- Superclass
- Interfaces count
- Interfaces
- Field count
- Fields
- Methods count
- Methods
- Attributes count
- Attributes

The JVM specification uses a *struct*-like format to show the class file's different components; see Listing 2-2.

Listing 2-2. *Class-file Struct*

```
Classfile {
    int                 magic,
    short               minor_version,
    short               major_version,
    short               constant_pool_count,
    cp_info             constant_pool[constant_pool_count-1],
    short               access_flags,
    short               this_class,
    short               super_class,
    short               interfaces_count,
```

```
    short               interfaces [interfaces_count],
    short               fields_count,
    field_info          fields [fields_count],
    short               methods_count,
    method_info         methods [methods_count],
    short               attributes_count
    attributes_info     attributes[attributes_count]
}
```

This has always seemed like a very cumbersome way of displaying the class file, so you can use an XML format that allows you to traverse in and out of the class file's inner structures much more quickly. It also makes the class-file information easier to understand as you try to unravel its meaning. The complete class-file structure, with all the XML nodes collapsed, is shown in Figure 2-3.

```
- <root>
    <MagicNumber>0xcafebabe</MagicNumber>
    <MinorVersion>0</MinorVersion>
    <MajorVersion>51</MajorVersion>
  + <ConstantPool>
    <AccessFlag>ACC_PUBLIC, ACC_SUPER</AccessFlag>
    <ThisClass>12</ThisClass>
    <SuperClass>13</SuperClass>
  + <Fields>
  + <Methods>
  </root>
```

Figure 2-3. *XML representation of* `Casting.class`

You look next at each of the different nodes and their form and function. In Chapter 6, you learn to create ClassToXML for all Java class files—the code in this chapter works on `Casting.class` only. To run the code for this chapter, first download the jCFL jar file from `www.freeinternals.org` and put it in your classpath. Then execute the following commands:

```
javac ClassToXML.java
java ClassToXML < Casting.class > Casting.xml
```

Magic Number

It's pretty easy to find the magic and version numbers, because they come at the start of the class file—you should be able to make them out in Figure 2-2. The magic number in hex is the first 4 bytes of the class file (0xCAFEBABE), and it tells the JVM that it's receiving a class file. Curiously, these are also the first four bytes in multiarchitecture binary (MAB) files on the NeXT platform. Some cross-pollination of staff must have occurred between Sun and NeXT during early implementations of Java.

0xCAFEBABE was chosen for a number of reasons. First, it's hard to come up with meaningful eight-letter words out of the letters *A* through *F*. According to James Gosling, Cafe Dead was the name of a café near their office where the Grateful Dead used to perform. And so 0xCAFEDEAD and shortly thereafter 0xCAFEBABE became part of the Java file format. My first reaction was to think it's a pity 0xGETALIFE isn't a legitimate hexadecimal string, but then I couldn't come up with better hexadecimal names either. And there are worse magic numbers out there, such as 0xFEEDFACE, 0xDEADBEEF, and possibly the worst, 0xDEADBABE, which are used at Motorola, IBM, and Sun, respectively.

Microsoft's CLR files have a similar header, BSJB, which was named after four of the original developers of the .Net platform: Brian Harry, Susan Radke-Sproull, Jason Zander, and Bill Evans. OK, maybe 0xCAFEBABE isn't so bad after all.

Minor and Major Versions

The minor and major version numbers are the next four bytes 0x0000 and 0x0033, see Listing 2-2, or minor version 0 and major version 51, which means the code was compiled by the JDK 1.7.0. These major and minor numbers are used by the JVM to make sure that it recognizes and fully understands the format of the class file. JVM's will refuse to execute any class file with a higher major and minor number.

The minor version is for small changes that require an updated JVM, the major number is for wholesale fundamental changes requiring a completely different and incompatible JVM.

Constant-Pool Count

All class and interface constants are stored in the constant pool. And surprise, surprise, the constant-pool count, taking up the next 2 bytes, tells you how many variable-length elements follow in the constant pool.

0x0035 or integer 53 is the number in the example. The JVM specification tells you that `constant_pool[0]` is reserved by the JVM. In fact, it doesn't even appear in the class file, so the constant pool elements are stored in `constant_pool[1]` to `constant_pool[52]`.

Constant Pool

The next item is the constant pool itself, which is of type cp_info; see Listing 2-3.

Listing 2-3. cp_info *Structure*

```
cp_info {
    byte tag,
    byte info[]
}
```

The constant pool is made up of an array of variable-length elements. It's full of symbolic references to other entries in the constant pool, later in the class file. The constant-pool count telling you how many variables are in the constant pool.

Every constant and variable name required by the class file can be found in the constant pool. These are typically strings, integers, floats, method names, and so on, all of which remain fixed. Each constant is then referenced by its constant-pool index everywhere else in the class file.

Each element of the constant pool (remember that there are 53 in the example) begins with a tag to tell you what type of constant is coming next. Table 2-1 lists the valid tags and their corresponding values used in the class file.

Table 2-1. *Constant-Pool Tags*

Constant Pool Tag	Value
Utf8	1
Integer	3
Float	4
Long	5
Double	6
Class	7
String	8
Fieldref	9
Methodref	10

Constant Pool Tag	Value
InterfaceMethodref	11
NameAndType	12

Many of the tags in the constant pool are symbolic references to other members of the constant pool. For example each `String` points at a `Utf8` tag where the string is ultimately stored. The `Utf8` has the data structure shown in Listing 2-4.

Listing 2-4. *`Utf8` Structure*

```
Utf8 {
    byte  tag,
    int length,
    byte  bytes[length]
}
```

I've collapsed these data structures wherever possible in my XML output of the constant pool (see Listing 2-5) so you can read it easily.

Listing 2-5. *Constant Pool for `Casting.class`*

```
<ConstantPool>
<ConstantPoolEntry>
<id>1</id>
<Type>Methodref</Type>
<ConstantPoolAddress>13,27</ConstantPoolAddress>
</ConstantPoolEntry>
<ConstantPoolEntry>
<id>2</id>
<Type>Fieldref</Type>
<ConstantPoolAddress>28,29</ConstantPoolAddress>
</ConstantPoolEntry>
<ConstantPoolEntry>
<id>3</id>
<Type>Class</Type>
<ConstantPoolAddress>30</ConstantPoolAddress>
</ConstantPoolEntry>
<ConstantPoolEntry>
<id>4</id>
<Type>Methodref</Type>
<ConstantPoolAddress>3,27</ConstantPoolAddress>
</ConstantPoolEntry>
<ConstantPoolEntry>
<id>5</id>
<Type>String</Type>
<ConstantPoolAddress>31</ConstantPoolAddress>
```

```
</ConstantPoolEntry>
<ConstantPoolEntry>
<id>6</id>
<Type>Methodref</Type>
<ConstantPoolAddress>3,32</ConstantPoolAddress>
</ConstantPoolEntry>
<ConstantPoolEntry>
<id>7</id>
<Type>Methodref</Type>
<ConstantPoolAddress>3,33</ConstantPoolAddress>
</ConstantPoolEntry>
<ConstantPoolEntry>
<id>8</id>
<Type>String</Type>
<ConstantPoolAddress>34</ConstantPoolAddress>
</ConstantPoolEntry>
<ConstantPoolEntry>
<id>9</id>
<Type>Methodref</Type>
<ConstantPoolAddress>3,35</ConstantPoolAddress>
</ConstantPoolEntry>
<ConstantPoolEntry>
<id>10</id>
<Type>Methodref</Type>
<ConstantPoolAddress>3,36</ConstantPoolAddress>
</ConstantPoolEntry>
<ConstantPoolEntry>
<id>11</id>
<Type>Methodref</Type>
<ConstantPoolAddress>37,38</ConstantPoolAddress>
</ConstantPoolEntry>
<ConstantPoolEntry>
<id>12</id>
<Type>Class</Type>
<ConstantPoolAddress>39</ConstantPoolAddress>
</ConstantPoolEntry>
<ConstantPoolEntry>
<id>13</id>
<Type>Class</Type>
<ConstantPoolAddress>40</ConstantPoolAddress>
</ConstantPoolEntry>
<ConstantPoolEntry>
<id>14</id>
<Type>Utf8</Type>
<ConstantPoolValue>ascStr</ConstantPoolValue>
</ConstantPoolEntry>
<ConstantPoolEntry>
<id>15</id>
<Type>Utf8</Type>
<ConstantPoolValue>Ljava/lang/String</ConstantPoolValue>
```

```
</ConstantPoolEntry>
<ConstantPoolEntry>
<id>16</id>
<Type>Utf8</Type>
<ConstantPoolValue>ConstantValue</ConstantPoolValue>
</ConstantPoolEntry>
<ConstantPoolEntry>
<id>17</id>
<Type>Utf8</Type>
<ConstantPoolValue>chrStr</ConstantPoolValue>
</ConstantPoolEntry>
<ConstantPoolEntry>
<id>18</id>
<Type>Utf8</Type>
<ConstantPoolValue><init></ConstantPoolValue>
</ConstantPoolEntry>
<ConstantPoolEntry>
<id>19</id>
<Type>Utf8</Type>
<ConstantPoolValue>V</ConstantPoolValue>
</ConstantPoolEntry>
<ConstantPoolEntry>
<id>20</id>
<Type>Utf8</Type>
<ConstantPoolValue>Code</ConstantPoolValue>
</ConstantPoolEntry>
<ConstantPoolEntry>
<id>21</id>
<Type>Utf8</Type>
<ConstantPoolValue>LineNumberTable</ConstantPoolValue>
</ConstantPoolEntry>
<ConstantPoolEntry>
<id>22</id>
<Type>Utf8</Type>
<ConstantPoolValue>main</ConstantPoolValue>
</ConstantPoolEntry>
<ConstantPoolEntry>
<id>23</id>
<Type>Utf8</Type>
<ConstantPoolValue>Ljava/lang/String</ConstantPoolValue>
</ConstantPoolEntry>
<ConstantPoolEntry>
<id>24</id>
<Type>Utf8</Type>
<ConstantPoolValue>StackMapTable</ConstantPoolValue>
</ConstantPoolEntry>
<ConstantPoolEntry>
<id>25</id>
<Type>Utf8</Type>
<ConstantPoolValue>SourceFile</ConstantPoolValue>
```

```
</ConstantPoolEntry>
<ConstantPoolEntry>
<id>26</id>
<Type>Utf8</Type>
<ConstantPoolValue>Casting</ConstantPoolValue>
</ConstantPoolEntry>
<ConstantPoolEntry>
<id>27</id>
<Type>NameAndType</Type>
<ConstantPoolAddress>18,19</ConstantPoolAddress>
</ConstantPoolEntry>
<ConstantPoolEntry>
<id>28</id>
<Type>Class</Type>
<ConstantPoolAddress>41</ConstantPoolAddress>
</ConstantPoolEntry>
<ConstantPoolEntry>
<id>29</id>
<Type>NameAndType</Type>
<ConstantPoolAddress>42,43</ConstantPoolAddress>
</ConstantPoolEntry>
<ConstantPoolEntry>
<id>30</id>
<Type>Utf8</Type>
<ConstantPoolValue>java/lang/StringBuilder</ConstantPoolValue>
</ConstantPoolEntry>
<ConstantPoolEntry>
<id>31</id>
<Type>Utf8</Type>
<ConstantPoolValue>ascii</ConstantPoolValue>
</ConstantPoolEntry>
<ConstantPoolEntry>
<id>32</id>
<Type>NameAndType</Type>
<ConstantPoolAddress>44,45</ConstantPoolAddress>
</ConstantPoolEntry>
<ConstantPoolEntry>
<id>33</id>
<Type>NameAndType</Type>
<ConstantPoolAddress>44,46</ConstantPoolAddress>
</ConstantPoolEntry>
<ConstantPoolEntry>
<id>34</id>
<Type>Utf8</Type>
<ConstantPoolValue>character</ConstantPoolValue>
</ConstantPoolEntry>
<ConstantPoolEntry>
<id>35</id>
<Type>NameAndType</Type>
<ConstantPoolAddress>44,47</ConstantPoolAddress>
```

```
</ConstantPoolEntry>
<ConstantPoolEntry>
<id>36</id>
<Type>NameAndType</Type>
<ConstantPoolAddress>48,49</ConstantPoolAddress>
</ConstantPoolEntry>
<ConstantPoolEntry>
<id>37</id>
<Type>Class</Type>
<ConstantPoolAddress>50</ConstantPoolAddress>
</ConstantPoolEntry>
<ConstantPoolEntry>
<id>38</id>
<Type>NameAndType</Type>
<ConstantPoolAddress>51,52</ConstantPoolAddress>
</ConstantPoolEntry>
<ConstantPoolEntry>
<id>39</id>
<Type>Utf8</Type>
<ConstantPoolValue>Casting</ConstantPoolValue>
</ConstantPoolEntry>
<ConstantPoolEntry>
<id>40</id>
<Type>Utf8</Type>
<ConstantPoolValue>java/lang/Object</ConstantPoolValue>
</ConstantPoolEntry>
<ConstantPoolEntry>
<id>41</id>
<Type>Utf8</Type>
<ConstantPoolValue>java/lang/System</ConstantPoolValue>
</ConstantPoolEntry>
<ConstantPoolEntry>
<id>42</id>
<Type>Utf8</Type>
<ConstantPoolValue>out</ConstantPoolValue>
</ConstantPoolEntry>
<ConstantPoolEntry>
<id>43</id>
<Type>Utf8</Type>
<ConstantPoolValue>Ljava/io/PrintStream</ConstantPoolValue>
</ConstantPoolEntry>
<ConstantPoolEntry>
<id>44</id>
<Type>Utf8</Type>
<ConstantPoolValue>append</ConstantPoolValue>
</ConstantPoolEntry>
<ConstantPoolEntry>
<id>45</id>
<Type>Utf8</Type>
<ConstantPoolValue>Ljava/lang/StringBuilder</ConstantPoolValue>
```

```
</ConstantPoolEntry>
<ConstantPoolEntry>
<id>46</id>
<Type>Utf8</Type>
<ConstantPoolValue>Ljava/lang/StringBuilder</ConstantPoolValue>
</ConstantPoolEntry>
<ConstantPoolEntry>
<id>47</id>
<Type>Utf8</Type>
<ConstantPoolValue>Ljava/lang/StringBuilder</ConstantPoolValue>
</ConstantPoolEntry>
<ConstantPoolEntry>
<id>48</id>
<Type>Utf8</Type>
<ConstantPoolValue>toString</ConstantPoolValue>
</ConstantPoolEntry>
<ConstantPoolEntry>
<id>49</id>
<Type>Utf8</Type>
<ConstantPoolValue>Ljava/lang/String</ConstantPoolValue>
</ConstantPoolEntry>
<ConstantPoolEntry>
<id>50</id>
<Type>Utf8</Type>
<ConstantPoolValue>java/io/PrintStream</ConstantPoolValue>
</ConstantPoolEntry>
<ConstantPoolEntry>
<id>51</id>
<Type>Utf8</Type>
<ConstantPoolValue>println</ConstantPoolValue>
</ConstantPoolEntry>
<ConstantPoolEntry>
<id>52</id>
<Type>Utf8</Type>
<ConstantPoolValue>Ljava/lang/String</ConstantPoolValue>
</ConstantPoolEntry>
</ConstantPool>
```

It's a simple yet elegant design when you take the time to examine the output of the class file. Take the first method reference, `constant_pool[1]`:

```
<ConstantPoolEntry>
<id>1</id>
<Type>Methodref</Type>
<ConstantPoolAddress>13,27</ConstantPoolAddress>
</ConstantPoolEntry>
```

This tells you to look for the class in `constant_pool[13]` as well as the class name and type in `constant_pool[27]`

```
<ConstantPoolEntry>
<id>13</id>
<Type>Class</Type>
<ConstantPoolAddress>40</ConstantPoolAddress>
</ConstantPoolEntry>
```

which points to `constant_pool[40]`:

```
<ConstantPoolEntry>
<id>40</id>
<Type>Utf8</Type>
<ConstantPoolValue>java/lang/Object</ConstantPoolValue>
</ConstantPoolEntry>
```

But you also have `constant_pool[27]` to resolve, which gives you the name and type of the method:

```
<ConstantPoolEntry>
<id>27</id>
<Type>NameAndType</Type>
<ConstantPoolAddress>18,19</ConstantPoolAddress>
</ConstantPoolEntry>
```

Elements 18 and 19 of the constant pool contain the method name and its descriptors. According to the JVM specification, method descriptors take the following form:

```
(ParameterDescriptor *) ReturnDescriptor
```

The return descriptor can be either V for void or one of the `FieldTypes` (see Table 2-2):

```
<ConstantPoolEntry>
<id>18</id>
<Type>Utf8</Type>
<ConstantPoolValue><init></ConstantPoolValue>
</ConstantPoolEntry>
<ConstantPoolEntry>
<id>19</id>
<Type>Utf8</Type>
<ConstantPoolValue>V</ConstantPoolValue>
</ConstantPoolEntry>
```

In this case, the name of the method is `<init>`, an internal JVM method that is in every class file; its method descriptor is `()V`, or `void`, for the field descriptor mapping (see Table 2-2).

So you can now re-create the method as follows:

```
void init()
```

Table 2-2. *Field Descriptors*

Descriptor	Name
B	Byte
C	Char
D	Double
F	Float
I	Int
J	Long
L<classname>	Class
S	Short
Z	Boolean
[	Array

You can try to unravel some other classes too. It may help if you work backward from the target class or method. Some of the strings are pretty unintelligible, but with a little practice the method signatures become clear.

The earliest types of obfuscators simply renamed these strings to something completely unintelligible. This stopped primitive decompilers but didn't harm the class file, because the JVM used a pointer to the string in the constant pool and not the string itself as long as you didn't rename internal methods such as `<init>` or destroy the references to any Java classes in an external library.

You already know what classes you need for your import statements from the following entries: `constant_pool[36, 37, 39, 46]`. Note that there are no interfaces or static final classes in the `Casting.java` example (see Listing 2-1). These would come up as field references in the constant pool, but so far the simple class parser is complete enough to handle any class file you care to throw at it.

Access Flags

Access flags contain bitmasks that tell you whether you're dealing with a class or an interface, and whether it's public, final, and so on. All interfaces are abstract.

There are eight access flag types (see Table 2-3), but more may be introduced in the future. `ACC_SYNTHETIC`, `ACC_ANNOTATION`, and `ACC_ENUM` were relatively recent additions in JDK 1.5.

Table 2-3. *Access Flag Names and Values*

FLAG NAME	Value	Description
ACC_PUBLIC	0x0001	Public class
ACC_FINAL	0x0010	Final class
ACC_SUPER	0x0020	Always set; used for compatibility with older Sun compilers
ACC_INTERFACE	0x0200	Interface class
ACC_ABSTRACT	0x0400	Always set for interfaces
ACC_SYNTHETIC	0x1000	Class generated by the compiler
ACC_ANNOTATION	0x2000	Code annotations; always an interface
ACC_ENUM	0x4000	Enumerated type class

Access flags are `or`'d together to come up with a description of the modifier before the `this` class or interface. `0x21` tells you that the `this` class in `Casting.class` is a public (and super) class, which you can verify is correct by going all the way back to the code in Listing 2-1:

```
<AccessFlags>0x21</AccessFlags>
```

The this Class and the Superclass

The next two values point at the constant pool index for the this class and the superclass.

```
<ThisClass>12</ThisClass>
<SuperClass>13</SuperClass>
```

If you follow the XML output in Listing 2-5, constant_pool[12] points at constant_pool[39]; here the Utf8 structure contains the string Casting, telling you that this is the Casting class. The superclass is in constant_pool[13], which points at constant_pool[40]; here the Utf8 structure contains java/lang/Object because every class has object as its superclass.

Interfaces and Interface Count

The Casting.java example in Listing 2-1 doesn't have any interfaces, so you have to look at a different example to get a better understanding of how interfaces are implemented in the class file (see Listing 2-6).

Listing 2-6. *Interface Example*

```
interface IProgrammer {
    public void code();
    public void earnmore();
}

interface IWriter {
    public void pullhairout();
    public void earnless();
}

public class Person implements IProgrammer, IWriter {

    public Person() {
         Geek g = new Geek(this);
         Author t = new Author(this);
    }

    public void code() { /* ..... */ }
    public void earnmore() { /* ..... */ }
    public void pullhairout() { /* ..... */ }
    public void earnless() { /* ..... */ }

}
```

```
class Geek {
    IProgrammer iprog = null;

    public Geek(IProgrammer iprog) {
         this.iprog = iprog;
         iprog.code();
         iprog.earnmore();
    }
}

class Author {
    IWriter iwriter = null;

    public Author(IWriter iwriter) {
         this.iwriter = iwriter;
         iwriter.pullhairout();
         iwriter.earnless();
    }
}
```

Listing 2-6 has two interfaces, `IProgrammer` and `IWriter`. Running ClassToXML against the class files gives the following information in the interfaces section:

```
<InterfaceCount>2</InterfaceCount>
<Interfaces>
  <Interface>8</Interface>
  <Interface>9</Interface>
</Interfaces>
```

This resolves to the `IProgrammer` and `IWriter` strings in the constant pool as follows:

```
<ConstantPoolEntry>
<id>8</id>
  <Type>Class</Type>
  <ConstantPoolAddress>27</ConstantPoolAddress>
</ConstantPoolEntry>
<ConstantPoolEntry>
<id>9</id>
  <Type>Class</Type>
  <ConstantPoolAddress>28</ConstantPoolAddress>
</ConstantPoolEntry>


<ConstantPoolEntry>
<id>27</id>
  <Type>Class</Type>
  <ConstantPoolAddress>27</ConstantPoolAddress>
</ConstantPoolEntry>
<ConstantPoolEntry>
<id>28</id>
```

```
  <Type>Class</Type>
  <ConstantPoolAddress>28</ConstantPoolAddress>
</ConstantPoolEntry>
```

Fields and Field Count

The `field_info` structure is shown in Listing 2-7.

Listing 2-7. *`field_info` Data Structure*

```
field_info {
        u2 access_flags;
        u2 name_index;
        u2 descriptor_index;
        u2 attributes_count;
        attribute_info attributes[attributes_count];
}
```

`Casting.class` as it stands has two static and final fields, `ascStr` and `chrStr` (see Listing 2-1). I also made them static and final, to force a `ConstantValue` field attribute.

Now, if you pull out the relevant section in the XML, you see that there are two fields (Listing 2-8). Let's focus on the first.

Listing 2-8. *`Casting.java` Field Information*

```
<FieldCount>2</FieldCount>
<Fields>
<Field>
<AccessFlags>ACC_STATIC, ACC_FINAL</AccessFlags>
<Name>ascStr</Name>
<Descriptor>java.lang.String</Descriptor>
<Attributes>
<Attribute>
<AttributeType>String</AttributeType>
<AttributeName>ascii</AttributeName>
</Attribute>
</Attributes>
</Field>
<Field>
<AccessFlags>ACC_STATIC, ACC_FINAL</AccessFlags>
<Name>chrStr</Name>
<Descriptor>java.lang.String</Descriptor>
<Attributes>
<Attribute>
<AttributeType>String</AttributeType>
<AttributeName>character</AttributeName>
</Attribute>
```

```
</Attributes>
</Field>
</Fields>
```

Field access flags (see Table 2-4) tell you whether the field is public, private, protected, static, final, volatile, or transient.

Table 2-4. *Field Access Flag Names and Values*

FLAG NAME	Value	Description
ACC_PUBLIC	0x0001	Public field
ACC_PRIVATE	0x0002	Private field
ACC_PROTECTED	0x0004	Protected field
ACC_STATIC	0x0008	Static field
ACC_FINAL	0x0010	Final field
ACC_VOLATILE	0x0040	Volatile field; can't be cached
ACC_TRANSIENT	0x0080	Transient field
ACC_ENUM	0x0100	Enum element

The first five and the last keywords should be obvious to anyone who has written Java. The volatile keyword tells a thread that the variable may be updated by another thread, and the transient keyword is used in object serialization. An access flag of 0x0018 in this example denotes a static final field.

Go back to Table 2-2 to refresh your mind before you unravel the different field descriptors:

```
<Field>
<AccessFlags>ACC_STATIC, ACC_FINAL</AccessFlags>
<Name>ascStr</Name>
<Descriptor>java.lang.String</Descriptor>
<Attributes>
<Attribute>
<AttributeType>String</AttributeType>
<AttributeName>ascii</AttributeName>
</Attribute>
</Attributes>
```

```
</Field>
```

The descriptor points back to the constant_pool[14] field ascStr, which has the field descriptor constant_pool[15] or Ljava/lang/String; this is an instance of a String class.

Field Attributes

The attribute count is, no surprise, the number of attributes, which is immediately followed by the attributes themselves. Attributes throughout the class file are in the format shown in Listing 2-9.

Listing 2-9. *attribute-info Structure*

```
attribute_info {
        u2 attribute_name_index;
        u4 attribute_length;
        u1 info[attribute_length];
}
```

Several different attribute types are found in the field data structure, the method data structure, and the attribute data structure—the final element of the class-file data structure. But there are really only two field attributes, ConstantValue and Synthetic, of interest here. ConstantValue is used for constant variables, such as those declared as static and final in the current example. The Synthetic variable was introduced in JDK 1.1 to support inner classes.

Signature and Deprecated attributes are also possible and users can also define their own attribute types, but they're irrelevant to the current discussion.

Listing 2-11. *Field Attribute Data*

```
<Attributes>
<Attribute>
<AttributeType>String</AttributeType>
<AttributeName>ascii</AttributeName>
</Attribute>
</Attributes>
```

The attribute for the first field (see Listing 2-11), is a constant that can be found in constant_pool[5] (see Listing 2-12), a string, which in turn points at the string "ascii ".

Listing 2-12. *Fields in the Constant Pool*

```
<ConstantPoolEntry>
<id>5</id>
<Type>String</Type>
<ConstantPoolAddress>31</ConstantPoolAddress>
</ConstantPoolEntry>
<ConstantPoolEntry>
<id>31</id>
<Type>Utf8</Type>
<ConstantPoolValue>ascii</ConstantPoolValue>
</ConstantPoolEntry>
```

You have now decompiled the first field into its original format:

```
static final String ascStr = "ascii ";
```

Methods and Method Count

And now for the most important part of the class file: the methods. All the source code is converted into bytecode and stored or contained in the `method_info` area. (Well, it's actually in the code attribute within the methods, but you're getting very close.) If someone can get at the bytecode, then they can try to convert it back into source. The `Methods` element is preceded by a method count and the data structure (see Listing 2-13) and is not dissimilar to the `field_info` structure in the previous section. Three types of attributes normally appear at the `method_info` level: `Code`, `Exceptions`, and once again `Synthetic` for inner classes.

Listing 2-13. `method_info` **Structure**

```
method_info {
        u2 access_flags;
        u2 name_index;
        u2 descriptor_index;
        u2 attributes_count;
        attribute_info attributes[attributes_count];
}
```

The methods in Listing 2-1's `Casting.class` are as shown in Listing 2-14.

Listing 2-14. `Casting.class` **Method Information**

```
<MethodCount>2</MethodCount>
<Methods>
<Method>
<Attributes>
<Attribute>
```

```
<AttributeName>Code:</AttributeName>
<Max_Stack>1</Max_Stack>
<Max_Locals>1</Max_Locals>
<Method_Args>1</Method_Args>
<Method_Code>
        0: aload_0
        1: invokespecial #1
        4: return
</Method_Code>
<Method_LineNumberTable>line 1: 0</Method_LineNumberTable>
</Attribute>
</Attributes>
<AccessFlags>public</AccessFlags>
<Name>Casting</Name>
<Descriptor>();</Descriptor>
</Method>
<Method>
<Attributes>
<Attribute>
<AttributeName>Code:</AttributeName>
<Max_Stack>3</Max_Stack>
<Max_Locals>2</Max_Locals>
<Method_Args>1</Method_Args>
<Method_Code>
        0: iconst_0
        1: istore_1
        2: iload_1
        3: sipush        128
        6: if_icmpge     51
        9: getstatic     #2
       12: new           #3
       15: dup
       16: invokespecial #4
       19: ldc           #5
       21: invokevirtual #6
       24: iload_1
       25: invokevirtual #7
       28: ldc           #8
       30: invokevirtual #6
       33: iload_1
       34: invokevirtual #9
       37: invokevirtual #10
       40: invokevirtual #11
       43: iload_1
       44: iconst_1
       45: iadd
       46: i2c
       47: istore_1
       48: goto          2
       51: return
```

```
</Method_Code>
<Method_LineNumberTable>
        line 8: 0
        line 9: 9
        line 8: 43
        line 11: 51
</Method_LineNumberTable>
<Method_StackMapTableEntries>2</Method_StackMapTableEntries>
<Method_StackMapTable>
        frame_type = 252 /* append */
        offset_delta = 2
        locals = [ int ]
        frame_type = 250 /* chop */
        offset_delta = 48</Method_StackMapTable>
</Attribute>
</Attributes>
<AccessFlags>public, static</AccessFlags>
<Name>main</Name>
<Descriptor>(java.lang.String[]);</Descriptor>
</Method>
</Methods>
```

Different access flags are set for each method depending on what modifiers were used in the original source; see Table 2-5. A number of restrictions exist, because some of the access flags are mutually exclusive—in other words, a method can't be declared as both ACC_PUBLIC and ACC_PRIVATE or even ACC_PROTECTED. However, you won't normally be disassembling illegal bytecodes, so you're unlikely to come across any such eventualities.

The first methods in the example is public; the second is a public static method.

Table 2-5. *Method Access Flags*

FLAG NAME	Value	Description
ACC_PUBLIC	0x0001	Class or interface
ACC_PRIVATE	0x0002	Class
ACC_PROTECTED	0x0004	Class
ACC_STATIC	0x0008	Static field
ACC_FINAL	0x0010	Final field

FLAG NAME	Value	Description
ACC_SYNCHRONIZED	0x0020	Class
ACC_BRIDGE	0x0040	Compiler generated
ACC_VARARGS	0x0080	Variable number of arguments
ACC_NATIVE	0x0100	Class or interface
ACC_ABSTRACT	0x0400	Abstract
ACC_STRICT	0x0800	Strict
ACC_SYNTHETIC	0x1000	Synthetic

You can now find the name and the method descriptors of the final method:

```
<Name>main</Name>
<Descriptor>(java.lang.String[]);</Descriptor>
```

You pull out the name and description of the method from `constant_pool[22]` and `constant_pool[23]`, as shown in Listing 2-15.

Listing 2-15. *`Casting.class` Method Name and Descriptor Constant-Pool Information*

```
<ConstantPoolEntry>
<id>22</id>
<Type>Utf8</Type>
<ConstantPoolValue>main</ConstantPoolValue>
</ConstantPoolEntry>
<ConstantPoolEntry>
<id>23</id>
<Type>Utf8</Type>
<ConstantPoolValue>Ljava/lang/String</ConstantPoolValue>
</ConstantPoolEntry>
```

You can now reassemble the method without any of the underlying code:

```
public static void main(java.lang.String args[]) {
 /*  */
}
```

or simply:

```
import java.lang.String;
...
public static void main(String args[]) {
 /*  */
}
```

The remaining methods fall out of the constant pool in a similar fashion.

Method Attributes

Attributes appear in the `field`, `method`, and `attributes` elements of the class-file structure. Each attribute begins with an `attribute_name_index` that references the constant pool and an attribute length. But *the* meat of the class file is in the method attributes (see Listing 2-16).

Listing 2-16. *Init Method Attributes*

```
<Attributes>
<Attribute>
<AttributeName>Code:</AttributeName>
<Max_Stack>1</Max_Stack>
<Max_Locals>1</Max_Locals>
<Method_Args>1</Method_Args>
<Method_Code>
        0: aload_0
        1: invokespecial #1
        4: return
</Method_Code>
<Method_LineNumberTable>line 1: 0</Method_LineNumberTable>
</Attribute>
</Attributes>
```

The attribute type in this example is a code attribute. The code attribute is shown in Listing 2-17.

Listing 2-17. *Code Attribute*

```
Code_attribute {
        u2 attribute_name_index;
        u4 attribute_length;
        u2 max_stack;
        u2 max_locals;
        u4 code_length;
        u1 code[code_length];
        u2 exception_table_length;
        {
                u2 start_pc;
```

```
            u2 end_pc;
            u2 handler_pc;
            u2 catch_type;
        } exception_table[exception_table_length];
        u2 attributes_count;
        attribute_info attributes[attributes_count];
}
```

The `attribute_length` is the length of the code attribute minus the first 6 bytes. The `attribute_type` and the `attribute_name` take up the first 6 bytes and aren't included in the `attribute_length`. The `max_stack` and `max_locals` give the maximum number of variables on the operand stack and local variable sections of the stack frame. This tells you how deep the stack will go and how many variables will be pushed on and off the stack.

The code length gives the size of the following code array. The code array is simply a series of bytes where each bytecode is a reserved byte value or opcode followed by zero or more operands—or, to put it another way:

```
opcode operand
```

Looking at the output (Listing 2-14) from running ClassToXML on `Casting.class`, you see that there are two methods, `main` and `init` which is the empty constructor that the Java compiler always adds when the developer chooses not to add their own constructor. Each method has its own Code array.

<init> method

Before I explain what bytecode maps onto which opcode, let's look at the simplest method to unravel, which is the first code segment:

```
2ab70001b1
```

When you convert this into opcodes and operands, it becomes

```
2a          aload 0
b70001      invokespecial #1
b1          return
```

`2a` becomes `aload 0`. This loads the local variable 0 onto the stack, required by `invokespecial`. `b70001` becomes `invokespecial #1`, where `invokespecial` is used to invoke a method in a limited number of cases such as an instance-initialization method (`<init>` to you and me), which is what you have here. `#1` is a reference to `constant_pool[1]`, which is a `CONSTANT_Methodref` structure. Listing 2-18 collects together all the related constant-pool entries for `constant_pool[1]`.

Listing 2-18. *<init> Method Constant-Pool Resolution*

```
<ConstantPoolEntry>
<id>1</id>
<Type>Methodref</Type>
<ConstantPoolAddress>13,27</ConstantPoolAddress>
</ConstantPoolEntry>

<ConstantPoolEntry>
<id>13</id>
<Type>Class</Type>
<ConstantPoolAddress>40</ConstantPoolAddress>
</ConstantPoolEntry>

<ConstantPoolEntry>
<id>40</id>
<Type>Utf8</Type>
<ConstantPoolValue>java/lang/Object</ConstantPoolValue>
</ConstantPoolEntry>

<ConstantPoolEntry>
<id>27</id>
<Type>NameAndType</Type>
<ConstantPoolAddress>18,19</ConstantPoolAddress>
</ConstantPoolEntry>

<ConstantPoolEntry>
<id>18</id>
<Type>Utf8</Type>
<ConstantPoolValue>init</ConstantPoolValue>
</ConstantPoolEntry>

<ConstantPoolEntry>
<id>19</id>
<Type>Utf8</Type>
<ConstantPoolValue>V</ConstantPoolValue>
</ConstantPoolEntry>
```

You can resolve the symbolic references by hand to

```
<Method java.lang.Object.<init>()V>
```

This is the empty constructor that the javac compiler adds to all classes that don't already have a constructor. The final `b1` opcode is a simple `return` statement. So the first method can be converted straight back into the following code, an empty constructor:

```
public class Casting()
{
       return;
```

```
}
```

main method

The second code attribute is less trivial. To get any further, you need to know what each hexadecimal value maps onto what opcode.

> **NOTE:** Although the example list is shorter than most other opcode lists (you're ignoring any opcodes above 201), it still runs on for several pages; you can reference it in Appendix A and at `www.apress.com`. Note that opcodes beyond 201 are reserved for future use, because they have no effect on the original bytecode in a class file and can be safely ignored.

You also need to know how each element of the Java language is compiled into bytecode so you can reverse the process. Then you can see how the remaining code attributes can be turned into opcodes and their operands.

The main method has the following 52-byte `byte_code` attribute, which is broken down in Listing 2-19 into opcodes and operands

```
033c1b110080a2002db20002bb000359b700041205b600061bb600071208b600061bb60009b6000a
b6000b1b0460923ca7ffd2b1
```

Listing 2-19. *Main Method*

```
<Method>
<Attributes>
<Attribute>
<AttributeName>Code:</AttributeName>
<Max_Stack>3</Max_Stack>
<Max_Locals>2</Max_Locals>
<Method_Args>1</Method_Args>
<Method_Code>
        0: iconst_0
         1: istore_1
         2: iload_1
         3: sipush        128
         6: if_icmpge     51
         9: getstatic     #2
        12: new           #3
        15: dup
        16: invokespecial #4
        19: ldc           #5
        21: invokevirtual #6
```

```
        24: iload_1
        25: invokevirtual #7
        28: ldc           #8
        30: invokevirtual #6
        33: iload_1
        34: invokevirtual #9
        37: invokevirtual #10
        40: invokevirtual #11
        43: iload_1
        44: iconst_1
        45: iadd
        46: i2c
        47: istore_1
        48: goto          2
        51: return
</Method_Code>
<Method_LineNumberTable>
        line 8: 0
        line 9: 9
        line 8: 43
        line 11: 51
</Method_LineNumberTable>
<Method_StackMapTableEntries>2</Method_StackMapTableEntries>
<Method_StackMapTable>
        frame_type = 252 /* append */
        offset_delta = 2
        locals = [ int ]
        frame_type = 250 /* chop */
        offset_delta = 48</Method_StackMapTable>
</Attribute>
</Attributes>
<AccessFlags>static</AccessFlags>
<Name>main</Name>
<Descriptor>(java.lang.String[]);</Descriptor>
</Method>
</Methods>
```

You can reverse engineer the opcodes and operands in a similar fashion to the previous method, as you can see in Table 2-6.

Table 2-6. *Main Code Attribute Breakdown*

PC	Bytecode	Opcode	Operand	Constant Pool Resolution (if applicable)
0	03	iconst_0		
1	3c	istore_1		

2	1b	iload_1		
3	110080	sipush	128	
6	a2002d	if_icmpge	51	
9	b20002	getstatic	#2	Field java/lang/System.out:Ljava/io/PrintStream;
12	bb0003	new	#3	class java/lang/StringBuilder
15	59	dup		
16	b70004	invokespecial	#4	Method java/lang/StringBuilder."<init>":()V
19	1205	ldc	#5	String ascii
21	b60006	invokevirtual	#6	Method java/lang/StringBuilder.append:(Ljava/lang/String;)Ljava/lang/StringBuilder;
24	1b	iload_1		
25	b60007	invokevirtual	#7	Method java/lang/StringBuilder.append:(I)Ljava/lang/StringBuilder;
28	1208	ldc	#8	String character
30	b60006	invokevirtual	#6	Method java/lang/StringBuilder.append:(Ljava/lang/String;)Ljava/lang/StringBuilder;
33	1b	iload_1		

PC	Bytecode	Opcode	Operand	Constant Pool Resolution (if applicable)
34	b60009	invokevirtual	#9	Method java/lang/StringBuilder.append:(C)Ljava/lang/StringBuilder;
37	b6000a	invokevirtual	#10	Method java/lang/StringBuilder.toString:()Ljava/lang/String;
40	b6000b	invokevirtual	#11	Method java/io/PrintStream.println:(Ljava/lang/String;)V
43	1b	iload_1		
44	04	iconst_1		
45	60	iadd		
46	92	i2c		
47	3c	istore_1		
48	a7ffd2	goto	2	
51	b1	return		

`iconst_0` and `istore_1` push the number 0 onto the stack, `sipush` pushes the number 128 onto the stack, and `if_icmpge` compares the two numbers and the `goto` program counter or `PC = 51` (that is, returns if the numbers are equal). This is the following code snippet from the `Casting.class` code:

```
for(char c=0; c < 128; c++) {
}
```

In the same manner, you can complete the analysis to return the complete main method. The aim of this book is to show you how to do that programmatically.

ClassToXML, available from the downloads area of the Apress site, outputs bytecode like a true disassembler. And now that you've seen how easy it is to create a disassembler, you can probably see why so many disassemblers have user interfaces.

Attributes and Attributes Count

The final two elements contain the number of class-file attributes and the remaining attributes, which are usually `SourceFile` and `InnerClasses`.

`SourceFile` is the name of the Java file that was used to originally generate the code. The `InnerClasses` attribute is a bit more complicated and is ignored by several decompilers that can't handle inner classes.

You're not limited to the `SourceFile` and `InnerClasses` attribute. New attributes can be defined here or in any of the field or methods attribute sections. Developers may want to store information in a custom attribute, perhaps using it for some low-level check or for storing encrypted code attributes to possibly prevent decompilation. Assuming your new code attribute follows the format of all other attributes, you can add any attribute you want, which will be ignored by the JVM. Each attribute needs 2 bytes that provide a number pointing into the constant pool to give the name of the attribute, `attribute_name_index`; and 4 bytes giving the length of the remaining bytes in the attribute, `attribute_length`.

Summary

You've finally come to the end of the guts of the class file and manually disassembled ClassToXML in the process (refer to the appropriate files on `www.apress.com`). I hope you begin to see how it all fits together. Although the design of the class file is neat and compact, because of the split between the initial and final compilation stages you have an awful lot of information to help you recover the source. For many years, programmers have been protected by the encoding that compiling to an executable usually offers, but splitting the compilation and carrying around so much information at the intermediate stage is asking for trouble.

Chapter 3 looks at unraveling the DEX file format to help you understand how to reverse-engineer that back into Java source code.

Chapter 3

Inside the DEX File

It might seem odd that we would need another virtual machine for Android phones and that the Java virtual machine (JVM) wouldn't be good enough. But for optimization and performance, the Dalvik virtual machine (DVM) is used on all Android phones. It was named after a place in the Icelandic homeland of one the original developers and is considerably different in design from the JVM. Instead of a push-pop stack machine, the DVM uses registers. The corresponding DVM bytecode or DEX files are also a completely different design than Java class files.

But all is not lost. There is more than enough information about the DEX file specification to repeat the same exercise you looked at for the class file in Chapter 2 and come to the same happy conclusion that lets you gain access to the DEX file bytecode and convert it back into Java source code, even if you are doing it manually in this chapter. The DEX file can be unraveled into its different sections: the `header` and the DEX version of the constant pool, which houses pointers for strings, fields, methods, and class information in its `data` section.

Ghost in the Machine, Part Deux

When you download an application from the Android Market or Amazon Marketplace onto your Android phone, you're downloading an Android package (APK) file. Each and every APK file is in a zip format. Change the `.apk` file extension to `.zip`, and unzipping the file gives you the resources, the images, the `AndroidManifest.xml` file, and the `classes.dex` file contained in the APK, in a structure similar to that shown in Figure 3-1.

Name	Date modified	Type	Size
META-INF	1/19/2012 5:04 AM	File folder	
res	1/19/2012 5:03 AM	File folder	
AndroidManifest	9/24/2011 9:50 PM	XML Document	6 KB
classes.dex	9/24/2011 9:50 PM	DEX File	223 KB
resources.arsc	9/24/2011 9:50 PM	ARSC File	63 KB

Figure 3-1. *Unzipped APK file*

Whereas a Java jar file has many class files, each APK file has only a single `classes.dex` file, as shown in Figure 3-2. According to Google, the APK format differs from the class-file format for performance and security reasons. But regardless of what the reasons are, from a reverse-engineering perspective it means your target is now the `classes.dex` file. You have moved completely away from the Java class-file format and now need to understand what is inside the `classes.dex` file so you can decompile it back into Java source.

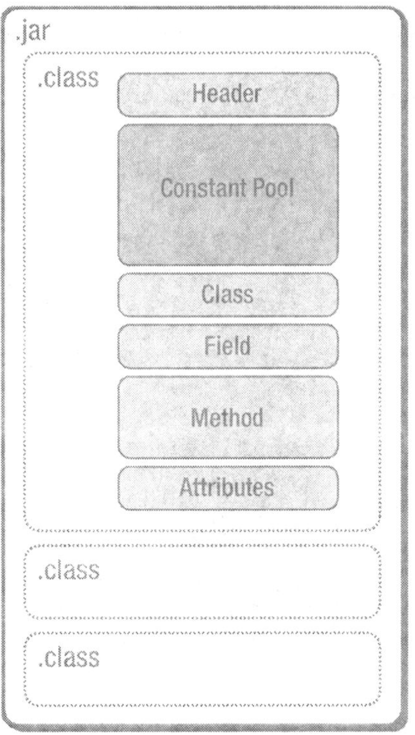

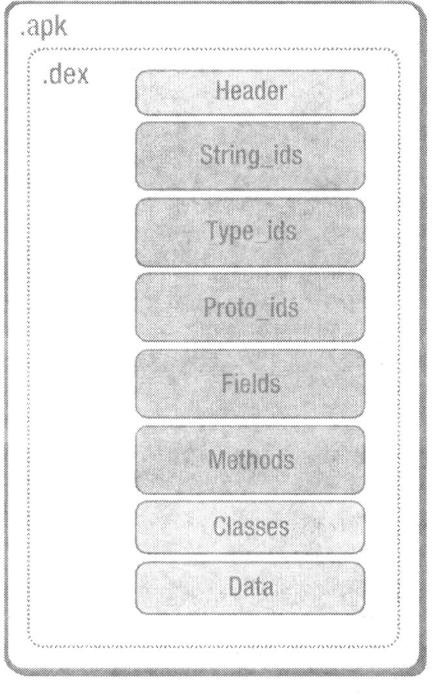

Figure 3-2. *Class file vs DEX file*

Chapter 4 looks at many Android and third-party tools that are available to help you pull apart APKs and classes.dex files. In this chapter, you manually create your own classes.dex disassembler.

Converting Casting.class

To begin, you need to convert your Casting.class file from Chapter 3 into a classes.dex file so you have something to work with. This classes.dex file will run on the command line on an Android phone, but it's not a classic APK file. However, the classes.dex format will be the same, so it's a good place to start your DEX file investigation.

You do this conversion using the dx program, which comes with the Android platform tools. Make sure the Casting.class file is in the casting folder, and execute the following command:

```
javac c:\apress\chap3\casting\Casting.java

dx --dex --output=c:\temp\classes.dex C:\apress\chap3\casting
```

Figure 3-3 shows the resulting classes.dex file for the Casting.java code in Listing 3-1, in hexadecimal format.

Listing 3-1. *Casting.java*

```
public class Casting {

 static final String ascStr = "ascii ";
 static final String chrStr = " character ";

 public static void main(String args[]){
   for(char c=0; c < 128; c++) {
          System.out.println("ascii " + (int)c + " character "+ c);
   }
 }
}
```

```
64 65 78 0A 30 33 35 00  62 8B 44 18 DA A9 21 CA
9C 4F B4 C5 21 D7 77 BC  2A 18 4A 38 0D A2 AA FE
50 04 00 00 70 00 00 00  78 56 34 12 00 00 00 00
00 00 00 00 A4 03 00 00  1A 00 00 00 70 00 00 00
0A 00 00 00 D8 00 00 00  07 00 00 00 00 01 00 00
03 00 00 00 54 01 00 00  09 00 00 00 6C 01 00 00
01 00 00 00 B4 01 00 00  7C 02 00 00 D4 01 00 00
72 02 00 00 7F 02 00 00  87 02 00 00 8A 02 00 00
98 02 00 00 9B 02 00 00  9E 02 00 00 A2 02 00 00
AD 02 00 00 B1 02 00 00  B5 02 00 00 CC 02 00 00
E0 02 00 00 F4 02 00 00  0F 03 00 00 23 03 00 00
26 03 00 00 2A 03 00 00  3F 03 00 00 47 03 00 00
4F 03 00 00 57 03 00 00  5F 03 00 00 65 03 00 00
6A 03 00 00 73 03 00 00  02 00 00 00 04 00 00 00
07 00 00 00 0A 00 00 00  0B 00 00 00 0C 00 00 00
0D 00 00 00 0E 00 00 00  0F 00 00 00 11 00 00 00
05 00 00 00 05 00 00 00  00 00 00 00 06 00 00 00
06 00 00 00 54 02 00 00  08 00 00 00 06 00 00 00
5C 02 00 00 09 00 00 00  06 00 00 00 64 02 00 00
0F 00 00 00 08 00 00 00  00 00 00 00 10 00 00 00
08 00 00 00 64 02 00 00  10 00 00 00 08 00 00 00
6C 02 00 00 02 00 05 00  13 00 00 00 02 00 05 00
15 00 00 00 07 00 03 00  17 00 00 00 02 00 04 00
01 00 00 00 02 00 06 00  16 00 00 00 03 00 05 00
18 00 00 00 04 00 04 00  01 00 00 00 06 00 04 00
01 00 00 00 06 00 01 00  12 00 00 00 06 00 02 00
12 00 00 00 06 00 03 00  12 00 00 00 06 00 00 00
19 00 00 00 02 00 00 00  01 00 00 00 04 00 00 00
00 00 00 00 03 00 00 00  00 00 00 00 92 03 00 00
8D 03 00 00 01 00 01 00  01 00 00 00 7D 03 00 00
04 00 00 00 70 10 03 00  00 00 0E 00 05 00 01 00
02 00 00 00 82 03 00 00  2C 00 00 00 12 00 13 01
80 00 35 10 28 00 62 01  02 00 22 02 06 00 70 10
04 00 02 00 1A 03 14 00  6E 20 07 00 32 00 0C 02
6E 20 06 00 02 00 0C 02  1A 03 00 00 6E 20 07 00
32 00 0C 02 6E 20 05 00  02 00 0C 02 6E 10 08 00
02 00 0C 02 6E 20 02 00  21 00 D8 00 00 01 8E 00
28 D7 0E 00 01 00 00 00  00 00 00 00 01 00 00 00
01 00 00 00 01 00 00 00  05 00 00 00 01 00 00 00
09 00 0B 20 63 68 61 72  61 63 74 65 72 20 00 06
3C 69 6E 69 74 3E 00 01  43 00 0C 43 61 73 74 69
6E 67 2E 6A 61 76 61 00  01 49 00 01 4C 00 02 4C
43 00 09 4C 43 61 73 74  69 6E 67 3B 00 02 4C 49
00 02 4C 4C 00 15 4C 6A  61 76 61 2F 69 6F 2F 50
72 69 6E 74 53 74 72 65  61 6D 3B 00 12 4C 6A 61
76 61 2F 6C 61 6E 67 2F  4F 62 6A 65 63 74 3B 00
12 4C 6A 61 76 61 2F 6C  61 6E 67 2F 53 74 72 69
6E 67 3B 00 19 4C 6A 61  76 61 2F 6C 61 6E 67 2F
53 74 72 69 6E 67 42 75  69 6C 64 65 72 3B 00 12
4C 6A 61 76 61 2F 6C 61  6E 67 2F 53 79 73 74 65
6D 3B 00 01 56 00 02 56  4C 00 13 5B 4C 6A 61 76
61 2F 6C 61 6E 67 2F 53  74 72 69 6E 67 3B 00 06
61 70 70 65 6E 64 00 06  61 73 63 53 74 72 00 06
61 73 63 69 69 20 00 06  63 68 72 53 74 72 00 04
6D 61 69 6E 00 03 6F 75  74 00 07 70 72 69 6E 74
6C 6E 00 08 74 6F 53 74  72 69 6E 67 00 01 00 07
0E 00 08 01 00 07 0E 5A  01 22 0D 4D 00 02 17 14
17 00 02 00 02 00 00 18  01 18 00 81 80 04 D4 03
01 09 EC 03 0E 00 00 00  00 00 00 00 01 00 00 00
00 00 00 00 01 00 00 00  1A 00 00 00 70 00 00 00
02 00 00 00 0A 00 00 00  D8 00 00 00 03 00 00 00
07 00 00 00 00 01 00 00  04 00 00 00 03 00 00 00
54 01 00 00 05 00 00 00  09 00 00 00 6C 01 00 00
06 00 00 00 01 00 00 00  B4 01 00 00 01 20 00 00
02 00 00 00 D4 01 00 00  01 10 00 00 04 00 00 00
54 02 00 00 02 20 00 00  1A 00 00 00 72 02 00 00
03 20 00 00 02 00 00 00  7D 03 00 00 05 20 00 00
01 00 00 00 8D 03 00 00  00 20 00 00 01 00 00 00
92 03 00 00 00 10 00 00  01 00 00 00 A4 03 00 00
```

Figure 3-3. *classes.dex*

To open the DEX file further, in this chapter you simulate the actions of a disassembler by breaking the DEX file into its parts. You do this by building your own primitive disassembler called DexToXML, which takes the DEX file and outputs the code into an easy-to-read XML format.

Breaking the DEX File into Its Constituent Parts

You can break the class file into the following constituent parts:

- header
- string_ids
- type_ids
- proto_ids
- field_ids
- method_ids
- class_defs
- data
- link_data

The header section contains a summary of the file's information, its sizes, and pointers or offsets to where the other information can be found. String_ids lists all the strings in the file, and the Java types are found in the type_ids section. You see later how the proto_ids for prototypes, field_ids, method_ids, and class_defs sections let you reverse-engineer the class names, method calls, and fields back into Java. The data section is the Android version of the constant pool. The link_data section is for statically linked files and isn't relevant to this discussion, so no related section is provided in this chapter.

The DEX file format specification (http://source.android.com/tech/dalvik/dex-format.html) uses a struct-like format to show the DEX file's components; see Listing 3-2.

Listing 3-2. *DEX File Struct*

```
Dexfile {
        header          header_item,
        string_ids      string_id_item[],
        type_ids        type_id_item[],
        proto_ids       proto_id_item[],
        field_ids       field_id_item[],
        method_ids      method_id_item[],
        class_defs      class_def_item[],
        data            ubyte[],
        link_data       ubyte[]
}
```

And as in the last chapter, you use an XML format because it allows you to traverse in and out of the DEX file's inner structures much more quickly. It also makes the DEX file information easier to understand as you unravel its meaning. The DEX file structure—with all the XML nodes collapsed—is shown in Listing 3-3.

Listing 3-3. *DexToXML*

```
<root>
<header />
<string_ids />
<type_ids />
<proto_ids />
<field_ids />
<method_ids />
<class_defs />
<data />
</root>
```

The following sections explain what is in each of the nodes.

The Header Section

The header section contains the top-level information for the remainder of the file. The structure of the DEX file is dramatically different than its original-format Java class file and resembles the metadata section of a Microsoft .Net PE file more than what you saw in the last chapter. The header preamble contains the magic number, checksum, signature, and size of the class file. The remaining information tells you how big the strings, types, protos, methods, and classes are and provides an address pointer or offset to where you can find the actual strings, types, protos, methods, and classes in the classes.dex file. There is also a pointer to the map info in the data section, which repeats much of the information in the header section.

Listing 3-4 uses a struct-like format to show how the header is laid out.

Listing 3-4. *Header Section Struct*

```
DexfileHeader{
        ubyte[8]           magic,
        int                checksum,
        ubyte[20]          signature,
        uint               file_size,
        uint               header_size,
        uint               endian_tag,
        uint               link_size,
        uint               link_off,
```

```
        uint            map_off,
        uint            string_ids_size,
        uint            string_ids_off,
        uint            type_ids_size,
        uint            type_ids_off,
        uint            proto_ids_size,
        uint            proto_ids_off,
        uint            field_ids_size,
        uint            field_ids_off,
        uint            method_ids_size,
        uint            method_ids_off,
        uint            class_defs_size,
        uint            class_defs_off,
        uint            data_size,
        uint            data_off
}
```

The `header` fields are detailed in Table 3-1.

Table 3-1. *Dex File* `Header`

Name	Format	Hex	Value	Comments
`magic`	8 bytes	`64 65 78 0A 30 33 35 00`	`dex\n035\0`	Similar to the CAFEBABE magic number in the class file
`checksum`	4 bytes	`62 8B 44 18`	`0x18448B62`	Checksum, not including magic. Little-endian.
`signature`	20 bytes	`DA A9 21 CA 9C 4F B4 C5 21 D7 77 BC 2A 18 4A 38 0D A2 AA FEW`	`0xDAA921CA 9C4FB4C5 21D777BC 2A184A38 0DA2AAFE`	SHA-1 signature not including the magic and checksum fields.
`file_size`	4 bytes	`50 04 00 00`	`0x450`	Little-endian.
`header_size`	4 bytes	`70 00 00 00`	`0x70`	Always 0x70; little-endian again.
`endian_tag`	4 bytes	`78 56 34 12`	`0x12345678`	`classes.dex` uses `little_endian` to store the data.

Name	Format	Hex	Value	Comments
link_size	4 bytes	00 00 00 00	0x0	Size of the link data at the end of the file.
link_offset	4 bytes	00 00 00 00	0x0	Address of the link_data section.
map_off	4 bytes	a4 03 00 00	0x3a4	Address of the map area in the data section.
string_ids_size	4 bytes	1a 00 00 00	0x1a or 26	Number of strings.
string_ids_off	4 bytes	70 00 00 00	0x70	Address of the strings section.
type_ids_size	4 bytes	0a 00 00 00	0xa or 10	Number of types.
type_ids_off	4 bytes	d8 00 00 00	0d8	Address of the types section.
proto_ids_size	4 bytes	07 00 00 00	0x7 or 7	Number of prototypes.
proto_ids_off	4 bytes	00 01 00 00	0x100	Address of the proto section.
fields_ids_size	4 bytes	03 00 00 00	0x3 or 3	Number of fields.
field_ids_off	4 bytes	54 01 00 00	0x154	Address of the fields section.
method_ids_size	4 bytes	09 00 00 00	0x9 or 9	Number of methods.
method_ids_off	4 bytes	6c 01 00 00	0x16c	Address of the methods section.
class_defs_size	4 bytes	01 00 00 00	0x1 or 1	Number of classes.

class_defs_off	4 bytes	b4 01 00 00	0x1b4	Address of the classes section.
data_size	4 bytes	7c 02 00 00	0x27c	676 bytes of data.
data_off	4 bytes	d4 01 00 00	0x1d4	Data section address.

The header section in the DEX file is highlighted in Figure 3-4, and you can just about follow where each field appears using Table 3-1. But reading hexadecimal requires a certain type of masochism, which is why DexToXML outputs the same data in a much easier to read XML format. The DexToXML header fields are shown in Listing 3-5.

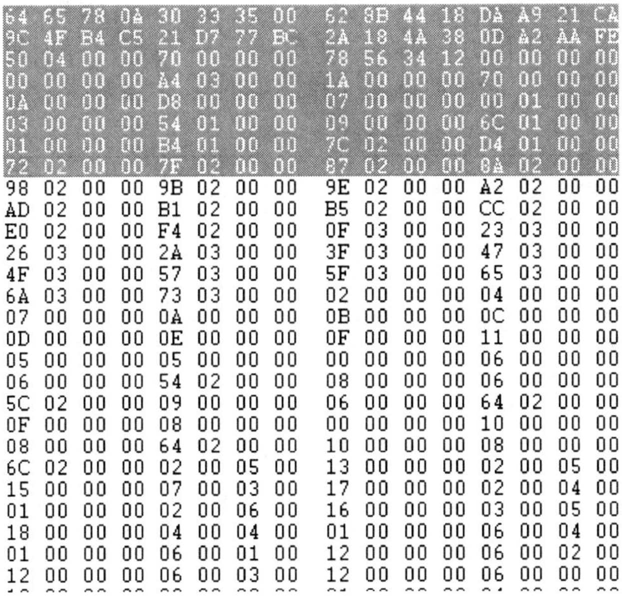

```
64 65 78 0A 30 33 35 00  62 8B 44 18 DA A9 21 CA
9C 4F B4 C5 21 D7 77 BC  2A 18 4A 38 0D A2 AA FE
50 04 00 00 70 00 00 00  78 56 34 12 00 00 00 00
00 00 00 00 A4 03 00 00  1A 00 00 00 70 00 00 00
0A 00 00 00 D8 00 00 00  07 00 00 00 00 01 00 00
03 00 00 00 54 01 00 00  09 00 00 00 6C 01 00 00
01 00 00 00 B4 01 00 00  7C 02 00 00 D4 01 00 00
72 02 00 00 7F 02 00 00  87 02 00 00 8A 02 00 00
98 02 00 00 9B 02 00 00  9E 02 00 00 A2 02 00 00
AD 02 00 00 B1 02 00 00  B5 02 00 00 CC 02 00 00
E0 02 00 00 F4 02 00 00  0F 03 00 00 23 03 00 00
26 03 00 00 2A 03 00 00  3F 03 00 00 47 03 00 00
4F 03 00 00 57 03 00 00  5F 03 00 00 65 03 00 00
6A 03 00 00 73 03 00 00  02 00 00 00 04 00 00 00
07 00 00 00 0A 00 00 00  0B 00 00 00 0C 00 00 00
0D 00 00 00 0E 00 00 00  0F 00 00 00 11 00 00 00
05 00 00 00 05 00 00 00  00 00 00 00 06 00 00 00
06 00 00 00 54 02 00 00  08 00 00 00 06 00 00 00
5C 02 00 00 09 00 00 00  06 00 00 00 64 02 00 00
0F 00 00 00 08 00 00 00  00 00 00 00 10 00 00 00
08 00 00 00 64 02 00 00  10 00 00 00 08 00 00 00
6C 02 00 00 02 00 05 00  13 00 00 00 02 00 05 00
15 00 00 00 07 00 03 00  17 00 00 00 02 00 04 00
01 00 00 00 02 00 06 00  16 00 00 00 03 00 05 00
18 00 00 00 04 00 04 00  01 00 00 00 06 00 04 00
01 00 00 00 06 00 01 00  12 00 00 00 06 00 02 00
12 00 00 00 06 00 03 00  12 00 00 00 06 00 00 00
```

Figure 3-4. *Header fields in* `classes.dex`

Listing 3-5. *DexToXML Output of the* `header` *Section*

```
<root>
<header>
   <magic>dex\n035\0</magic>
   <checksum>628B4418</checksum>
   <signature>DAA921CA9C4FB4C521D777BC2A184A380DA2AAFE</signature>
   <file_size>0x00000450</file_size>
   <header_size>112</header_size>
   <endian_tag>0x12345678</endian_tag>
   <link_size>0</link_size>
   <link_offset>0x00000000</link_offset>
   <map_offset>0x000003A4</map_offset>
   <string_ids_size>26</string_ids_size>
   <string_ids_offset>0x00000070</string_ids_offset>
   <type_ids_size>10</type_ids_size>
   <type_ids_offset>0x000000D8</type_ids_offset>
   <proto_ids_size>7</proto_ids_size>
   <proto_ids_offset>0x00000100</proto_ids_offset>
   <field_ids_size>3</field_ids_size>
   <field_ids_offset>0x00000154</field_ids_offset>
   <method_ids_size>9</method_ids_size>
   <method_ids_offset>0x0000016C</method_ids_offset>
   <class_defs_size>1</class_defs_size>
   <class_defs_offset>0x000001B4</class_defs_offset>
   <data_size>0x0000027C</data_size>
   <data_offset>0x000001D4</data_offset>
</header>
<string_ids />
<type_ids />
<proto_ids />
<field_ids />
<method_ids />
<class_defs />
<data />
<link_data />
</root>
```

Several of these fields require further explanation: `magic`, `checksum`, `header_size`, and `Endian_tag`. The remaining fields in the `header` section are sizes and offsets into other sections.

Magic

The DEX file magic number is the first 8 bytes and is always `64 65 78 0A 30 33 35 00` in hex or the string `dex\n035\0`. The specification mentions that a newline and `\0` are there to prevent certain types of corruption. The `035` is expected to change over time like the major and minor version in the class file.

Checksum

The checksum is an Adler32 checksum of the file, not including the magic number. In the `classes.dex` file in Figure 3-4, the hexadecimal on the first line in the second block is `62 8B 44 18`. But the data is stored little-endian, so the real checksum is reversed and is the value `0x18448B62`.

Header_size

`Header` size is the same for all `classes.dex` files: `0x70`.

Endian_tag

The `endian_tag` in all `classes.dex` files is `0x12345678`, which tells you that the data is stored little-endian (reversed). This won't necessarily always be the case for future DEX files. But for the time being, you can assume it's little-endian.

The string_ids Section

You know from the `header` section that there are `<string_ids_size>26</string_ids_size>` strings in this `classes.dex` file, which you can find at the following address: `<string_ids_offset>0x00000070</string_ids_offset>`. Conveniently, this is at the end of the `header` section. But you already knew that from the header size: `<header_size>0x00000070</header_size>`.

Each of these 26 entries in the `classes.dex` file is an 8 byte address offset or `string_data_off` that points at the actual string in the `data` section. In Figure 3-5, you can see that the first `string_ids` entry is `72 02 00 00`. Remembering that the storage is little-endian, this tells you that the first string can be found at address `0x00000272`, further down the file in the `data` section. The last strings entry is `73 03 00 00`, which tells you that the last string is at an offset or address of `0x00000373`.

```
  0: 64 65 78 0A 30 33 35 00  62 8B 44 18 DA A9 21 CA
 10: 9C 4F B4 C5 21 D7 77 BC  2A 18 4A 38 0D A2 AA FE
 20: 50 04 00 00 70 00 00 00  78 56 34 12 00 00 00 00
 30: 00 00 00 00 A4 03 00 00  1A 00 00 00 70 00 00 00
 40: 0A 00 00 00 D8 00 00 00  07 00 00 00 00 01 00 00
 50: 03 00 00 00 54 01 00 00  09 00 00 00 6C 01 00 00
 60: 01 00 00 00 B4 01 00 00  7C 02 00 00 D4 01 00 00
 70: 72 02 00 00 7F 02 00 00  87 02 00 00 8A 02 00 00
 80: 98 02 00 00 9B 02 00 00  9E 02 00 00 A2 02 00 00
 90: AD 02 00 00 B1 02 00 00  B5 02 00 00 CC 02 00 00
 A0: E0 02 00 00 F4 02 00 00  0F 03 00 00 23 03 00 00
 B0: 26 03 00 00 2A 03 00 00  3F 03 00 00 47 03 00 00
 C0: 4F 03 00 00 57 03 00 00  5F 03 00 00 65 03 00 00
 D0: 6A 03 00 00 73 03 00 00  02 00 00 00 04 00 00 00
 E0: 07 00 00 00 0A 00 00 00  0B 00 00 00 0C 00 00 00
 F0: 0D 00 00 00 0E 00 00 00  0F 00 00 00 11 00 00 00
100: 05 00 00 00 05 00 00 00  00 00 00 00 06 00 00 00
110: 06 00 00 00 54 02 00 00  08 00 00 00 06 00 00 00
120: 5C 02 00 00 09 00 00 00  06 00 00 00 64 02 00 00
130: 0F 00 00 00 08 00 00 00  00 00 00 00 10 00 00 00
140: 08 00 00 00 64 02 00 00  10 00 00 00 08 00 00 00
150: 6C 02 00 00 02 00 05 00  13 00 00 00 02 00 05 00
160: 15 00 00 00 07 00 03 00  17 00 00 00 02 00 04 00
170: 01 00 00 00 02 00 06 00  16 00 00 00 03 00 05 00
180: 18 00 00 00 04 00 04 00  01 00 00 00 06 00 04 00
190: 01 00 00 00 06 00 01 00  12 00 00 00 06 00 02 00
1A0: 12 00 00 00 06 00 03 00  12 00 00 00 06 00 00 00
1B0: 19 00 00 00 02 00 00 00  01 00 00 00 04 00 00 00
1C0: 00 00 00 00 03 00 00 00  00 00 00 00 92 03 00 00
1D0: 8D 03 00 00 01 00 01 00  01 00 00 00 7D 03 00 00
1E0: 04 00 00 00 70 10 03 00  00 00 0E 00 05 00 01 00
1F0: 02 00 00 00 82 03 00 00  2C 00 00 00 12 00 13 01
200: 80 00 35 10 28 00 62 01  02 00 22 02 06 00 70 10
210: 04 00 02 00 1A 03 14 00  6E 20 07 00 32 00 0C 02
```

Figure 3-5. *`string_ids` section of `classes.dex`*

Listing 3-6 shows the `strings_ids` section in XML format as you continue to build out the XML representation of the file.

Listing 3-6. *DexToXML `string_ids` Section*

```
<root>
<header />
<string_ids>
   <string>
       <id>0</id>
       <address>0x00000272</address>
   </string>
   <string>
       <id>1</id>
       <address>0x0000027F</address>
   </string>
```

```
<string>
    <id>2</id>
    <address>0x00000287</address>
</string>
<string>
    <id>3</id>
    <address>0x0000028A</address>
</string>
<string>
    <id>4</id>
    <address>0x00000298</address>
</string>
<string>
    <id>5</id>
    <address>0x0000029B</address>
</string>
<string>
    <id>6</id>
    <address>0x0000029E</address>
</string>
<string>
    <id>7</id>
    <address>0x000002A2</address>
</string>
<string>
    <id>7</id>
    <address>0x000002A2</address>
</string>
<string>
    <id>8</id>
    <address>0x000002AD</address>
</string>
<string>
    <id>9</id>
    <address>0x000002B1</address>
</string>
<string>
    <id>10</id>
    <address>0x000002B5</address>
</string>
<string>
    <id>11</id>
    <address>0x000002CC</address>
</string>
<string>
    <id>12</id>
    <address>0x000002E0</address>
</string>
<string>
    <id>13</id>
```

```
        <address>0x000002F4</address>
    </string>
    <string>
        <id>13</id>
        <address>0x000002F4</address>
    </string>
    <string>
        <id>14</id>
        <address>0x0000030F</address>
    </string>
    <string>
        <id>15</id>
        <address>0x00000323</address>
    </string>
    <string>
        <id>16</id>
        <address>0x00000326</address>
    </string>
    <string>
        <id>17</id>
        <address>0x0000032A</address>
    </string>
    <string>
        <id>18</id>
        <address>0x0000033F</address>
    </string>
    <string>
        <id>19</id>
        <address>0x00000347</address>
    </string>
    <string>
        <id>20</id>
        <address>0x0000034F</address>
    </string>
    <string>
        <id>21</id>
        <address>0x00000357</address>
    </string>
    <string>
        <id>22</id>
        <address>0x0000035F</address>
    </string>
    <string>
        <id>23</id>
        <address>0x00000365</address>
    </string>
    <string>
        <id>24</id>
        <address>0x0000036A</address>
    </string>
```

```
    <string>
        <id>25</id>
        <address>0x00000373</address>
    </string>
</string_ids>
......
</root>
```

Unlike in the class file, the strings aren't intermixed in the constant pool. The `string_ids` section consists entirely of pointers to the strings stored in the `data` section. The strings can be found in the `data` section beginning at `0x00000272` and are also presented in Listing 3-7.

Listing 3-7. *Strings in the* `data` *Section*

```
string[0]:  character
string[1]: <init>
string[2]: C
string[3]: Casting.java
string[4]: I
string[5]: L
string[6]: LC
string[7]: LCasting;
string[8]: LI
string[9]: LL
string[10]: Ljava/io/PrintStream;
string[11]: Ljava/lang/Object;
string[12]: Ljava/lang/String;
string[13]: Ljava/lang/StringBuilder;
string[14]: Ljava/lang/System;
string[15]: V
string[16]: VL
string[17]: [Ljava/lang/String;
string[18]: append
string[19]: ascStr
string[20]: ascii
string[21]: chrStr
string[22]: main
string[23]: out
string[24]: println
string[25]: toString
```

The type_ids Section

The `header` section tells you there are 10 `type_ids` that start at an offset of 0x000000D8 (Listing 3-8). The first `type_id`, as you can see in Figure 3-6, is `02 00 00 00`. That points to `string_id[2]`, which points to `C` in the `data` section (see `strings_ids`). The remaining `type_ids` fall out in a similar fashion.

```
  0: 64 65 78 0A 30 33 35 00  62 8B 44 18 DA A9 21 CA
 10: 9C 4F B4 C5 21 D7 77 BC  2A 18 4A 38 0D A2 AA FE
 20: 50 04 00 00 70 00 00 00  78 56 34 12 00 00 00 00
 30: 00 00 00 00 A4 03 00 00  1A 00 00 00 70 00 00 00
 40: 0A 00 00 00 D8 00 00 00  07 00 00 00 00 01 00 00
 50: 03 00 00 00 54 01 00 00  09 00 00 00 6C 01 00 00
 60: 01 00 00 00 B4 01 00 00  7C 02 00 00 D4 01 00 00
 70: 72 02 00 00 7F 02 00 00  87 02 00 00 8A 02 00 00
 80: 98 02 00 00 9B 02 00 00  9E 02 00 00 A2 02 00 00
 90: AD 02 00 00 B1 02 00 00  B5 02 00 00 CC 02 00 00
 A0: E0 02 00 00 F4 02 00 00  0F 03 00 00 23 03 00 00
 B0: 26 03 00 00 2A 03 00 00  3F 03 00 00 47 03 00 00
 C0: 4F 03 00 00 57 03 00 00  5F 03 00 00 65 03 00 00
 D0: 6A 03 00 00 73 03 00 00  02 00 00 00 04 00 00 00
 E0: 07 00 00 00 0A 00 00 00  0B 00 00 00 0C 00 00 00
 F0: 0D 00 00 00 0E 00 00 00  0F 00 00 00 11 00 00 00
100: 05 00 00 00 05 00 00 00  00 00 00 00 06 00 00 00
110: 06 00 00 00 54 02 00 00  08 00 00 00 06 00 00 00
120: 5C 02 00 00 09 00 00 00  06 00 00 00 64 02 00 00
130: 0F 00 00 00 08 00 00 00  00 00 00 00 10 00 00 00
140: 08 00 00 00 64 02 00 00  10 00 00 00 08 00 00 00
150: 6C 02 00 00 02 00 05 00  13 00 00 00 02 00 05 00
160: 15 00 00 00 07 00 03 00  17 00 00 00 02 00 04 00
170: 01 00 00 00 02 00 06 00  16 00 00 00 03 00 05 00
180: 18 00 00 00 04 00 04 00  01 00 00 00 06 00 04 00
190: 01 00 00 00 06 00 01 00  12 00 00 00 06 00 02 00
1A0: 12 00 00 00 06 00 03 00  12 00 00 00 06 00 00 00
1B0: 19 00 00 00 02 00 00 00  01 00 00 00 04 00 00 00
1C0: 00 00 00 00 03 00 00 00  00 00 00 00 92 03 00 00
1D0: 8D 03 00 00 01 00 01 00  01 00 00 00 7D 03 00 00
1E0: 04 00 00 00 70 10 03 00  00 00 0E 00 05 00 01 00
1F0: 02 00 00 00 82 03 00 00  2C 00 00 00 12 00 13 01
```

Figure 3-6. *type_ids section of classes.dex*

Listing 3-8. *DexToXML type_ids Section*

```
<root>
<header />
<string_ids />
<type_ids>
   <type>
      <id>0</id>
      <string_id>2</string_id>
   </type>
   <type>
      <id>1</id>
      <string_id>4</string_id>
   </type>
   <type>
      <id>3</id>
      <string_id>10</string_id>
   </type>
```

```
    <type>
        <id>4</id>
        <string_id>11</string_id>
    </type>
    <type>
        <id>5</id>
        <string_id>12</string_id>
    </type>
    <type>
        <id>6</id>
        <string_id>13</string_id>
    </type>
    <type>
        <id>7</id>
        <string_id>14</string_id>
    </type>
    <type>
        <id>8</id>
        <string_id>15</string_id>
    </type>
    <type>
        <id>9</id>
        <string_id>17</string_id>
    </type>
</type_ids>
...
</root>
```

As you saw in the last section, the strings are found in the `data` section at the offset or address given in the `string_ids` section. I've pulled out the strings that are `type_ids` so you can more easily follow the reverse-engineering process; see Listing 3-9.

Listing 3-9. *Types in the `data` Section*

```
type[0]: C
type[1]: I
type[2]: LCasting;
type[3]: Ljava/io/PrintStream;
type[4]: Ljava/lang/Object;
type[5]: Ljava/lang/String;
type[6]: Ljava/lang/StringBuilder;
type[7]: Ljava/lang/System;
type[8]: V
type[9]: [Ljava/lang/String;
```

The proto_ids Section

`Proto_ids` contain the prototype methods in `Casting.java`. The DVM uses the `Proto_ids` together with the relevant `type_ids` to assemble the `method_ids`. Figure 3-7 shows once again where these are located in the `classes.dex` file.

Each `proto_id` has three parts, shown in the `ProtoID` struct in Listing 3-10. These are pointers to the `string_id` for the short description or ShortyDescriptor (see Table 2-2) of the `method` parameter, a pointer to the `type_id` for the return type, and an address offset into the `data` section to find the parameter list.

```
  0: 64 65 78 0A 30 33 35 00  62 8B 44 18 DA A9 21 CA
 10: 9C 4F B4 C5 21 D7 77 BC  2A 18 4A 38 0D A2 AA FE
 20: 50 04 00 00 70 00 00 00  78 56 34 12 00 00 00 00
 30: 00 00 00 00 A4 03 00 00  1A 00 00 00 70 00 00 00
 40: 0A 00 00 00 D8 00 00 00  07 00 00 00 00 01 00 00
 50: 03 00 00 00 54 01 00 00  09 00 00 00 6C 01 00 00
 60: 01 00 00 00 B4 01 00 00  7C 02 00 00 D4 01 00 00
 70: 72 02 00 00 7F 02 00 00  87 02 00 00 8A 02 00 00
 80: 98 02 00 00 9B 02 00 00  9E 02 00 00 A2 02 00 00
 90: AD 02 00 00 B1 02 00 00  B5 02 00 00 CC 02 00 00
 A0: E0 02 00 00 F4 02 00 00  0F 03 00 00 23 03 00 00
 B0: 26 03 00 00 2A 03 00 00  3F 03 00 00 47 03 00 00
 C0: 4F 03 00 00 57 03 00 00  5F 03 00 00 65 03 00 00
 D0: 6A 03 00 00 73 03 00 00  02 00 00 00 04 00 00 00
 E0: 07 00 00 00 0A 00 00 00  0B 00 00 00 0C 00 00 00
 F0: 0D 00 00 00 0E 00 00 00  0F 00 00 00 11 00 00 00
100: 05 00 00 00 05 00 00 00  00 00 00 00 06 00 00 00
110: 06 00 00 00 54 02 00 00  08 00 00 00 06 00 00 00
120: 5C 02 00 00 09 00 00 00  06 00 00 00 64 02 00 00
130: 0F 00 00 00 08 00 00 00  00 00 00 00 10 00 00 00
140: 00 00 00 00 64 02 00 00  10 00 00 00 08 00 00 00
150: 6C 02 00 00 02 00 05 00  13 00 00 00 02 00 05 00
160: 15 00 00 00 07 00 03 00  17 00 00 00 02 00 04 00
170: 01 00 00 00 02 00 06 00  16 00 00 00 03 00 05 00
180: 18 00 00 00 04 00 04 00  01 00 00 00 06 00 04 00
190: 01 00 00 00 06 00 01 00  12 00 00 00 06 00 02 00
1A0: 12 00 00 00 06 00 03 00  12 00 00 00 06 00 00 00
1B0: 19 00 00 00 02 00 00 00  01 00 00 00 04 00 00 00
1C0: 00 00 00 00 03 00 00 00  00 00 00 00 92 03 00 00
1D0: 8D 03 00 00 01 00 01 00  01 00 00 00 7D 03 00 00
1E0: 04 00 00 00 70 10 03 00  00 00 0E 00 05 00 01 00
```

Figure 3-7. *proto_ids section of classes.dex*

Listing 3-10. *proto_id Struct*

```
ProtoID{
uint    shorty_idx,
uint    return_type_idx,
uint    parameters_off
}
```

In this example, there are seven `proto_ids` according to the `header` file. These are shown in DexToXML in Listing 3-11; the prototypes themselves are shown in Listing 3-12.

Listing 3-11. *DexToXML* `proto_ids` *Section*

```
<root>
<header />
<string_ids />
<type_ids />
<proto_ids>
   <proto>
       <id>0</id>
       <string_id>5</string_id>
       <type_id>5</type_id>
       <address>0x0</address>
   </proto>
   <proto>
       <id>1</id>
       <string_id>6</string_id>
       <type_id>6</type_id>
       <address>0x254</address>
   </proto>
   <proto>
       <id>2</id>
       <string_id>8</string_id>
       <type_id>6</type_id>
       <address>0x25c</address>
   </proto>
   <proto>
       <id>3</id>
       <string_id>9</string_id>
       <type_id>6</type_id>
       <address>0x264</address>
   </proto>
   <proto>
       <id>4</id>
       <string_id>15</string_id>
       <type_id>8</type_id>
       <data_off>0x0</data_off>
   </proto>
   <proto>
       <id>5</id>
       <string_id>10</string_id>
       <type_id>8</type_id>
       <address>0x264</address>
   </proto>
   <proto>
       <id>6</id>
       <string_id>10</string_id>
```

```
        <type_id>8</type_id>
        <address>0x26c</address>
    </proto>
</proto_ids>
....
</root>
```

Listing 3-12 shows the prototypes from the `data` section.

Listing 3-12. ***Prototypes in the*** `data` ***Section***

```
proto[0]: Ljava/lang/String; proto(  )
proto[1]: Ljava/lang/StringBuilder; proto( C )
proto[2]: Ljava/lang/StringBuilder; proto( I )
proto[3]: Ljava/lang/StringBuilder; proto( Ljava/lang/String; )
proto[4]: V proto(  )
proto[5]: V proto( Ljava/lang/String; )
Proto[6]: V proto( Ljava/lang/String; )
```

The field_ids Section

Next up are the `field_ids`. Each `field_id` has three parts: the name of the class, the type of the field, and the name of the field. Listing 3-13 shows this in a struct format.

Listing 3-13. `field_id` ***Struct***

```
FieldID{
ushort  class_idx,
ushort  type_idx,
uint     name_idx
}
```

Figure 3-8 shows the location of the `field_ids` section in the `classes.dex` file.

```
  0: 64 65 78 0A 30 33 35 00  62 8B 44 18 DA A9 21 CA
 10: 9C 4F B4 C5 21 D7 77 BC  2A 18 4A 38 0D A2 AA FE
 20: 50 04 00 00 70 00 00 00  78 56 34 12 00 00 00 00
 30: 00 00 00 00 A4 03 00 00  1A 00 00 00 70 00 00 00
 40: 0A 00 00 00 D8 00 00 00  07 00 00 00 00 01 00 00
 50: 03 00 00 00 54 01 00 00  09 00 00 00 6C 01 00 00
 60: 01 00 00 00 B4 01 00 00  7C 02 00 00 D4 01 00 00
 70: 72 02 00 00 7F 02 00 00  87 02 00 00 8A 02 00 00
 80: 98 02 00 00 9B 02 00 00  9E 02 00 00 A2 02 00 00
 90: AD 02 00 00 B1 02 00 00  B5 02 00 00 CC 02 00 00
 A0: E0 02 00 00 F4 02 00 00  0F 03 00 00 23 03 00 00
 B0: 26 03 00 00 2A 03 00 00  3F 03 00 00 47 03 00 00
 C0: 4F 03 00 00 57 03 00 00  5F 03 00 00 65 03 00 00
 D0: 6A 03 00 00 73 03 00 00  02 00 00 00 04 00 00 00
 E0: 07 00 00 00 0A 00 00 00  0B 00 00 00 0C 00 00 00
 F0: 0D 00 00 00 0E 00 00 00  0F 00 00 00 11 00 00 00
100: 05 00 00 00 05 00 00 00  00 00 00 00 06 00 00 00
110: 06 00 00 00 54 02 00 00  08 00 00 00 06 00 00 00
120: 5C 02 00 00 09 00 00 00  06 00 00 00 64 02 00 00
130: 0F 00 00 00 08 00 00 00  00 00 00 00 10 00 00 00
140: 08 00 00 00 64 02 00 00  10 00 00 00 08 00 00 00
150: 6C 02 00 00 02 00 05 00  13 00 00 00 02 00 05 00
160: 15 00 00 00 07 00 03 00  17 00 00 00 02 00 04 00
170: 01 00 00 00 02 00 06 00  16 00 00 00 03 00 05 00
180: 18 00 00 00 04 00 04 00  01 00 00 00 06 00 04 00
190: 01 00 00 00 06 00 01 00  12 00 00 00 06 00 02 00
1A0: 12 00 00 00 06 00 03 00  12 00 00 00 06 00 00 00
1B0: 19 00 00 00 02 00 00 00  01 00 00 00 04 00 00 00
1C0: 00 00 00 00 03 00 00 00  00 00 00 00 92 03 00 00
1D0: 8D 03 00 00 01 00 01 00  01 00 00 00 7D 03 00 00
1E0: 04 00 00 00 70 10 03 00  00 00 0E 00 05 00 01 00
1F0: 02 00 00 00 82 03 00 00  2C 00 00 00 12 00 13 01
200: 80 00 35 10 28 00 62 01  02 00 22 02 06 00 70 10
210: 04 00 02 00 1A 03 14 00  6E 20 07 00 32 00 0C 02
220: 6E 20 06 00 02 00 0C 02  1A 03 00 00 6E 20 07 00
```

Figure 3-8. *`field_ids` section of `classes.dex`*

In this example, there are three `fields_ids` according to the `header` file. These are shown in DexToXML in Listing 3-14, and the fields themselves are shown in Listing 3-15.

Listing 3-14. *DexToXML `field_ids` Section*

```
<root>
<header />
<string_ids />
<type_ids />
<proto_ids />
<fields>
   <field>
       <id>0</id>
       <type_id>2</type_id>
```

```
        <type_id>5/type_id>
        <string_id>19</string_id>
    </field>
    <field>
        <id>1</id>
        <type_id>2</type_id>
        <type_id>5</type_id>
        <string_id>21</string_id>
    </field>
    <field>
        <id>2/id>
        <type_id>7</type_id>
        <type_id>3</type_id>
        <string_id>23</string_id>
    </field>
</fields>
...
</root>
```

In this section, you can assemble the fields from the information in the previous `string_ids` and `type_ids` sections. For `field [0]`, you can see that the name of the class is `type_id[2]` or `Casting`, the type of the field is `type_id[5]` or `string`, and the name of the field is `string_id[19]` or `ascStr`:

```
type_id[2] = LCasting;
type_id[5] = Ljava/lang/String;
string_id[19] = ascStr
```

Listing 3-15 shows this and the similarly resolved remaining fields.

Listing 3-15. ***Fields Information***

```
field_ids[0]: Casting.ascStr:Ljava/lang/String;
field_ids[1]: Casting.chrStr:Ljava/lang/String;
field_ids[2]: java.lang.System.out:Ljava/io/PrintStream;
```

The method_ids Section

Each `method_id` has three parts: the name of the class, the prototype of the method from the `proto_ids` section, and the name of the method. Listing 3-16 shows this in a struct format.

Listing 3-16. *`method_id`* ***Struct***

```
MethodIDStruct{
ushort  class_idx,
ushort  proto_idx,
uint      name_idx
}
```

Figure 3-9 shows the location of the `method_ids` section in the `classes.dex` file.

```
  0: 64 65 78 0A 30 33 35 00  62 8B 44 18 DA A9 21 CA
 10: 9C 4F B4 C5 21 D7 77 BC  2A 18 4A 38 0D A2 AA FE
 20: 50 04 00 00 70 00 00 00  78 56 34 12 00 00 00 00
 30: 00 00 00 00 A4 03 00 00  1A 00 00 00 70 00 00 00
 40: 0A 00 00 00 D8 00 00 00  07 00 00 00 00 01 00 00
 50: 03 00 00 00 54 01 00 00  09 00 00 00 6C 01 00 00
 60: 01 00 00 00 B4 01 00 00  7C 02 00 00 D4 01 00 00
 70: 72 02 00 00 7F 02 00 00  87 02 00 00 8A 02 00 00
 80: 98 02 00 00 9B 02 00 00  9E 02 00 00 A2 02 00 00
 90: AD 02 00 00 B1 02 00 00  B5 02 00 00 CC 02 00 00
 A0: E0 02 00 00 F4 02 00 00  0F 03 00 00 23 03 00 00
 B0: 26 03 00 00 2A 03 00 00  3F 03 00 00 47 03 00 00
 C0: 4F 03 00 00 57 03 00 00  5F 03 00 00 65 03 00 00
 D0: 6A 03 00 00 73 03 00 00  02 00 00 00 04 00 00 00
 E0: 07 00 00 00 0A 00 00 00  0B 00 00 00 0C 00 00 00
 F0: 0D 00 00 00 0E 00 00 00  0F 00 00 00 11 00 00 00
100: 05 00 00 00 05 00 00 00  00 00 00 00 06 00 00 00
110: 06 00 00 00 54 02 00 00  08 00 00 00 06 00 00 00
120: 5C 02 00 00 09 00 00 00  06 00 00 00 64 02 00 00
130: 0F 00 00 00 08 00 00 00  00 00 00 00 10 00 00 00
140: 08 00 00 00 64 02 00 00  10 00 00 00 08 00 00 00
150: 6C 02 00 00 02 00 05 00  13 00 00 00 02 00 05 00
160: 15 00 00 00 07 00 03 00  17 00 00 00 02 00 04 00
170: 01 00 00 00 02 00 06 00  16 00 00 00 03 00 05 00
180: 18 00 00 00 04 00 04 00  01 00 00 00 06 00 04 00
190: 01 00 00 00 06 00 01 00  12 00 00 00 06 00 02 00
1A0: 12 00 00 00 06 00 03 00  12 00 00 00 06 00 00 00
1B0: 19 00 00 00 02 00 00 00  01 00 00 00 04 00 00 00
1C0: 00 00 00 00 03 00 00 00  00 00 00 00 92 03 00 00
1D0: 8D 03 00 00 01 00 01 00  01 00 00 00 7D 03 00 00
1E0: 04 00 00 00 70 10 03 00  00 00 0E 00 05 00 01 00
1F0: 02 00 00 00 82 03 00 00  2C 00 00 00 12 00 13 01
200: 80 00 35 10 28 00 62 01  02 00 22 02 06 00 70 10
210: 04 00 02 00 1A 03 14 00  6E 20 07 00 32 00 0C 02
220: 6E 20 06 00 02 00 0C 02  1A 03 00 00 6E 20 07 00
230: 32 00 0C 02 6E 20 05 00  02 00 0C 02 6E 10 08 00
240: 02 00 0C 02 6E 20 02 00  21 00 D8 00 00 01 8E 00
250: 28 D7 0E 00 01 00 00 00  00 00 00 00 01 00 00 00
```

Figure 3-9. *`method_ids` section of `classes.dex`*

In this example, there are nine `method_ids` according to the `header` file. These are shown in DexToXML in Listing 3-17, and the methods themselves are shown in Listing 3-18.

Listing 3-17. *DexToXML `method_ids` Section*

```
<root>
<header />
<string_ids />
<type_ids />
```

```
<proto_ids />
<fields />
<methods>
   <method>
       <id>0</id>
       <type_id>2</type_id>
       <proto_id>4</proto_id>
       <string_id>1</string_id>
   </method>
   <method>
       <id>1</id>
       <type_id>2</type_id>
       <proto_id>6</proto_id>
       <string_id>22</string_id>
   </method>
   <method>
       <id>2</id>
       <type_id>3</type_id>
       <proto_id>5</proto_id>
       <string_id>24</string_id>
   </method>
   <method>
       <id>3</id>
       <type_id>4</type_id>
       <proto_id>4</proto_id>
       <string_id>1</string_id>
   </method>
   <method>
       <id>4</id>
       <type_id>6</type_id>
       <proto_id>4</proto_id>
       <string_id>1</string_id>
   </method>
   <method>
       <id>5</id>
       <type_id>6</type_id>
       <proto_id>1</proto_id>
       <string_id>18</string_id>
   </method>
   <method>
       <id>6</id>
       <type_id>6</type_id>
       <proto_id>2</proto_id>
       <string_id>18</string_id>
   </method>
   <method>
       <id>7</id>
       <type_id>6</type_id>
       <proto_id>3</proto_id>
       <string_id>18</string_id>
```

```
    </method>
    <method>
        <id>8</id>
        <type_id>6</type_id>
        <proto_id>0</proto_id>
        <string_id>25</string_id>
    </method>
</methods>
</root>
```


You can manually assemble the methods from the information in the previous sections without having to go to the data section. For method [0], the name of the class is type_id[2] or LCasting, the prototype of the method is proto_id[4] or V proto (), and the name of the method is string_id[1[<init>:

```
type_id[2] = LCasting;
proto_id[4] = V proto( )
string_id[1] = <init>
```

Listing 3-18 shows this and the similarly resolved remaining methods.

Listing 3-18. *Methods*

```
method[0]: Casting.<init> (<init>()V)
method[1]: Casting.main (main([Ljava/lang/String;)V)
method[2]: java.io.PrintStream.println (println(Ljava/lang/String;)V)
method[3]: java.lang.Object.<init> (<init>()V)
method[4]: java.lang.StringBuilder.<init> (<init>()V)
method[5]: java.lang.StringBuilder.append (append(C)Ljava/lang/StringBuilder;)
method[6]: java.lang.StringBuilder.append (append(I)Ljava/lang/StringBuilder;)
method[7]: java.lang.StringBuilder.append
(append(Ljava/lang/String;)Ljava/lang/StringBuilder;)
method[8]: java.lang.StringBuilder.toString (toString()Ljava/lang/String;)
```

The class_defs Section

Each class_def has eight parts: the id of the class, the access_flags of the class, a type_id for the superclass, an address for the interfaces list, a string_id for the source file name, another address for any annotations (which aren't relevant for reverse-engineering source code), an address for the class data (where you can find more class information), and a final address where you can find the data with the initial values of any static fields. Listing 3-19 shows this in a struct format.

Listing 3-19. *class_defs Struct*

```
ClassDefsStruct {
uint class_idx,
uint access_flags,
uint superclass_idx,
uint interfaces_off,
uint source_file_idx,
uint annotations_off,
uint class_data_off,
uint static_values_off,
}
```

Figure 3-10 shows the location of the `class_defs` section in the `classes.dex` file.

```
 B0: 26 03 00 00 2A 03 00 00  3F 03 00 00 47 03 00 00
 C0: 4F 03 00 00 57 03 00 00  5F 03 00 00 65 03 00 00
 D0: 6A 03 00 00 73 03 00 00  02 00 00 00 04 00 00 00
 E0: 07 00 00 00 0A 00 00 00  0B 00 00 00 0C 00 00 00
 F0: 0D 00 00 00 0E 00 00 00  0F 00 00 00 11 00 00 00
100: 05 00 00 00 05 00 00 00  00 00 00 00 06 00 00 00
110: 06 00 00 00 54 02 00 00  08 00 00 00 06 00 00 00
120: 5C 02 00 00 09 00 00 00  06 00 00 00 64 02 00 00
130: 0F 00 00 00 08 00 00 00  00 00 00 00 10 00 00 00
140: 08 00 00 00 64 02 00 00  10 00 00 00 08 00 00 00
150: 6C 02 00 00 02 00 05 00  13 00 00 00 02 00 05 00
160: 15 00 00 00 07 00 03 00  17 00 00 00 02 00 04 00
170: 01 00 00 00 02 00 06 00  16 00 00 00 03 00 05 00
180: 18 00 00 00 04 00 04 00  01 00 00 00 06 00 04 00
190: 01 00 00 00 06 00 01 00  12 00 00 00 06 00 02 00
1A0: 12 00 00 00 06 00 03 00  12 00 00 00 06 00 00 00
1B0: 19 00 00 00 02 00 00 00  01 00 00 00 04 00 00 00
1C0: 00 00 00 00 03 00 00 00  00 00 00 00 92 03 00 00
1D0: 8D 03 00 00 01 00 01 00  01 00 00 00 7D 03 00 00
1E0: 04 00 00 00 70 10 03 00  00 00 0E 00 05 00 01 00
1F0: 02 00 00 00 82 03 00 00  2C 00 00 00 12 00 13 01
200: 80 00 35 10 28 00 62 01  02 00 22 02 06 00 70 10
210: 04 00 02 00 1A 03 14 00  6E 20 07 00 32 00 0C 02
220: 6E 20 06 00 02 00 0C 02  1A 03 00 00 6E 20 07 00
230: 32 00 0C 02 6E 20 05 00  02 00 0C 02 6E 10 08 00
240: 02 00 0C 02 6E 20 02 00  21 00 D8 00 00 01 8E 00
250: 28 D7 0E 00 01 00 00 00  00 00 00 00 01 00 00 00
260: 01 00 00 00 01 00 00 00  05 00 00 00 01 00 00 00
270: 09 00 0B 20 63 68 61 72  61 63 74 65 72 20 00 06
```

Figure 3-10. *class_defs section of classes.dex*

In this example there is only one class, shown in DexToXML in Listing 3-20.

Listing 3-20. *DexToXML* `class_defs` *Section*

```
<root>
<header />
<string_ids />
<type_ids />
<proto_ids />
<fields />
<methods />
<classes>
   <class>
       <id>0</id>
       <type_id>2</type_id>
       <access_flags>
          <access_flag>public</access_flag>
       </access_flags>
       <type_id>4</type_id>
       <address>0x0</address>
       <string_id>3</string_id>
       <address>0x0</address>
       <address>0x00000392</address>
       <address>0x0000038D</address>
   </class>
</classes>
...
</root>
```

In `classes.dex`, the `access_flags` value for the class `Casting` is `0x00000001`. Table 3-2 lists the conversions for access flags; in this case, the access flag is `public`.

Table 3-2. *Access Flags*

Name	Value	For Classes	For Fields	For Methods
ACC_PUBLIC	0x1	public	public	public
ACC_PRIVATE	0x2	private	private	private
ACC_PROTECTED	0x4	protected	protected	protected
ACC_STATIC	0x8	static	static	static
ACC_FINAL	0x10	final	final	final
ACC_SYNCHRONIZED	0x20			synchronized

Name	Value	For Classes	For Fields	For Methods
ACC_VOLATILE	0x40		volatile	
ACC_BRIDGE	0x40			
ACC_TRANSIENT	0x80		transient	
ACC_VARARGS	0x80			Variable method args
ACC_NATIVE	0x100			native
ACC_INTERFACE	0x200	interface		
ACC_ABSTRACT	0x400	abstract		abstract
ACC_STRICT	0x800			strictfp
ACC_SYNTHETIC	0x1000			
ACC_ANNOTATION	0x2000			
ACC_ENUM	0x4000			
(Unused)	0x8000			
ACC_CONSTRUCTOR	0x10000			constructor
ACC_DECLARED_SYNCHRONIZED	0x20000			

By manually assembling the Java code you can see that the class is defined as public class Casting from type_id[2], the superclass is java/Lang/Object from type_id[4], and the source file is Casting.java from string_id[3]:

```
access_flags = public
type_id[2] = LCasting;
type_id[4] = Ljava/lang/Object;
string_id[3] = Casting.java
```

The data Section

You're now in the data section, which is the real meat of classes.dex. The earlier information has led to this point. And you have a choice as you parse the remainder of the file: you can either parse it sequentially or begin following the addresses in the data offsets to find the bytecodes you want to decompile.

The most obvious thing to do is to follow the data offsets, so let's try that approach. First on the agenda is class_data_item from class_defs, given that you're looking for the bytecode. The class_data_item section contains information about the fields and methods; this is followed by the code_item section, which has the bytecode.

class_data_item

From disassembling class_defs, you know that the address of the only class in this file, Casting.java, is 0x392. The information is in a class_data_item structure, similar to Listing 3-21.

Listing 3-21. *class_data_item* ***Struct***

```
ClassDataItemStruct {
uleb128                               static_fields_size,
uleb128                               instance_fields_size,
uleb128                               direct_method_size,
uleb128                               virtual_method_size,
encoded_field[static_fields_size]     static_fields,
encoded_field[instance_fields_size]   instance_fields,
encoded_method[direct_fields_size]    direct_methods,
encoded_method[virtual_fields_size]   virtual_methods
}
```

Uleb128 is an unsigned little-endian base 128 encoding format for storing large integers. To convert an integer to uleb128, you convert it to binary, pad it to a multiple of 7 bits, split it into seven bit groups, add a high 1 bit on all but the last group to form bytes (that is, 8 bits), convert to hexadecimal, and then flip the result to be little-endian. This makes a lot more sense if you look at an example. The following example comes from Wikipedia (http://en.wikipedia.org/wiki/LEB128):

```
10011000011101100101         In raw binary
010011000011101100101        Padded to a multiple of 7 bits
0100110  0001110  1100101    Split into 7-bit groups
00100110 10001110 11100101   Add high 1 bits on all but last group to form
bytes
0x26     0x8E     0xE5              In hexadecimal
```

```
0xE5 0x8E 0x26                    Output stream
```

Thanks to the small integer in the example, the conversion is much easier: `0x2` in uleb128 is `2`.

There are two other structures for `encoded_field` and `encoded_method`, which take the format shown in Listings 3-22 and 3-23. `Field_idx_diff` is unusual in that although the first entry is the direct `field_id[]` reference, any subsequent `field_id[]` entries are listed as the difference from the previous listed `field_id`. `Method_idx_diff` follows the same pattern.

Listing 3-22. *encoded_field* **Struct**

```
EncodedFieldStruct{
        uleb128     field_idx_diff, (explain that it's diff and directly for the
first)
        uleb128     access_flags
}
```

Listing 3-23. *encoded_method* **Struct**

```
EncodedMethodStruct{
        uleb128     method_idx_diff, (explain that it's diff and directly for the
first)
        uleb128     access_flags,
        uleb128     code_off
}
```

Figure 3-11 shows where you are in the `classes.dex` file: right in the middle of the `data` section.

```
360: 6D 61 69 6E 00 03 6F 75  74 00 07 70 72 69 6E 74
370: 6C 6E 00 08 74 6F 53 74  72 69 6E 67 00 01 00 07
380: 0E 00 08 01 00 07 0E 5A  01 22 0D 4D 00 02 17 14
390: 17 00 02 00 02 00 00 18  01 18 00 81 80 04 D4 03
3A0: 01 09 EC 03 0E 00 00 00  00 00 00 00 01 00 00 00
3B0: 00 00 00 00 01 00 00 00  1A 00 00 00 70 00 00 00
3C0: 02 00 00 00 0A 00 00 00  D8 00 00 00 03 00 00 00
3D0: 07 00 00 00 00 01 00 00  04 00 00 00 03 00 00 00
3E0: 54 01 00 00 05 00 00 00  09 00 00 00 6C 01 00 00
3F0: 06 00 00 00 01 00 00 00  B4 01 00 00 01 20 00 00
400: 02 00 00 00 D4 01 00 00  01 10 00 00 04 00 00 00
410: 54 02 00 00 02 20 00 00  1A 00 00 00 72 02 00 00
420: 03 20 00 00 02 00 00 00  7D 03 00 00 05 20 00 00
430: 01 00 00 00 8D 03 00 00  00 20 00 00 01 00 00 00
440: 92 03 00 00 00 10 00 00  01 00 00 00 A4 03 00 00
```

Figure 3-11. `class_data_item` **section of** `classes.dex`

Listing 3-24 shows the DexToXML output for the `class_defs` section.

Listing 3-24. *DexToXML* `class_defs`

```
<root>
<header />
<string_ids />
<type_ids />
<proto_ids />
<fields />
<methods />
<classes />
<data>
   <class_data_items>
       <class_data_item>
          <static_field_size>2</static_field_size>
          <instance_field_size>0</instance_field_size>
          <direct_method_size>2</direct_method_size>
          <virtual_method_size>0</virtual_method_size>
          <static_fields>
              <static_field>
                 <id>0</id>
                 <field_id>0</field_id>
                 <access_flags>
                     <access_flag>static</access_flag>
                     <access_flag>final</access_flag>
                 </access_flags>
              </static_field>
              <static_field>
                 <id>1</id>
                 <field_id>1</field_id>
                 <access_flags>
                     <access_flag>static</access_flag>
                     <access_flag>final</access_flag>
                 </access_flags>
              </static_field>
          </static_fields>
          <instance_methods />
          <direct_methods>
              <direct_method>
                 <id>0</id>
                 <method_id>0</method_id>
                 <access_flags>
                     <access_flag>public</access_flag>
                     <access_flag>constructor</access_flag>
                 </access_flags>
                 <address>0x1d4</address>
              </direct_method>
              <direct_method>
                 <id>1</id>
                 <method_id>1</method_id>
                 <access_flags>
```

```
                    <access_flag>public</access_flag>
                    <access_flag>static</access_flag>
                </access_flags>
                <address>0x1ec</address>
            </direct_method>
        </direct_methods>
        <virtual_methods />
    </data>
</root>
```

Manually assembling the information, you can see the static field and method information shown here:

```
static_field[0]
        field[0]: Casting.ascStr:Ljava/lang/String;
        access_flags = static & final
static_field[1]
        field[1]: Casting.chrStr:Ljava/lang/String;
        access_flags = static & final
direct_method[0]
        method[0]: Casting.<init> (<init>()V)
        access_flags = public & constructor
        code_offset = 0x00001d4
direct_method[1]
        method[1]: Casting.main (main([Ljava/lang/String;)V)
        access_flags = public & static
        code_offset = 0x00001ec
```

You now have all the information about the methods and fields in your class; in case it's not obvious, you're re-creating the `Casting.java` code from the outside in. You should also take special note of the `code_offset`, because that's where the bytecode resides that will be used to re-create the source code. That's where you're going next.

code_item

`class_data_item` told you that `code_item` begins at `0x1d4` for the first `<init>` method and `0x1ec` for the main method. The information is in a `code_item` structure, similar to Listing 3-25.

Listing 3-25. *code_item* **Struct**

```
CodeItemStruct {
ushort                                  registers_size,
ushort                                  ins_size,
ushort                                  outs_size,
ushort                                  tries_size,
uint                                    debug_info_off,
```

```
uint                                    insns_size,
ushort[insns_size]                      insns,
ushort                                  padding,
try_item[tries_size]                    tries,
encoded_catch_handler_list              handlers
}
```

It took some time getting here, but pay special attention to the `insns` element in `CodeItemStruct`: that is where `classes.dex` stores the bytecode instructions.

Figure 3-12 shows the location of the `code_item` sections (`init` and `main`) in the `classes.dex` file. This highlighted area is for both `code_items`, which are stored one after the other.

```
  0: 64 65 78 0A 30 33 35 00  62 8B 44 18 DA A9 21 CA
 10: 9C 4F B4 C5 21 D7 77 BC  2A 18 4A 38 0D A2 AA FE
 20: 50 04 00 00 70 00 00 00  78 56 34 12 00 00 00 00
 30: 00 00 00 00 A4 03 00 00  1A 00 00 00 70 00 00 00
 40: 0A 00 00 00 D8 00 00 00  07 00 00 00 00 01 00 00
 50: 03 00 00 00 54 01 00 00  09 00 00 00 6C 01 00 00
 60: 01 00 00 00 B4 01 00 00  7C 02 00 00 D4 01 00 00
 70: 72 02 00 00 7F 02 00 00  87 02 00 00 8A 02 00 00
 80: 98 02 00 00 9B 02 00 00  9E 02 00 00 A2 02 00 00
 90: AD 02 00 00 B1 02 00 00  B5 02 00 00 CC 02 00 00
 A0: E0 02 00 00 F4 02 00 00  0F 03 00 00 23 03 00 00
 B0: 26 03 00 00 2A 03 00 00  3F 03 00 00 47 03 00 00
 C0: 4F 03 00 00 57 03 00 00  5F 03 00 00 65 03 00 00
 D0: 6A 03 00 00 73 03 00 00  02 00 00 00 04 00 00 00
 E0: 07 00 00 00 0A 00 00 00  0B 00 00 00 0C 00 00 00
 F0: 0D 00 00 00 0E 00 00 00  0F 00 00 00 11 00 00 00
100: 05 00 00 00 05 00 00 00  00 00 00 00 06 00 00 00
110: 06 00 00 00 54 02 00 00  08 00 00 00 06 00 00 00
120: 5C 02 00 00 09 00 00 00  06 00 00 00 64 02 00 00
130: 0F 00 00 00 08 00 00 00  00 00 00 00 10 00 00 00
140: 08 00 00 00 64 02 00 00  10 00 00 00 08 00 00 00
150: 6C 02 00 00 02 00 05 00  13 00 00 00 02 00 05 00
160: 15 00 00 00 07 00 03 00  17 00 00 00 02 00 04 00
170: 01 00 00 00 02 00 06 00  16 00 00 00 03 00 05 00
180: 18 00 00 00 04 00 04 00  01 00 00 00 06 00 04 00
190: 01 00 00 00 06 00 01 00  12 00 00 00 06 00 02 00
1A0: 12 00 00 00 06 00 03 00  12 00 00 00 06 00 00 00
1B0: 19 00 00 00 02 00 00 00  01 00 00 00 04 00 00 00
1C0: 00 00 00 00 03 00 00 00  00 00 00 00 92 03 00 00
1D0: 8D 03 00 00 01 00 01 00  01 00 00 00 7D 03 00 00
1E0: 04 00 00 00 70 10 03 00  00 00 0E 00 05 00 01 00
1F0: 02 00 00 00 82 03 00 00  2C 00 00 00 12 00 13 01
200: 80 00 35 10 28 00 62 01  02 00 22 02 06 00 70 10
210: 04 00 02 00 1A 03 14 00  6E 20 07 00 32 00 0C 02
220: 6E 20 06 00 02 00 0C 02  1A 03 00 00 6E 20 07 00
230: 32 00 0C 02 6E 20 05 00  02 00 0C 02 6E 10 08 00
240: 02 00 0C 02 6E 20 02 00  21 00 D8 00 00 01 8E 00
250: 28 D7 0E 00 01 00 00 00  00 00 00 00 01 00 00 00
260: 01 00 00 00 01 00 00 00  05 00 00 00 01 00 00 00
270: 09 00 0B 20 63 68 61 72  61 63 74 65 72 20 00 06
280: 3C 69 6E 69 74 3E 00 01  43 00 0C 43 61 73 74 69
290: 6E 67 2E 6A 61 76 61 00  01 49 00 01 4C 00 02 4C
```

Figure 3-12. *`code_item` section of `classes.dex`*

Listing 3-26 shows the DexToXML output for each code_item section.

Listing 3-26. *DexToXML* *code_item*

```
<root>
<header />
<string_ids />
<type_ids />
<proto_ids />
<fields />
<methods />
<classes />
<data>
   <class_data_items />
   <code_items>
       <code_item>
          <id>0</id>
          <registers_size>1</registers_size>
          <ins_size>1</ins_size>
          <outs_size>1</outs_size>
          <tries_size>0</tries_size>
          <debug_info_off>0x37d</debug_info_off>
          <insns_size>4</insns_size>
          <insns>
              <insn>invoke-direct {v0},java/lang/Object/<init>   ;
<init>()V</insn>
              <insn>return-void</insn>
          </insns>
          <padding />
          <handlers />
       </code_item>
       <code_item>
          <id>1</id>
          <registers_size>5</registers_size>
          <ins_size>1</ins_size>
          <outs_size>2</outs_size>
          <tries_size>0</tries_size>
          <debug_info_off>0x382</debug_info_off>
          <insns_size>44</insns_size>
          <insns>
         <insn>const/4  v0,0</insn>
         <insn>const/16    v1,128</insn>
         <insn>if-ge  v0,v1,l252</insn>
         <insn>sget-object   v1,java/lang/System.out
        Ljava/io/PrintStream;</insn>
         <insn>new-instance v2,java/lang/StringBuilder</insn>
         <insn>invoke-direct {v2},java/lang/StringBuilder/<init>   ;
        <init>()V</insn>
         <insn>const-string   v3,"ascii "</insn>
```

```
        <insn>invoke-virtual {v2,v3},java/lang/StringBuilder/append    ;
       append(Ljava/lang/String;)Ljava/lang/StringBuilder;</insn>
        <insn>move-result-object    v2</insn>
        <insn>invoke-virtual {v2,v0},java/lang/StringBuilder/append    ;
       append(I)Ljava/lang/StringBuilder;</insn>
        <insn>move-result-object    v2</insn>
        <insn>const-string   v3," character "</insn>
        <insn>invoke-virtual {v2,v3},java/lang/StringBuilder/append    ;
       append(Ljava/lang/String;)Ljava/lang/StringBuilder;</insn>
        <insn>move-result-object    v2</insn>
        <insn>invoke-virtual {v2,v0},java/lang/StringBuilder/append    ;
       append(C)Ljava/lang/StringBuilder;</insn>
        <insn>move-result-object    v2</insn>
        <insn>invoke-virtual {v2},java/lang/StringBuilder/toString    ;
       toString()Ljava/lang/String;</insn>
        <insn>move-result-object    v2</insn>
        <insn>invoke-virtual {v1,v2},java/io/PrintStream/println  ;
       println(Ljava/lang/String;)V</insn>
        <insn>add-int/lit8 v0,v0,1</insn>
        <insn>int-to-char v0,v0</insn>
        <insn>goto  l1fe</insn>
        <insn>return-void</insn>
         </insns>
         <padding />
         <handlers />
      </code_item>
   </code_items>
</data>
</root>
```

NOTE: Table A-2, "DVM bytecode to opcode mapping," in the appendix lists the DVM opcodes you can use to convert the hex code to the equivalent opcode or bytecode and complete the disassembly. Refer to that when making your conversions.

You know that the first method in Listing 3-26, `<init>`, has four instructions, based on `<insns_size />`. You can see from the hex file that the four hex codes are `7010 0300 0000 0e00`. You can manually convert this into the following:

```
7010 invoke-direct 10 string[16]: VL
0003 method[3]: java.lang.Object.<init> (<init>()V)
0000 no argument
0e00 return-void
```

This is the empty constructor that the javac compiler adds to all classes that don't already have a constructor. So, your first method can be converted straight back into the following code, which is an empty constructor:

```
public class Casting()
{
}
```

Summary

This completes your unraveling of the `classes.dex` file. The complete DexToXML parser code is on the Apress website (`www.apress.com`). It includes other sections such as `map_data` and `debug_info`, which are also in the `classes.dex` file but aren't relevant to the decompilation process. The next chapter discusses all the tools and techniques available in the world of Android disassembly, decompilation, and obfuscation. You return to DexToXML and DexToSource, your Android decompiler, in Chapter 5 and 6.

Chapter 4

Tools of the Trade

This chapter looks at some of the tools as well as some simple techniques that hackers use to reverse-engineer the underlying source code from an Android package file (APK). It also takes a brief look at the major open source and commercial obfuscators, because obfuscation is far and away the most popular tool for protecting source code. In addition, the chapter covers the theory behind these obfuscators so you're better informed about what you're buying.

Let's begin the chapter by looking at how someone might crack your Android APK file. That way, you can begin to avoid some of the most obvious pitfalls when you're attempting to protect your code.

Downloading the APK

It has been no secret for many years that Java code can be decompiled or reverse-engineered into something that's often very close to the original code. But it's never been a burning issue since browser applets went out of favor years ago. The reason for that is plain and simple: access. Most Java code on the Internet lives on servers and not in the browser. Some desktop applications are written in Java Swing, such as Corel's WordPerfect. But these are notable exceptions, and most Java code lives on web servers behind firewalls. So, you would have to hack into a server to get access to the class files before you could decompile them. This is an unlikely scenario; and frankly, if someone has gained access to your class files by hacking into your server, then you have worse things to worry about than them decompiling your code.

But this is no longer the case on Android phones. In Chapter 3, you saw how Java code is compiled down into a `classes.dex` file. The `classes.dex` file is then bundled together with all the other resources, such as images, strings, files, and so on, into the APK that your customer downloads onto their phone. Your Android app is client side; given the right knowledge, anyone can gain access to the APK and, ultimately, your code.

There are three ways to gain access to an APK: by backing it up onto an SD card; via Internet forums; and by using Android's platform tools, which come with the Android SDK. These options are discussed in the following sections.

Backing Up the APK

Perhaps the simplest way to gain access to an APK is to use a backup tool to download the APK onto a micro SD card for later examination on a PC. The steps are as follows:

1. Download and install the free edition of ASTRO File Manager from the Android Market.
2. Insert micro SD card into phone
3. Open ASTRO, and press the Menu button on the phone.
4. Choose Tools ➤ Application Manager/Backup.
5. Select the check box beside the target APK, and click Backup, see Figure 4-1.
6. Close ASTRO File Manager.
7. Remove the micro SD Card, and plug it into the computer. Alternatively, if you don't have an SD card, e-mail the APK to yourself.

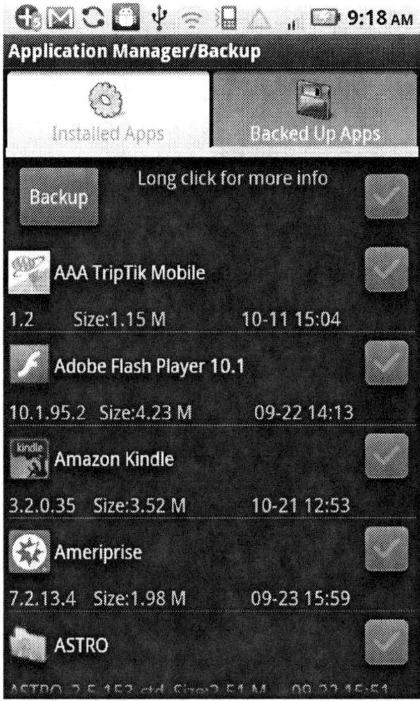

Figure 4-1. *Backing up an APK using ASTRO File Manager*

Forums

If you're looking for one of the more popular APKs, it's probably readily available on Web. For example, the XDA Developers forum at `http://forum.xda-developers.com` is a place where developers share old and new APKs.

Platform Tools

If you develop Android apps, then it's more likely that you're going to want to use the Android platform tools to gain access to the APK. This is trivial way to download an APK, but only when you've gained root or admin access to the phone, which is known as *rooting* the phone. In my not-so-scientific opinion, Android phones are more likely to be rooted or jailbroken than iPhones or Windows mobile phones because of the open source nature of the Android platform. Open source attracts more developers who typically want to know (or have the option to know, if they ever have time) how their phone works by pulling the software or hardware apart. Others may simply want to tether their phone and get free Wi-Fi, which the carriers discourage.

Rooting is easy on the Android and has been encouraged by Google since the early days with its unlocked Nexus phone line. The next section shows how easy it is to root a phone; I can't cover every device and Android version, but they all follow a similar pattern. The hardest thing about rooting a phone is often getting the right USB driver for your device.

Keep in mind that there are risks involved when rooting your phone. Among other things, doing so may invalidate the warranty; so if anything goes wrong, you may be left with a dead device.

Rooting the Phone

There are a number of different options when it comes to rooting your phone. The best approach for your phone depends on the phone type as well as the version of Android running on the phone. The most straightforward way is to download Z4Root, SuperOneClick, or Universal Androot Android app from the XDA Developers forums and install it on your phone. For a while, Z4Root was available in the Android market; but, not surprisingly, it and other APKs that will root your phone can no longer be found there.

Z4Root worked well on early Droids running Android 2.2 (Froyo) and used the RageAgainstTheCage virus to gain root access. This was fixed by Google in Android 2.3 (Gingerbread). But GingerBreak was then created to allow hackers to gain access to phones running Gingerbread. And on and on it goes to the present day, with Superboot now available to gain root access to Android 4.0 (Ice Cream Sandwich) phones.

Let's look at how Z4Root works on Android 2.2.1 or Froyo. Although it's an early version of Android, the process is the same when using GingerBreak on Gingerbread or Honeycomb or Superboot on Ice Cream Sandwich.

The steps to install Z4Root on your Android 2.2.1 phone are as follows:

1. Back up your phone.
2. Download the APK from `http://forum.xda-developers.com`. If you have a virus scanner on your PC, it will pop up a message saying you've downloaded a file with the RageAgainstTheCage virus, which is the exploit that Z4Root uses to hack the phone.
3. Copy the APK onto an SD card from your computer.

4. Put the SD card into your phone, and install Z4Root using ASTRO File Manager.

5. Follow the steps in Z4Root, as shown in Figures 4-2 and 4-3. Choose Root on the first screen; then, choose Temporary Root to root your phone until your phone is rebooted, or choose Permanent Root to keep it rooted. It can take several minutes for Z4Root to root your phone, but if it's successful, the device will reboot and the phone will be rooted.

Figure 4-2. *Z4Root install*

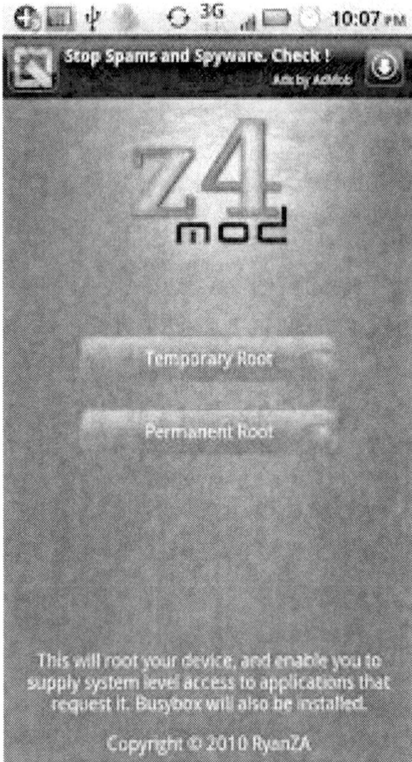

Figure 4-3. *Choosing a temporary or permanent root in Z4Root*

If you run Z4Root after the phone has been rooted, it offers you the option to unroot the phone. This is useful in case you need to replace your phone and don't want to invalidate the warranty (see Figure 4-4).

Figure 4-4. *Disabling root using Z4Root*

The RageAgainstTheCage virus that Z4Root uses spawns numerous adb (Android Debug Bridge) processes until the phone maxes out on the number of processes it can handle. Z4Root kills the last process; then, due to a bug in Android 2.2.1, the last adb process remains running as root and also allows adb to run as root when rebooted, so the phone is compromised.

Installing and Using the Platform Tools

To see if your phone has been successfully rooted, you need to install the Android SDK from `http://developer.android.com`. You can find lots of goodies in the `platform-tools` and `tools` directories of the SDK, including the Dalvik Debug Monitor Service (DDMS), which lets you debug the phone as well as take screen captures; phone emulators; and the dedexer tool, which helps you see inside the `classes.dex` file.

The adb tool, briefly mentioned earlier, connects your computer to the phone. Using adb, you can connect to the phone or tablet and execute Unix commands from its command line; see Listing 4-1, shown using a Windows 7 machine. If you get the # prompt after running the `su` command, as shown, then your phone is successfully rooted.

Listing 4-1. *Rooted Phone*

```
C:\Users\godfrey>adb devices
List of devices attached
0A3A9B900A01F014        device
C:\Users\godfrey>adb shell
$ su
su
#
```

A rooted phone connected to a computer gives you easy access to all the APKs on the phone. You can find your target APK by executing the command `ls /data/app` or `ls /data/app-private` for the paid or protected apps on your device using the adb shell; see Listing 4-2.

Listing 4-2. *Finding the APK to Download*

```
c:\android\android-sdk\platform-tools>adb shell
$ su
# ls /data/app
com.apps.aaa.roadside-1.apk
com.pyxismobile.Ameriprise.ui.activity-1.zip
com.s1.citizensbank-1.zip
com.hungerrush.hungryhowies-1.apk
com.huntington.m-1.apk
com.netflix.mediaclient-1.apk
com.priceline.android.negotiator-1.apk
com.google.android.googlequicksearchbox-1.apk
# ls /data/app-private
com.s1.citizensbank-1.apk
com.pyxismobile.Ameriprise.ui.activity-1.apk
```

If you see a `.zip` file in the `/data/app` directory, then the APK is in the `/data/app-private` directory.

Exit the adb shell, and, from your computer's command line, use the `adb pull` command to copy the APK to your local folder; see Listing 4-3.

Listing 4-3. *Using the* `adb pull` *Command*

```
c:\android\android-sdk\platform-tools>adb pull data/app/com.riis.mobile.apk
```

Decompiling an APK

In Chapter 3, you saw that the format of `classes.dex` is a distinct break from the Java class-file format. But currently there are no `classes.dex` decompilers—only Java class-file decompilers. You have to wait until Chapters 5 and 6 to build your own decompiler. In the meantime, you can use dex2jar to convert the `classes.dex` back into a class file.

dex2jar is a tool for converting Android's `.dex` format to Java's `.class` format. It converts from one binary format to another binary format, not to source. and is available from `http://code.google.com/p/dex2jar`. Once you convert to a class-file format, you still need to use a Java decompiler like JD-GUI to see the Java source.

From the command line, run the following commands on your APK:

```
c:\temp>dex2jar com.riis.mobile.apk
c:\temp>jd-gui com.riis.mobile.apk.dex2jar
```

Alternatively, you can use apktool from Ryszard Wiśniewski, which is available from `http://code.google.com/p/android-apktool`. On Windows, after installing apktool, you can decompile an APK with a right-click of the mouse. apktool unzips the APK, runs baksmali (a disassembler), decodes the `AndroidManifest.xml` file using AXMLPrinter2, converts `classes.dex` to a jar file using dex2jar, and then pops up the Java code in JD-GUI.

What's in an APK File?

APKs are in a zipped format. You can unzip the file by changing the extension to `.zip` and using your favorite unzipping tool. (Many tools, such as 7-Zip, will recognize that it's a zip file and upzip it without your needing to change the extension.) The contents of such a zip file are shown in Figure 4-5.

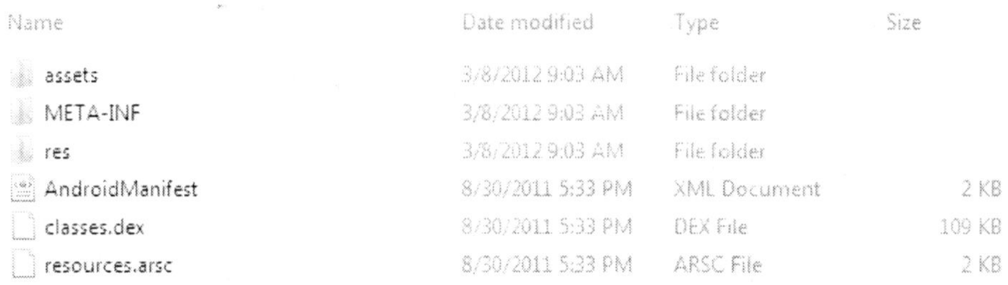

Name	Date modified	Type	Size
assets	3/8/2012 9:03 AM	File folder	
META-INF	3/8/2012 9:03 AM	File folder	
res	3/8/2012 9:03 AM	File folder	
AndroidManifest	8/30/2011 5:33 PM	XML Document	2 KB
classes.dex	8/30/2011 5:33 PM	DEX File	109 KB
resources.arsc	8/30/2011 5:33 PM	ARSC File	2 KB

Figure 4-5. *Content of an unzipped APK file*

The `META-INF` directory includes a `manifest.mf` or manifest file, which contains a manifest digest for all the files. `cert.rsa` has the certificate used to sign the files, and `cert.sf` has the list of resources in the APK along with the SHA-1 digest for each of the files. The `res` directory contains all the APK resources, such as XML layout-definition files and related images, and `assets` contains images and HTML, CSS, and JavaScript files. `AndroidManifest.xml` contains the name, version number, and access rights of the APK. This is usually in a binary format and needs to be converted to a readable format using AXMLPrinter2. Finally you have the `classes.dex` file with the compiled Java class files; and `resources.asrc`, which contains any precompiled resources not in the resources directory. AXMLPrinter2 is available at `http://code.google.com/p/android4me`. Listing 4-4 shows how to use it to decode the `AndroidManifest.xml` file.

Listing 4-4. *`AXMLPrinter2.jar` Command*

```
java -jar AXMLPrinter2.jar AndroidManifest.xml > AndroidManifest_decoded.xml
```

Listing 4-5 shows an `AndroidManifest`.xml file after it has been decoded using AXMLPrinter2.

Listing 4-5. *Decoded `AndroidManifest.xml`*

```
<?xml version="1.0" encoding="utf-8"?>
<manifest
   xmlns:android="http://schemas.android.com/apk/res/android"
   android:versionCode="1"
   android:versionName="1.0"
   package="com.riis.agile.agileandbeyond.android"
   >
   <application
       android:label="@7F070000"
       android:icon="@7F020015"
       android:name=".OpenSourceBridgeApplication"
```

```
        android:debuggable="true"
        >
        <activity
            android:theme="@android:01030006"
            android:label="@7F070000"
            android:name=".LaunchActivity"
            >
            <intent-filter
                >
                <action
                    android:name="android.intent.action.MAIN"
                    >
                </action>
                <category
                    android:name="android.intent.category.LAUNCHER"
                    >
                </category>
            </intent-filter>
        </activity>
        <activity
            android:theme="@android:01030006"
            android:label="@7F070000"
            android:name=".ScheduleActivity"
            >
        </activity>
    </application>
    <uses-sdk
        android:minSdkVersion="3"
        >
    </uses-sdk>
</manifest>
```

There can be other directories in an APK. If the file is a HTML5/CSS app, then it will have an assets library with the HTML pages and JavaScript code. If the APK uses other Java libraries or any C++ code in a native library, there will be `.jar` and `.so` files in a `lib` folder.

Random APK Issues

Of a random sample of 50 APKs that I downloaded, only 1 had any sort of protection. This is likely to change as the issue of decompiling Android code becomes better understood. This section outlines some of the issues I encountered in my sample. All company names, web service URLs, and API keys or login information have been modified to protect the innocent.

Web Service Keys and Logins

Although many Android apps are stand-alone, many are classic client-side applications that communicate via web-service keys to back-end systems. Listing 4-6 shows decompiled source code with an API key to the production web service as well as help and support information. This might not be enough to hack into the web service, but it's an invitation for the hacker to explore the API some more.

Listing 4-6. *Exposed Web-Service API Keys*

```
public class PortalInfoBuilder
{
  public static List a(Context paramContext)
  {
    ArrayList localArrayList = new ArrayList();
    Boolean localBoolean = Boolean.valueOf(0);
    PortalInfo localPortalInfo = new PortalInfo("Production",
          "https://runapiportal.riis.com/portal.svc",
                "d3IWwZ9TjkoNFtNYtwsLYM+gk/Q=", localBoolean);
    localPortalInfo.b("https://support.riis.com/riis_payroll//%d/help.htm");
    localPortalInfo.c("http://www.riis.com/ /guided_tours.xml");
    boolean bool = localArrayList.add(localPortalInfo);
    return localArrayList;
  }
}
```

Listing 4-7 shows an API that is protected by a username and password. But by decompiling the APK, the hacker gains access to the any information streamed by the API. In this case, the API didn't check to see if the browser was from a mobile device and the information could be repurposed from a web site. If the information served up by your API is valuable, then it's better to hide the usernames and passwords; you see how to do this in the "Protecting Your Source" section later in this chapter.

Listing 4-7. *Exposed API Username and Password*

```
  private String Digest(ArrayList<String> paramArrayList)
  {
   // setup
    String str5 = "CB8F9322-0C1C-4B28A4:" + str2 + ":" + "cxYacuzafrabru5a1beb";
    String str7 = "POST:" + "https://www.riis.com/api/";
  }
```

Listing 4-8 shows the same username and password, which were duplicated in a configuration file for no good reason. Make sure all usernames and passwords are properly protected wherever they appear before you release an app.

Listing 4-8. *Exposed Web Service Username and Password*

```
public static final String USER_NAME = "CB8F9322-0C1C-4B28A4";
public static final String PASSWORD = " cxYacuzafrabru5a1beb";
```

Database Schemas

Another area of concern is databases, where sensitive information is often stored. Decompiling the APK allows the hacker to see the database schema information for a SQLite or other database that is stored on the phone. A number of APKs store an individual's credit-card information in the local database. Gaining access to that data might require someone to either steal your phone or create an Android virus, which may not be very likely; but again, it's another piece of information that shouldn't be exposed.

Listing 4-9 shows some database schema information for a phone app, and Listing 4-10 shows information for an HTML5 app that stores credit-card information locally.

Listing 4-9. *Creating Schemas and Database Location Information*

```
public class DB
{
  public static final String ACTIVATION_CODE = "activationcode";
  public static final String ALLOWEDIT = "allowedit";
  private static final String ANYWHERE_CREATE = "create table %s
        (_id integer primary key autoincrement, description text,
                phoneNumber text not null, isActive text not null);";
  private static final String ANYWHERE_TABLE = "anywhere";
  private static final String AV_CREATE = "create table SettingValues
        (_id integer primary key autoincrement, keyname text not null,
                attribute text not null, value text not null);";
  private static final String AV_TABLE = "SettingValues";
  private static final String CALLCENTER_CREATE = "create table callcenters
        (_id integer primary key autoincrement, ServiceUserId text not null,
                Name text, PhoneNumber text, Extension text,
                Available text not null, LogoffAllowed text not null);";
  private static final String DATABASE_NAME = "settings.db";
  private static final int DATABASE_VERSION = 58;
}
```

Listing 4-10. *Storing Credit-Card Information*

```
// ****************************** Credit Cards Table

api.createCustCC = function (email,name,obj){
var rtn=-1;
try{
   api.open();
   conn.execute('INSERT INTO CustomerCC (Email,CCInfo,Name)
        VALUES(?,?,?)',email,JSON.stringify(obj),name);
                   rtn=conn.lastInsertRowId;
}
```

HTML5/CSS

A significant number of Android APKs are originally written in HTML5/CSS. Using tools such as PhoneGap, the HTML5/CSS files are converted into APKs and then uploaded into the Android market. The Java code in these apps is a framework that simply calls the HTML5 app from within an Android frame. Unzipping the APK you can find the original JavaScript in the `assets` folder.

Sometimes JavaScript contains even more dangerous information than Java source code, because the comments typically aren't removed before the APK is created. Using a JavaScript compressor helps solve this issue (see the "Obfuscators" section later in this chapter).

Fake Apps

Decompiling APKs doesn't often result in 100% of the code being reverse-engineered. dex2jar often fails to completely convert `classes.dex` to the Java jar files. But with some effort, it's possible to tweak the resulting Java source to get it to recompile into a stolen or hijacked APK that can then be resubmitted to the Android market under a different name. Fake apps can also be created to capture usernames and passwords from banking applications or any application that requires a login.

The most famous fake app to date was a phony Netflix app that collected Netflix account information. That particular example didn't use any decompiled code, but a hijacked app that looked like the real app would offer a level of sophistication that would fool most people into giving up login information. Fake apps would also be good vehicles for uploading malware onto the phone or device with little chance of being detected, because there is no preapproval on the Android market. Note, though, that the wonderfully name Android Bouncer is now catching some of these fake apps.

Disassemblers

If you spend any time with Android bytecode, you gradually notice different patterns and language constructs. With practice and a lot of patience, bytecode becomes just another language.

So far, you've seen two disassemblers: dx, which comes as part of the Android SDK; and DexToXML, which disassembles `classes.dex` into an XML structure. You used Android's dx tool in Chapter 3 to compile `Casting.class` into a `classes.dex` format, but it can also disassemble the `classes.dex` file into text.

Let's take a brief look at the dx output and some other alternatives to show whether they're better than DexToXML. To begin, don't forget about hexadecimal editors, which often provide all the information a hacker needs.

Hex Editors

For many years, hackers have been using hexadecimal editors and other more sophisticated tools such as Numega's SoftICE and more recently Hex-Rays' IDA to get around licensing schemes on time-bombed versions of all kinds of software. Cracking demonstration versions of the games that came with almost every computer magazine in the late 1980s and 1990s was a rite of passage for many of my fellow programmers.

Typically, programmers tried to protect their games and utilities by checking to see if the date was 30 days after the installation date. After 30 days, the evaluation copy ceased to run. If you just couldn't afford to buy the real thing, you'd set the time on your computer to be permanently a couple of days before the evaluation expired. Or, if you were clever, you'd realize that the developer had to store the install date somewhere: if you were lucky, it was somewhere simple like in the `.ini` file or the registry, and you could permanently set it to some far-off future date such as 1999.

The rite of passage was truly complete when you could just about read assembler; set a breakpoint to narrow in on the security functions; and find the piece of code that checked the evaluation date and disable it or create a serial number or key that the program would accept, so the evaluation copy became a fully functional version of the software.

There were countless more sophisticated mechanisms for protecting more expensive programs; the dongle used on many expensive CAD programs immediately springs to mind. Usually, most protection mechanisms did little more than keep the average person from disabling or cracking them. The tool of choice for attacking such mechanisms in the Java world is the hexadecimal editor.

Far from learning from the past, most programmers are condemned to repeat it. The vast majority of license-protection examples out there rely on something as simple as a conditional jump. In Listing 4-11, the modified sample code from Google shows how to expire a demo at the end 2012.

Listing 4-11. *Timebombed Trial App Code*

```
if (new Date().after(new GregorianCalendar(2012,12,31).getTime())) {
    AlertDialog.Builder ad = new AlertDialog.Builder(SomeActivity.this);
    ad.setTitle("App Trial Expired");
    ad.setMessage("Please download Full App from Android Market.");
    ad.setPositiveButton("Get from Market", new
DialogInterface.OnClickListener() {
    public void onClick(DialogInterface dialog, int whichButton) {
        Intent i = new Intent(Intent.ACTION_VIEW,
Uri.parse("http://market.android.com/search?q=pname:com.riis.app_full"));
        startActivity(i);
        finish();
      }
}).show();
}
```

Using the information in Chapter 3 makes it possible to find the Android bytecode. Then a quick peek and a poke, changing `after` to `before` using a hexadecimal editor, turns the trial app into a full version. Some hexadecimal editors such as IDA make this very simple to do; see Figure 4-6.

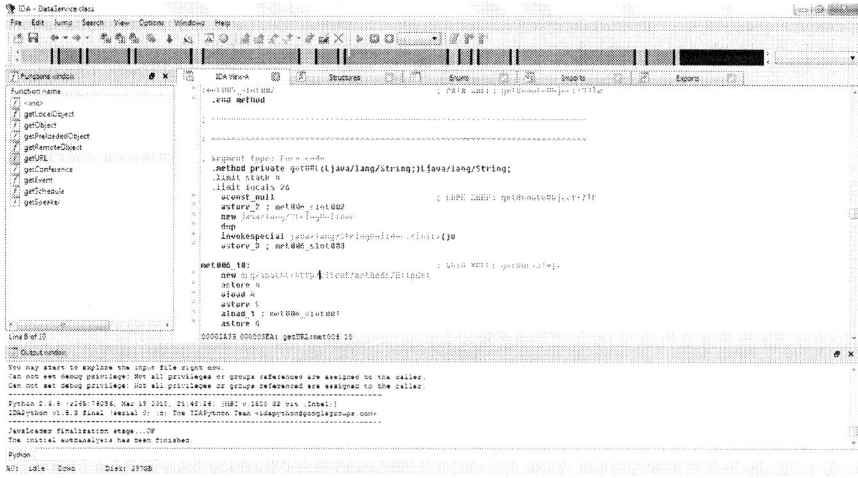

Figure 4-6. *IDA hexadecimal editor*

dx and dexdump

Dx is part of the Android SDK and can be found in the `platform-tools` directory along with dexdump. The dx command with the verbose option completely unravels any `classes.dex` file and is currently the best disassembler if you're trying to see inside `classes.dex`. The following command outputs a disassembled version of `classes.dex`: it compiles the `Casting.class` file in the `casting` directory and outputs `casting.dump`:

```
dx --dex --verbose-dump --dump-to=c:\temp\casting.dump c:\temp\casting
```

Listing 4-12 shows the output of the header section for the file.

***Listing 4-12.** Dx Output of the Header Section of* `classes.dex`

```
000000: 6465 780a 3033 |magic: "dex\n035\0"
000006: 3500           |
000008: 628b 4418      |checksum
00000c: daa9 21ca 9c4f |signature
000012: b4c5 21d7 77bc |
000018: 2a18 4a38 0da2 |
00001e: aafe           |
000020: 5004 0000      |file_size:       00000450
000024: 7000 0000      |header_size:     00000070
000028: 7856 3412      |endian_tag:      12345678
00002c: 0000 0000      |link_size:       0
000030: 0000 0000      |link_off:        0
000034: a403 0000      |map_off:         000003a4
000038: 1a00 0000      |string_ids_size: 0000001a
00003c: 7000 0000      |string_ids_off:  00000070
000040: 0a00 0000      |type_ids_size:   0000000a
000044: d800 0000      |type_ids_off:    000000d8
000048: 0700 0000      |proto_ids_size:  00000007
00004c: 0001 0000      |proto_ids_off:   00000100
000050: 0300 0000      |field_ids_size:  00000003
000054: 5401 0000      |field_ids_off:   00000154
000058: 0900 0000      |method_ids_size: 00000009
00005c: 6c01 0000      |method_ids_off:  0000016c
000060: 0100 0000      |class_defs_size: 00000001
000064: b401 0000      |class_defs_off:  000001b4
000068: 7c02 0000      |data_size:       0000027c
00006c: d401 0000      |data_off:        000001d4
```

Dexdump is the Android SDK equivalent of javap, the Java class-file disassembler. The dexdump command to produce the output in Listing 4-13 is as follows:

```
dexdump -d -h classes.dex
```

Listing 4-13. *Plain Dexdump Output with Disassembled File Header*

```
Processing 'classes.dex'...
Opened 'classes.dex', DEX version '035'
Class #0 header:
class_idx           : 2
access_flags        : 1 (0x0001)
superclass_idx      : 4
interfaces_off      : 0 (0x000000)
source_file_idx     : 3
annotations_off     : 0 (0x000000)
class_data_off      : 914 (0x000392)
static_fields_size  : 2
instance_fields_size: 0
direct_methods_size : 2
virtual_methods_size: 0

Class #0            -
  Class descriptor  : 'LCasting;'
  Access flags      : 0x0001 (PUBLIC)
  Superclass        : 'Ljava/lang/Object;'
  Interfaces        -
  Static fields     -
    #0              : (in LCasting;)
      name          : 'ascStr'
      type          : 'Ljava/lang/String;'
      access        : 0x0018 (STATIC FINAL)
    #1              : (in LCasting;)
      name          : 'chrStr'
      type          : 'Ljava/lang/String;'
      access        : 0x0018 (STATIC FINAL)
  Instance fields   -
  Direct methods    -
    #0              : (in LCasting;)
      name          : '<init>'
      type          : '()V'
      access        : 0x10001 (PUBLIC CONSTRUCTOR)
      code          -
      registers     : 1
      ins           : 1
      outs          : 1
      insns size    : 4 16-bit code units
0001d4:                                        |[0001d4] Casting.<init>:()V
0001e4: 7010 0300 0000                            |0000: invoke-direct {v0},
                                     Ljava/lang/Object;.<init>:()V //
method@0003
0001ea: 0e00                                   |0003: return-void
      catches       : (none)
      positions     :
        0x0000 line=1
```

```
      locals        :
        0x0000 - 0x0004 reg=0 this LCasting;

    #1              : (in LCasting;)
      name          : 'main'
      type          : '([Ljava/lang/String;)V'
      access        : 0x0009 (PUBLIC STATIC)
      code          -
      registers     : 5
      ins           : 1
      outs          : 2
      insns size    : 44 16-bit code units
0001ec:                                        |[0001ec]
Casting.main:([Ljava/lang/String;)V
0001fc: 1200                                   |0000: const/4 v0, #int 0 // #0
0001fe: 1301 8000                              |0001: const/16 v1, #int 128 //
#80
000202: 3510 2800                              |0003: if-ge v0, v1, 002b //
+0028
000206: 6201 0200                              |0005: sget-object v1,
Ljava/lang/System;.out:Ljava/io/PrintStream; // field@0002
00020a: 2202 0600                              |0007: new-instance v2,
Ljava/lang/StringBuilder; // type@0006
00020e: 7010 0400 0200                         |0009: invoke-direct {v2},
Ljava/lang/StringBuilder;.<init>:()V // method@0004
000214: 1a03 1400                              |000c: const-string v3, "ascii "
// string@0014
000218: 6e20 0700 3200                         |000e: invoke-virtual {v2, v3},
Ljava/lang/StringBuilder;.append:(Ljava/lang/String;)Ljava/lang/StringBuilder;
// method@0007
00021e: 0c02                                   |0011: move-result-object v2
000220: 6e20 0600 0200                         |0012: invoke-virtual {v2, v0},
Ljava/lang/StringBuilder;.append:(I)Ljava/lang/StringBuilder; // method@0006
000226: 0c02                                   |0015: move-result-object v2
000228: 1a03 0000                              |0016: const-string v3, "
character " // string@0000
00022c: 6e20 0700 3200                         |0018: invoke-virtual {v2, v3},
Ljava/lang/StringBuilder;.append:(Ljava/lang/String;)Ljava/lang/StringBuilder;
// method@0007
000232: 0c02                                   |001b: move-result-object v2
000234: 6e20 0500 0200                         |001c: invoke-virtual {v2, v0},
Ljava/lang/StringBuilder;.append:(C)Ljava/lang/StringBuilder; // method@0005
00023a: 0c02                                   |001f: move-result-object v2
00023c: 6e10 0800 0200                         |0020: invoke-virtual {v2},
Ljava/lang/StringBuilder;.toString:()Ljava/lang/String; // method@0008
000242: 0c02                                   |0023: move-result-object v2
000244: 6e20 0200 2100                         |0024: invoke-virtual {v1, v2},
Ljava/io/PrintStream;.println:(Ljava/lang/String;)V // method@0002
00024a: d800 0001                              |0027: add-int/lit8 v0, v0, #int
1 // #01
```

```
00024e: 8e00                                   |0029: int-to-char v0, v0
000250: 28d7                                   |002a: goto 0001 // -0029
000252: 0e00                                   |002b: return-void
      catches       : (none)
      positions     :
        0x0000 line=8
        0x0005 line=9
        0x0027 line=8
        0x002b line=11
      locals        :

  Virtual methods   -
  source_file_idx   : 3 (Casting.java)
```

dedexer

Dedexer is an open source disassembler tool from Gabor Paller, who is an engineer in Hungary. It's available at `http://dedexer.sourceforge.net`. Dedexer works as an excellent alternative to dx. Listing 4-14 shows the Dedexer `dex.log` output file after executing the following:

```
java -jar ddx1.18.jar -o -d c:\temp casting\classes.dex
```

Listing 4-14. *Dedexer Header Section Output*

```
00000000 :  64 65 78 0A
       30 33 35 00
       magic: dex\n035\0
00000008 :  62 8B 44 18
       checksum
0000000C :  DA A9 21 CA
       9C 4F B4 C5
       21 D7 77 BC
       2A 18 4A 38
       0D A2 AA FE
       signature
00000020 :  50 04 00 00
       file size: 0x00000450
00000024 :  70 00 00 00
       header size: 0x00000070
00000028 :  78 56 34 12
       00 00 00 00
       link size: 0x00000000
00000030 :  00 00 00 00
       link offset: 0x00000000
00000034 :  A4 03 00 00
       map offset: 0x000003A4
00000038 :  1A 00 00 00
       string ids size: 0x0000001A
```

```
0000003C :  70 00 00 00
       string ids offset: 0x00000070
00000040 :  0A 00 00 00
       type ids size: 0x0000000A
00000044 :  D8 00 00 00
       type ids offset: 0x000000D8
00000048 :  07 00 00 00
       proto ids size: 0x00000007
0000004C :  00 01 00 00
       proto ids offset: 0x00000100
00000050 :  03 00 00 00
       field ids size: 0x00000003
00000054 :  54 01 00 00
       field ids offset: 0x00000154
00000058 :  09 00 00 00
       method ids size: 0x00000009
0000005C :  6C 01 00 00
       method ids offset: 0x0000016C
00000060 :  01 00 00 00
       class defs size: 0x00000001
00000064 :  B4 01 00 00
       class defs offset: 0x000001B4
00000068 :  7C 02 00 00
       data size: 0x0000027C
0000006C :  D4 01 00 00
       data offset: 0x000001D4
00000070 :  72 02 00 00
```

baksmali

Backsmali is Icelandic for *disassembler* and continues the Icelandic theme of names associated with the Dalvik virtual machine, which you may remember was named after an Icelandic village where the one of original programmers' (Dan Bornstein) ancestors hailed from. Baksmali was written by someone called JesusFreke and is available at `http://code.google.com/p/smali` along with *smali*, which is *assembler* in Icelandic. Listing 4-15 shows the baksmali output for `classes.dex` when the following command is executed:

```
java -jar baksmali-1.3.2.jar -o c:\temp casting\classes.dex
```

Listing 4-15. *Casting.smali*

```
.class public LCasting;
.super Ljava/lang/Object;
.source "Casting.java"


# static fields
```

```
.field static final ascStr:Ljava/lang/String; = "ascii "

.field static final chrStr:Ljava/lang/String; = " character "


# direct methods
.method public constructor <init>()V
    .registers 1

    .prologue
    .line 1
    invoke-direct {p0}, Ljava/lang/Object;-><init>()V

    return-void
.end method

.method public static main([Ljava/lang/String;)V
    .registers 5
    .parameter

    .prologue
    .line 8
    const/4 v0, 0x0

    :goto_1
    const/16 v1, 0x80

    if-ge v0, v1, :cond_2b

    .line 9
    sget-object v1, Ljava/lang/System;->out:Ljava/io/PrintStream;

    new-instance v2, Ljava/lang/StringBuilder;

    invoke-direct {v2}, Ljava/lang/StringBuilder;-><init>()V

    const-string v3, "ascii "

    invoke-virtual {v2, v3}, Ljava/lang/StringBuilder;-
>append(Ljava/lang/String;)Ljava/lang/StringBuilder;

    move-result-object v2

    invoke-virtual {v2, v0}, Ljava/lang/StringBuilder;-
>append(I)Ljava/lang/StringBuilder;

    move-result-object v2

    const-string v3, " character "
```

```
    invoke-virtual {v2, v3}, Ljava/lang/StringBuilder;-
>append(Ljava/lang/String;)Ljava/lang/StringBuilder;

    move-result-object v2

    invoke-virtual {v2, v0}, Ljava/lang/StringBuilder;-
>append(C)Ljava/lang/StringBuilder;

    move-result-object v2

    invoke-virtual {v2}, Ljava/lang/StringBuilder;->toString()Ljava/lang/String;

    move-result-object v2

    invoke-virtual {v1, v2}, Ljava/io/PrintStream;->println(Ljava/lang/String;)V

    .line 8
    add-int/lit8 v0, v0, 0x1

    int-to-char v0, v0

    goto :goto_1

    .line 11
    :cond_2b
    return-void
.end method
```

Decompilers

Since the early 1990s, at least a dozen decompilers have been released: Mocha, WingDis, Java Optimize and Decompile Environment (JODE), SourceAgain, DejaVu, Jad, Homebrew, JReveal, DeCafe, JReverse, jAscii, and JD-GUI. There are also a number of programs—Jasmine and NMI, for example—that provide a front end to Jad or Mocha for the command-line impaired. Some, like the one that is perhaps the most famous, Mocha, are hopelessly out of date; and most decompilers other than JD-GUI and Jad are no longer available. The following sections review some of them.

Mocha

Many of the earliest decompilers have long since disappeared; Jive never even saw the light of day. Mocha's life, like that of its author, Hanpeter Van Vliet, was short. The original beta from June 1996 had a sister program, Crema, which cost $39; it protected class files from being decompiled by Mocha using obfuscation.

As one of the earliest decompilers, Mocha is a simple command-line tool with no front-end GUI. It uses JDK 1.02 and was distributed as a zip file of classes, which were obfuscated by Crema. Mocha is primed to recognize and ignore class files obfuscated by Crema. Not surprisingly, jar files aren't supported by Mocha, because they didn't exist when Mocha was originally written. And like all early decompilers, Mocha can't decompile inner classes, which only appeared in the JDK 1.1.

To decompile a file using Mocha, make sure the `mocha.zip` file is in your classpath, and decompile using the following command:

```
java mocha.Decompiler [-v] [-o] Casting.class
```

The decompiler was only released as a beta; its author met with an untimely demise before he could turn it into what you could call production quality. Mocha's flow analysis is incomplete, and it fails on a number of Java constructs. Several individuals have tried to patch Mocha in the past, but these efforts have been largely wasted. It makes much more sense these days to use either JD-GUI or Jad.

Just before he passed away from cancer at the age of only 34, Hanpeter sold the code for Mocha and Crema to Borland; some of the Crema obfuscation code made it into early versions of JBuilder. Just a few weeks after Hanpeter's death on New Year's Eve 1996, Mark LaDue's HoseMocha appeared, which allowed anyone to protect their files from being decompiled with Mocha without having to pay for Crema.

Jad

Jad is fast, free, and very effective, and was one of the first decompilers to handle inner classes properly. It's the work of Pavel Kouznetsov, a graduate from the Faculty of Applied Mathematics at Moscow State Aviation School, who was living in Cyprus when Jad was released. It's available from `www.varaneckas.com/jad` and is probably the simplest command-line tool to use in this chapter.

The last available version of Jad is v1.58, from 2001. According to the FAQ, the major known bug is that it doesn't handle inline functions very well; this shouldn't be an issue because most compilers leave it to the JIT engines to perform inlining.

In most cases, all you need to do is type the following:

```
jad target.class
```

For a one-man show, Jad is remarkably complete. Its most interesting feature is that it can annotate source code with the relevant parts of a class file's bytecode so you can see where each part of the decompiled code came from. This is a great tool for understanding bytecode; Listing 4-16 shows an example.

Listing 4-16. *`Casting.class` Decompiled by Jad*

```
// Decompiled by Jad v1.5.8g. Copyright 2001 Pavel Kouznetsov.
// Jad home page: http://www.kpdus.com/jad.html
// Decompiler options: packimports(3)
// Source File Name:   Casting.java

import java.io.PrintStream;

public class Casting
{

    public Casting()
    {
    }

    public static void main(String args[])
    {
        for(char c = '\0'; c < 128; c++)
            System.out.println((new StringBuilder()).append("ascii
").append(c).append(" character ").append(c).toString());

    }

    static final String ascStr = "ascii ";
    static final String chrStr = " character ";
}
```

JD-GUI

In 2012, JD-GUI is the de facto Java decompiler. It was written by Emmanual Dupuy, of Paris, and is available from `http://java.decompiler.free.fr`.

Drag and drop your Java class files, and they're immediately decompiled. JD-GUI also has an eclipse plugin, JD-Eclipse, as well as a core library that can be integrated with other applications.

JD-GUI was written for JDK 1.5 and has all of the modern constructs up to that point. It also works seamlessly with jar files. Figure 4-7 shows JD-GUI in action.

Figure 4-7. *`Casting.class` decompiled by JD-GUI*

dex2jar

Dex2jar is a tool for converting Android's `.dex` format to Java's `.class` format—just one binary format to another binary format, not to Java source. You still have to run a Java decompiler on the resulting jar file to view the source. Dex2jar is available from `http://code.google.com/p/dex2jar/` and was written by Panxiaobo, a graduate of Zhejiang University of Science and Technology who is currently working for a computer security company in China.

Dex2jar isn't perfect: it fails to convert a not-insignificant number of methods in a `classes.dex` file. But if it wasn't for dex2jar and, to a lesser extent, undx, (See section below) there wouldn't be any Android decompilation.

To convert an APK file to a jar file for further decompilation, run the following command:

```
c:\temp>dex2jar com.riis.mobile.apk
c:\temp>jd-gui com.riis.mobile.apk.dex2jar
```

undx

Undx is another, lesser-known DEX-file-to-class-file converter. It was originally written by Marc Schoenefeld in 2009 and was available at www.illegalaccess.org. It now seems to be a dead project and predates the move of dexdump in the Android SDK folder from tools to the platform-tools directory.

apktool

Apktool is a frightening addition to the decompiler's arsenal. Once it's installed, a right-click of a mouse will unzip the APK, run baksmali followed by AXMLPrinter2 and dex2jar, and launch JD-GUI—it completely automates the process of decompiling an APK. This moves the decompilation process from an art to a mouse-click and allows anyone who can install ASTRO File Manager the ability to see an APK's source. Apktool is available from http://code.google.com/p/android-apktool/.

Protecting Your Source

Now that you understand the problem and have seen how effective dex2jar and JD-GUI can be, you're probably wondering if there's any way code can be protected. If you're at the point of asking why you should write Android apps, this is the section for you.

The following quote will help define what I mean when I talk about protecting your source:

> *[We want] to protect [the] code by making reverse engineering so technically difficult that it becomes impossible or at the very least economically inviable.*
>
> —Christian Collberg, Clark Thomborson, and Douglas Low[1]

You probably have a foot in one of two camps: programmers may be interested in understanding how others achieve interesting effects, but from a business point of view nobody wants someone else to rebadge their code and sell it to third parties as their own. Even worse, under certain circumstances, decompiling Android code can allow someone to attack other parts of your systems by gaining access to back-end web-service APIs.

---

1 "A Taxonomy of Obfuscating Transformations," Computer Science Technical Reports 148 (1997), https://researchspace.auckland.ac.nz/handle/2292/3491.

You've seen in the previous chapters that for a number of reasons, Android `classes.dex` files contain an unusually large amount of symbolic information. And as you've seen, DEX files that aren't protected in some way return code that is almost identical to the original—except, of course, for a complete lack of programmer comments. This section looks at the steps you can take to limit the amount of information in the dex file and make the decompiler's job as difficult as possible.

The ideal solution would be a black-box application that would take a DEX file as input and output an equivalent protected version. Unfortunately, as yet, nothing out there can offer complete protection.

It's difficult to define criteria for evaluating each currently available protection strategy. But you can measure just how effective each tool or technique is using the following three criteria:

- How confused is the decompiler (potency)?
- Can it repel all attempts at decompilation (resilience)?
- What is the application overhead (cost)?

If the performance of the code is badly degraded, then that's probably too high a cost. Or if you convert your code into server-side code using web services, for example, then that will incur a much greater ongoing cost than a stand-alone application.

Let's look at the open source and commercial obfuscators and other tools available on the market and how effective they are at protecting your code. Chapter 1 looked at legal means of protecting your code. The following is a technical list of ways to protect your Android source code:

- Writing two versions of the Android app
- Obfuscation
- Web services and server-side execution
- Fingerprinting your code
- Native methods

Writing Two Versions of the Android App

Standard marketing practice in the software industry, especially on the Web, is to allow users to download a fully functional evaluation copy of the software that stops working after a certain period of time or number of uses. The theory behind this try-as-you-buy system is that after the allotted time, say 30 days, the user has become so accustomed to your program that they happily pay for a full version.

But most software developers realize that these full-version evaluation programs are a double-edged sword. They show the full functionality of the program but are often very difficult to protect, no matter what language you're talking about. Earlier in this chapter, you saw seen how handy hexadecimal editors are at ripping through licensing schemes, whether written in C++, Visual Basic, or Java.

Many different types of protection schemes are employed, but in the world of Java you have only one very simple protection tool:

```
if boolean = true
      execute
else
      exit
```

These types of schemes have been cracked since the first time they appeared in VB shareware. The protection is modified by flipping a bit in the hexadecimal editor to

```
if boolean = false
      execute
else
      exit
```

How much better it would be to write a demonstration applet or application that gives the potential customer a taste of the product without giving away the goods. Consider crippling the demo by removing all but the basic functionality while leaving in the menu options. If that's too much, then think about using a third-party vendor such as WebEx or Citrix so the potential customer gets to see your application but never has a chance to run it against a decompiler.

Of course, this doesn't stop anyone from decompiling a legitimate copy of the fully functional version after they've bought it, removing any licensing schemes, and then passing the app on to other third parties. But they will have to pay to get that far, and often that is enough of an impediment that hackers look elsewhere.

Obfuscation

A dozen or so Java obfuscators have seen the light of day. Most of the earlier versions of this type of technology are now difficult to locate. You can still find traces of them on the Web if you look hard enough, but apart from one or two notable exceptions, Java obfuscators have mostly faded into obscurity.

This leaves the interesting problem of how to tell whether any of the remaining handful of obfuscators are any good. Perhaps something very useful in the original obfuscators has been lost that would have protected your code but couldn't hold on long enough when the market took a turn for the worse. You need to understand what obfuscation means, because otherwise you have no way of knowing whether one obfuscator is better than another (unless market demand is your deciding factor).

> *When obfuscation is outlawed, only outlaws will sifjdifdm wofiefiemf eifm.*
>
> —Paul Tyma, PreEmptive Software

This section looks at obfuscation theory. I'll borrow from Collberg, Thomborson, and Low to help shed some light on where I stand. In their paper, the authors split obfuscation into three distinct areas:

- Layout obfuscation
- Control obfuscation
- Data obfuscation

Table 4-1 lists a reasonably complete set of obfuscations separated into these three types and in some cases further classified. Some transformation types from the paper that are particularly ineffective for Java are omitted from the table.

Table 4-1. *Obfuscation Transformations*

Obfuscation Type	Classification	Transformation
Layout		Scramble identifiers.
Control	Computations	Insert dead or irrelevant code.
		Extend a loop condition.
		Reducible to non-reducible.
		Add redundant operands.
		Remove programming

		idioms.
		Parallelize code.
	Aggregations	Inline and outline methods.
		Interleave methods.
		Clone methods.
		Loop transformations.
	Ordering	Reorder statements.
		Reorder loops.
		Reorder expressions.
Data	Storage and encoding	Change encoding.
		Split variables.
		Convert static data to procedural data.
	Aggregation	Merge scalar variables.
		Factor a class.
		Insert a bogus class.
		Refactor a class.
		Split an array.

		Merge arrays.
		Fold an array.
		Flatten an array.
	Ordering	Reorder methods and instance variables.
		Reorder arrays.

Most Java obfuscators only perform layout obfuscation, with some limited data and control obfuscation. This is partly due to the Java verification process throwing out any illegal bytecode syntax. The Java Verifier is very important if you write mostly applets because remote code is always verified. These days, when there are fewer and fewer applets, the main reason Java obfuscators don't feature more high-level obfuscation techniques is that the obfuscated code has to work on a variety of Java virtual machines (JVMs).

Although the JVM specification is pretty well defined, each JVM has its own slightly different interpretation of the specification, leading to lots of idiosyncrasies when it comes to how a JVM will handle bytecode that can no longer be represented by Java source. JVM developers don't pay much attention to testing this type of bytecode, and your customers aren't interested in whether the bytecode is syntactically correct—they just want to know why it won't run on their platform.

Remember that there is certain degree of tightrope-walking in advanced forms of obfuscation—what I call *high-mode obfuscation*—so you need to be very careful about what these programs can do to your bytecode. The more vigorous the obfuscation, the more difficult the code is to decompile, but the more likely it is to crash a DVM.

The best obfuscators perform multiple transformations without breaking the DVM. Not surprisingly, the obfuscation companies err on the side of caution, which inevitably means less protection for your source code.

Layout Obfuscations

Most obfuscators work by obscuring the variable names or scrambling the identifiers in a class file to try and make the decompiled source code useless. As you saw in Chapter 3, this doesn't stop the bytecode from being executed because the DEX file uses pointers to the methods names and variables in the data section rather than the actual names.

Obfuscated code mangles the source-code output from a decompiler by renaming the variables in the constant pool with automatically generated garbage variables while leaving the code syntactically correct. This then ends up in the data section of a DEX file. In effect, the process removes all clues that a programmer gives when naming variables (most good programmers choose meaningful variable names). It also means the decompiled code requires some rework before the code can be recompiled, because of duplicate names.

Most capable programmers can make their way through obfuscated code, with or without the aid of hints from the variable names. With due care and attention, perhaps the aid of a profiler to understand the program flow, and maybe a disassembler to rename the variables, most obfuscated code can be changed back into something that's easier to handle no matter how significant the obfuscation.

Early obfuscators such as JODE replaced method names with `a`, `b`, `c`, `d` ... `z()`. Crema's identifiers were much more unintelligible, using Java-like keywords to confuse the reader (see Listing 4-17). Several other obfuscators went one step further by using Unicode-style names, which had the nice side effect of crashing many of the existing decompilers.

Listing 4-17. *Crema-Protected Code*

```
private void _mth015E(void 867 % static 931){
  void short + = 867 % static 931.openConnection();
  short +.setUseCaches(true);
  private01200126013D = new DataInputStream(short +.getInputStream());
  if(private01200126013D.readInt() != 0x5daa749)
        throw new Exception("Bad Pixie header");
  void do const throws = private01200126013D.readShort();
  if(do const throws != 300)
        throw new Exception("Bad Pixie version " + do const throws);
  _fld015E = _mth012B();
  for = _mth012B();
  _mth012B();
  _mth012B();
  _mth012B();
  short01200129 = _mth012B();
  _mth012B();
```

```
  _mth012B();
  _mth012B();
  _mth012B();
  void |= = _mth012B();
  _fld013D013D012Oimport = new byte[|=];
  void void = |= / 20 + 1;
  private = false;
  void = = getGraphics();
  for(void catch 11 final = 0; catch 11 final < |=;){
        void while if = |= - catch 11 final;
        if(while if > void)
             while if = void;
        private01200126013D.readFully(_fld013D013D0120import, catch 11 final,
while if);
        catch 11 final += while if;
        if(= != null){
             const = (float)catch 11 final / (float)|=;
             =.setColor(getForeground());
             =.fillRect(0, size().height - 4, (int)(const * size().width), 4);
        }
  }
}
```

Most obfuscators are much better at reducing the size of a class file than protecting the source. But PreEmptive Software holds a patent that breaks the link between the original source and obfuscated code and goes some way toward protecting your code. All the methods are renamed to a, b, c, d, and so on. But unlike other programs, PreEmptive renames as many methods as possible using operator overloading. Overloaded methods have the same name but different numbers of parameters, so more than one method can be renamed a():

```
getPayroll()                                   becomes   a()
makeDeposit(float amount)              becomes   a(float a)
sendPayment(String dest)               becomes   a(String a)
```

An example from PreEmptive is shown in Listing 4-18.

Listing 4-18. *Operator Overloading*

```
// Before Obfuscation

private void calcPayroll(RecordSet rs) {

    while (rs.hasMore()) {
        Employee employee = rs.getNext(true);
        employee.updateSalary();
        DistributeCheck(employee);
    }
}
```

```
// After Obfuscation

private void a(a rs) {

    while (rs.a()) {
        a = rs.a(true);
        a.a();
        a(a);
    }
}
```

Giving multiple names to the different methods can be very confusing. True, the overloaded methods are difficult to understand, but they aren't impossible to comprehend. They too can be renamed into something easier to read. Having said that, operator overloading has proved to be one of the best layout-obfuscation techniques to beat because it breaks the link between the original and the obfuscated Java code.

Control Obfuscations

The concept behind control obfuscations is to confuse anyone looking at decompiled source by breaking up the control flow of the source. Functional blocks that belong together are broken apart, and functional blocks that don't belong together are intermingled to make the source much more difficult to understand.

Collberg et al's paper broke down control obfuscations into a further three classifications: *computation, aggregation*, and *ordering*. Let's look at some of the most important of these obfuscations or transformations in a little more detail.

Computation Obfuscation

Let's look at computation obfuscation, which attempts to hide the control flow and sprinkles in additional code to throw hackers off the scent.

(1) Inserting Dead or Irrelevant Code

You can insert dead code or dummy code to confuse your attacker; it can be extra methods or simply a few lines of irrelevant code. If you don't want the performance of your original code to be affected, then add the code in such a way that it's never executed. But be careful, because many decompilers and even obfuscators remove code that never gets called.

Don't limit yourself to inserting Java code—there's no reason you can't insert irrelevant bytecode. Mark Ladue wrote a small program called HoseMocha that altered a class file by adding a `pop` bytecode instruction at the end of every method. As far as most JVMs were concerned, this instruction was irrelevant and was ignored. But Mocha couldn't handle it and crashed. No doubt if Mocha's author had survived, the problem could have been easily fixed, but he didn't.

(2) Extending Loop Conditions

You can obfuscate code by making loop conditions much more complicated. You do this by extending the loop condition with a second or third condition that doesn't do anything. It shouldn't affect the number of times the loop is executed or decrease the performance. Try to use bitshift or ? operators in your extended condition for some added spice.

(3) Transforming Reducible to Non-Reducible

The holy grail of obfuscation is to create obfuscated code that can't be converted back into its original format. To do this, you need to break the link between the bytecode and the original Java source. The obfuscator transforms the bytecode control flow from its original reducible flow to something irreducible. Because Java bytecode in some ways is more expressive than Java, you can use the Java bytecode `goto` statement to help.

Let's revisit an old computing adage, which states that using the `goto` statement is the biggest sin that can be committed by any self-righteous computer programmer. Edsger W. Dijkstra's paper "Go To Statement Considered Harmful" (http://dl.acm.org/citation.cfm?doid=362929.362947) was the beginning of this particular religious fervor. The anti-`goto` statement camp produced enough anti-`goto` sentiment in its heyday to put it right up there with the best iPhone versus Android flame wars.

Common sense says it's perfectly acceptable to use the `goto` statement under certain limited circumstances. For example, you can use `goto` to replace how Java uses the `break` and `continue` statements. The issue is in using `goto` to break out of a loop or having two `goto` statements operate within the same scope. You may or may not have seen it in action, but bytecode uses the `goto` statement extensively as a means to control the code flow. But the scopes of two `goto`*s* never cross. The Fortran statement in Listing 4-18 illustrates a `goto` statement breaking out of a control loop.

Listing 4-18. *Breaking Out of a Control Loop Using a* `goto` *Statement*

```
        do 40 i = 2,n
                if(dx(i).le.dmax) goto 50
        dmax = dabs(dx(i))
40      continue
50      a = 1
```

One of the principal arguments against using this type of coding style is that it can make it almost impossible to model the control flow of a program and introduces an arbitrary nature into the program—which almost by definition is a recipe for disaster. The control flow has become *irreducible*.

As a standard programming techniques, it's a very bad idea to attempt to do this because not only is it likely to introduce unforeseen side effects—it's no longer possible to reduce the flow into a single flow graph—but it also makes the code unmanageable.

But there is an argument that this is the perfect tool for protecting bytecode if you can assume that the person who is writing the protection tool to produce the illegal `goto`s knows what they're doing and won't introduce any nasty side effects. It certainly makes the bytecode much harder to reverse-engineer because the code flow does indeed become irreducible; but it's important that any new constructs added be as similar as possible to the original.

A few words of warning before I leave this topic. Although a traditionally obfuscated class file is almost certainly functionally the same as its original counterpart, the same can't be said of a rearranged version. You have to place a large amount of trust in the protection tool, or it will be blamed for odd intermittent behavior. If possible, always test your transformed code on your target devices.

(4) Adding Redundant Operands

Another approach is to add extra insignificant terms to some of your basic calculations and round up the result before you use the result. For example, the code in Listing 4-19 prints "k = 2".

Listing 4-19. *Before Redundant Operands*

```
import java.io.*;

public class redundantOperands {
  public static void main(String argv[]) {
        int i=1;
        int j=2;
        int k;
```

```
        k = i * j;
        System.out.println("k = " + k);
  }
}
```

Add some redundant operands to the code, as shown in Listing 4-20, and the result will be exactly the same because you cast k to an integer before you print it.

Listing 4-20. *After Redundant Operands*

```
import java.io.*;

public class redundantOperands {

  public static void main(String argv[]) {
        int i = 1, j = 2;
        double x = 0.0007, y = 0.0006, k;

        k = (i * j) + (x * y);
        System.out.println(" k = " + (int)k);
  }
}
```

(5) Removing Programming Idioms (or Writing Sloppy Code)

Most good programmers amass a body of knowledge over their careers. For increased productivity, they use the same components, methods, modules, and classes over and over again in a slightly different way each time. Like osmosis, a new language gradually evolves until everyone decides to do some things in more or less the same way. Martin Fowler et al's book *Refactoring: Improving the Design of Existing Code* (Addison-Wesley, 1999) is an excellent collection of techniques that take existing code and refactor it into shape.

But this type of language standardization creates a series of idioms that give the hacker way too many helpful hints, even if they can only decompile part of your code. So throw out all your programming knowledge, stop using design patterns or classes that you know have been borrowed by lots of other programmers, and *defactor* your existing code.

Writing sloppy code, or defactoring the code, is easy. It's a heretical approach that gets under my skin and ultimately affects the performance and long-term maintenance of code, but it may work well if you use some sort of automated defactoring tool.

(6) Parallelizing Code

Converting your code to threads can significantly increase its complexity. The code doesn't necessarily have to be thread-compatible, as you can see in the HelloThread example in Listing 4-21. The flow of control has shifted from a sequential model to a quasi-parallel model, with each thread being responsible for printing a different word.

Listing 4-21. *Adding Threads*

```
import java.util.*;

public class HelloThread extends Thread
{
   private String theMessage;

   public HelloThread(String message) {
      theMessage = message;
      start();
   }

   public void run() {
    System.out.println(theMessage);
   }

   public static void main(String []args)
   {
      new HelloThread("Hello, ");
      new HelloThread("World");
   }
}
```

The downside of this approach is the programming overhead involved to make sure the threads are timed correctly and any interprocess communication is working correctly so the program executes as intended. The upside is that it in a real-world example, it can take significantly longer to realize that the code can be collapsed into a sequential model.

Aggregation Obfuscation

In aggregation obfuscation, you take code that should belong together and split it up. You also merge methods that wouldn't normally or logically belong together.

(1) Inlining and Outlining Methods

Inlining methods—replacing every method call with the actual body of the method—is often used to optimize code because doing so removes the overhead of the call. In Java code, this has the side effect of ballooning the code, often making it much more daunting to understand. You can also balloon the code by creating a dummy method that takes some of the inlined methods and outlines them into a dummy method that looks like it's being called but doesn't actually do anything.

Mandate's OneClass obfuscator took this transformation to the extreme by inlining every class in an application into a single Java class. But like all early obfuscation tools, OneClass is no longer with us.

(2) Interleaving Methods

Although it's a relatively simple task to interleave two methods, it's much more difficult to break them apart. Listing 4-22 shows two independent methods; in Listing 4-23, I've interleaved the code together so the methods appear to be connected. This example assumes you want to show the balance and e-mail the invoice, but there is no reason it couldn't be interleaved to allow you to only email the invoice.

Listing 4-22. *showBalance and emailInvoice*

```
void showBalance(double customerAmount, int daysOld) {
  if(daysOld > 60) {
        printDetails(customerAmount * 1.2);
  } else {
        printDetails(customerAmount);
  }
}
void emailInvoice(int customerNumber) {
  printBanner();
  printItems(customerNumber);
  printFooter();
}
```

Listing 4-23. *showBalanceEmailInvoice*

```
void showBalanceEmailInvoice(double customerAmount, int daysOld, int
customerNumber) {
  printBanner();
  if(daysOld > 60) {
        printItems(customerNumber);
        printDetails(customerAmount * 1.2);
  } else {
        printItems(customerNumber);
```

```
        printDetails(customerAmount);
    }
    printFooter();
}
```

(3) Cloning Methods

You can clone a method so that the same code but different methods are called under nearly identical circumstances. You could call one method over another based on the time of day to give the appearance that there are external factors when there really aren't. Use a different style in the two methods, or use cloning in conjunction with the interleaving transformation so the two methods look very different but really perform the same function.

(4) Loop Transformations

Compiler optimizations often perform a number of loop optimizations. You can perform the same optimizations by hand or code them in a tool to obfuscate the code. *Loop unrolling* reduces the number of times a loop is called, and *loop fission* converts a single loop into multiple loops. For example, if you know `maxNum` is divisible by 5, you can unroll the `for` loop as shown in Listing 4-23. Listing 4-24 shows an example of loop fission.

Listing 4-23. *Loop Unrolling*

```
// Before
for (int i = 0; i<maxNum; i++){
    sum += val[i];
}
// After
for (int i = 0; i<maxNum; i+=5){
    sum += val[i] + val[i+1] + val[i+2] + val[i+3] + val[i+4];
}
```

Listing 4-24. *Loop Fission*

```
// Before
for (x=0; x < maxNum; x++){
  i[x] += j[x] + k[x];
}
// After
for (x=0; x < maxNum; x++) i[x] += j[x];
for (x=0; x < maxNum; x++) i[x] += k[x];
```

Ordering Obfuscation

With this technique, you reorder variables and expressions into odd combinations and formats to create confusion in the decompiler's mind.

(1) Reordering Expressions

Reordering statements and expressions has a very minor effect on obfuscating the code. But there is one example where reordering the expressions at a bytecode level can have a much more significant impact when it once again breaks the link between bytecode and Java source.

PreEmptive software uses a concept known as transient variable caching (TVC) to reorder a bytecode expression. TVC is a straightforward technique that has been implemented in DashO. Say you want to swap two variables, x and y. The easiest way to accomplish this is to use a temporary variable, as shown in Listing 4-24. Otherwise you may end up with both variables containing the same value.

Listing 4-24. *Variable Swapping*

```
temp = x;
x = y;
y = temp;
```

This produces the bytecode in Listing 4-25 to complete the variable swap.

Listing 4-25. *Variable Swapping in Bytecode*

```
iload_1
istore_3
iload_2
istore_1
iload_3
istore_2
```

But the stack behavior of the JVM means there isn't any need for a temporary variable. The temporary or transient variable is cached on the stack, and the stack now doubles as a memory location. You can remove the load and store operations for the temporary variable, as shown in Listing 4-26.

Listing 4-26. *Variable Swapping in Bytecode Using DashO's TVC*

```
iload_1
iload_2
istore_1
istore_2
```

(2) Reordering Loops

You can transform a loop, making it go backward (see Listing 4-27). This probably won't do much in the way of optimization, but it's one of the simpler obfuscation techniques.

Listing 4-27. *Loop Reversals*

```
// Before
x = 0;
while (x < maxNum){
  i[x] += j[x];
        x++;
}
// After
x = maxNum;
while (x > 0){
  x--;
  i[x] += j[x];
}
```

Data Obfuscations

Collberg et al's paper breaks data obfuscations into a further three different classifications: *storage and encoding, aggregation,* and *ordering*. Many of the transformations you've looked at so far exploit the fact that there are standard conventions to how programmers write code. Turn these conventions on their head, and you have the basis of a good obfuscation process or tool. The more transformations you employ, the less likely it will be that anyone or any tool can understand the original source. This section looks at data obfuscations that reshape the data into less natural forms.

(1) Storage and Encoding

Storage and encoding looks at unusual ways of storing the data by encoding it in bitmasks or by splitting variables. The data should always end up the same as it was originally. It's often difficult to understand someone else's or even your own code 6 to 12 months after it was written, but if it's stored in these novel ways then this type of encoding makes it a lot harder to understand.

(2) Changing Encoding

Collberg et al's paper shows a simple encoding example: an integer variable `int i = 1` is transformed to `i' = x*i + y`. If you choose `x = 8` and `y =3`, you get the transformation shown in Listing 4-28.

Listing 4-28. *Variable Obfuscations*

```
// Before
int i = 1;
while (i < 1000) {
  val = A[i];
  i++;
}
```

```
// After
int i = 11;
while (i<8003) {
  val = A[(i-3)/8];
  i+=8;
}
```

(3) Splitting Variables

Variables can also be split into two or more parts to create a further level of obfuscation. Collberg suggests a lookup table. For example, if you're trying to define the Boolean value of `a= true`, then you split the variable into `a1=0` and `a2=1` and do a lookup on the table in Table 4-2 to convert it back into the Boolean value.

Table 4-2. *Boolean Split*

a1	a2	A
1	0	false
0	1	true

(4) Converting Static to Procedural Data

An interesting if not very practical transformation is to hide the data by converting it from static data to procedural data. For example, the copyright information in a string could be generated programmatically in your code, possibly using a combination interleave transformations as discussed earlier. The method to output the copyright notice could use a lookup-table method or combine the string from several different variables spread throughout the application.

(5) Aggregation

In data aggregation, you hide the data structures by merging variables, putting variables into arrays of unrelated variables, and adding threads where they aren't needed.

(6) Merging Scalar Variables

Variables can be merged together or converted to different bases and then merged. The variables values can be stored in a series of bits and pulled out using a variety of bitmask operators.

(7) Class Transformations

One of my favorite transformations is to use threads to confuse a hacker who is trying to steal code. There is an overhead because threads are harder to understand and harder to get right. If someone is dumb enough to try to decompile code instead of writing their own code, then the likelihood is that they'll be scared off by lots of threads.

Sometimes threads aren't practical because the overhead is just too big; the next best obfuscation is to use a series of class transformations. The complexity of a class increases with the depth of a class. Many of the transformations I've discussed go against the programmer's natural sense of what's good and right in the world, but if you use inheritance and interfaces to the extreme, then you'll be glad to hear that this creates deep hierarchies that the hacker will need time to understand.

You also don't have to defactor (see the section "Removing Programming Idioms") if you don't want to; you can refactor too. Refactor two similar classes into a parent class, but leave behind a buggy version of one or more of the refactored classes. You can also refactor two dissimilar classes into a parent class.

(8) Array Transformations

Like variables, arrays can be split, merged, or interleaved into a single array; folded into multiple dimensions; or flattened into a one- or two-dimensional array. A straightforward approach is to split an array into two separate arrays, one containing even and the other the odd indices of the array. A programmer who uses a two-dimensional array does so for a purpose; changing the dimension of the array creates a significant impediment in trying to understand your code.

Ordering

Ordering data declarations removes a lot of the pragmatic information in any decompiled code. Typically, data is declared at the beginning of a method or just before it's first referenced. Spread the data declarations throughout your code, while still keeping the data elements in the appropriate scope

Obfuscation Conclusion

The best obfuscator would use a number of the techniques this section has looked at. But you don't need to buy an obfuscator—you can add lots of these transformations yourself. The aim is to confuse the would-be decompiler as much as possible by removing as much information as you can. You can do this programmatically or as you write your code. Some of the transformations ask the developer to simulate what happens in an optimization stage of a compiler; others are simply bad coding practice to throw the hacker off the scent.

A couple of caveats before you leave this section. First, remember that if you obfuscate your code by using the same identifier multiple times in the constant pool, you might want to talk to PreEmptive Software first because it holds the patent on this technique. Second, you take your chances with any form of high-mode obfuscation because usually you won't have the luxury of insisting that your code be run only on certain specific phone or device.

Finally, writing really bad code makes your code very difficult to read. Be careful that you don't throw the baby out with the bath water. Obfuscated code is hard to maintain and, depending on the transformation, could destroy the performance of your code. Be careful what transformations you apply. Automating defactoring so it can be refactored automatically will help you in the long run. Both ProGuard and DashO let you revert your obfuscations if you need to do it.

Web Services

Sometimes the simplest ideas are the most effective. One of the simpler ideas for protecting code is to split your Android source code and keep much of the functionality on a remote server away from any prying eyes. The downloaded APK is then a straightforward GUI front end without any interesting code. The server code doesn't have to be written in Java, and the web service can be written in a lightweight RESTful API. But as you saw earlier in this chapter, be careful to hide any usernames and passwords so hackers don't attack your web service. There are some drawbacks to splitting your code though, as it won't work if the device is offline.

Fingerprinting Your Code

Although it doesn't actually protect your code, putting a digital fingerprint in your software allows you to later prove that *you* wrote *your* code. Ideally, this fingerprint—usually a copyright notice—acts like a software watermark that you can retrieve at any time even if your original code went through a number of changes or manipulations before it made it into someone else's Java application or applet. As I've said several times, there is no 100% surefire way of protecting your code, but that might not matter if you can recover some losses by proving you wrote the original code.

If you're confused, note that digitally fingerprinting your code is completely different than signing your applet or application. Signed applets don't have any effect when it comes to protecting your code. Signing an applet helps the person downloading or installing the software decide whether to trust an applet by looking at the digital certificate associated with the software. It's a protection mechanism for someone using your software to certify that this application was written by XYZ Widget Corp. The user can then decide whether they trust XYZ Widget Corp before they continue downloading the applet or launching the application. A digital fingerprint, on the other hand, is typically recovered using a decoding tool. It helps protect the developer's copyright, not the end user's hard drive.

Several attempts at fingerprinting attempt to protect the entire application using, for example, a defined coding style. More primitive types of fingerprinting encode the fingerprint into a dummy method or variable name. This method name or variable may be made up of a variety of parameters such as the date, developer's name, name of the application, and so on. But this approach can create a Catch-22. Suppose you put a dummy variable in your code and someone just happens to cut and paste the decompiled method, complete with the dummy variable, into their program. How can you know it's your code without decompiling their code and probably breaking the law in the process?

Most decompilers and even some obfuscators strip this information, because it doesn't play an active role as the code is interpreted or executed. Ultimately, you need to be able to convince the decompiler or obfuscator that any protected method is part of the original program by invoking the dummy method or using a fake conditional clause that will never be true so the method will never get called:

```
if(false) then{
  invoke dummy method
}
```

A smart individual can see a dummy method even if the decompiler can't see that the previous clause will never be true. They will come to the conclusion that the dummy method is probably some sort of fingerprint. So, you need to attach the fingerprint information at the method level for a more robust fingerprint.

Finally, you don't want the fingerprint to damage the functionality or performance of your application. As you've seen, the Java Verifier often plays a significant role in determining what protection mechanisms you can apply to your code, so you need to make sure your fingerprint doesn't stop your bytecode from making it through the Verifier.

Let's use this discussion to define the criteria for a good digital-fingerprinting system:

- It doesn't use dead-code dummy methods or dummy variables.
- The fingerprint needs to work even if only part of the program is stolen.
- The performance of the application shouldn't be affected. The end user shouldn't notice a difference between the fingerprinted and non-fingerprinted code.
- The fingerprinted code should be functionally equivalent to the original code.
- The fingerprint must be robust or obscure enough to survive a decompilation attack as well as any obfuscation tools. Otherwise it can simply be removed.
- The bytecode should be syntactically correct to get past the Java Verifier.
- The class file needs to be able to survive someone else fingerprinting the code with their own fingerprint.
- You need a corresponding decoding tool to recover and view the fingerprint using, preferably, a secret key. The fingerprint shouldn't be visible to the naked eye or other hackers.

You don't need to be worried about whether the fingerprint is highly visible. On the one hand, if it's both visible and robust, then it's likely to scare off the casual hacker. But then, the more seasoned attacker will know exactly where to attack. If the casual hacker doesn't know the application is protected, then there's no up-front deterrent to look elsewhere. PreEmptive's DashO has a fingerprinting option.

Native Methods

An approach to help obscure critical information, such as login usernames and passwords, is to move the passwords to a native library. Native code decompiles into assembly code, which is much harder to read and can only be disassembled, not decompiled.

The Android Native Development Kit (NDK) is a companion tool to the Android SDK that lets a developer create portions of their app in native code. To create a native library that uses the Java Native Interface (JNI), create a folder called jni at the root of the project. The JNI file can be called decompilingandroid-jni.c. It must have the suffix -jni.c for the NDK to pick it up. Listing 4-29 is an example of a simple method in decompilingandroid-jni.c to return a string.

Listing 4-29. *Native Method decompilingandroid-jni.c*

```
jstring Java_com_riis_decompilingandroid_getPassword(JNIEnv* env, jobject thiz)
{
  return (*env)->NewStringUTF(env, "password");
}
```

The reference to this method is handled in com.riis.decompilingandroid:

```
static
{
  // Load JNI library
  System.loadLibrary("decompilingandroid-jni");
}

/* Native methods that is implemented by the
 * 'decompilingandroid-jni' native library, which is packaged
 * with this application.
 */
public native String getPassword();
```

The return type is jstring, and the method name is prefaced with Java_ followed by the classpath, class name, and method. This full name is important for the JNI to map this method to the com.riis.example class.

Create a make file called Android.mk that describes the native sources to the NDK build:

```
LOCAL_PATH := $(call my-dir)
include $(CLEAR_VARS)
LOCAL_MODULE    := decompilingandroid-jni
LOCAL_SRC_FILES := decompilingandroid-jni.c
include $(BUILD_SHARED_LIBRARY)
```

Build your native code by running the ndk-build script from your project's directory. The ndk-build script is installed as part of the NDK SDK and must to be run under the Linux, OS X, or Windows (with Cygwin) platform:

```
cd <project>
<ndk>/ndk-build
```

If the build is successful, you end up with the following file:

```
<project>/libs/armeabi/libdecompilingandroid-jni.so
```

Simply moving the static string into a native library doesn't necessarily eliminate the problem of insecure strings. In the previous example, the string "password" can be easily found by viewing `libdecompilingandroid-jni.so` in a text editor. To secure the password even further, break it up into multiple chunks and concatenate the results back together. Listing 4-30 is an example of breaking up the `cxYacuzafrabru5a1beb` web service API password.

Listing 4-30. *Hiding Passwords from Disassemblers*

```
char str[80];
char *str1 = "bru";
char *str2 = "1beb";
char *str3 = "5a";
char *str4 = "fra";
char *str5 = "cxY";
char *str6 = "uza";
char *str7 = "ac";

strcpy(str, str5);
strcat(str, str7);
strcat(str, str6);
strcat(str, str4);
strcat(str, str1);
strcat(str, str3);
strcat(str, str2);

return (*env)->NewStringUTF(env, str);
```

Native code will only run on a specific processor that it was targeted for at compile time. Every Android device runs on an ARM processer except a few that aren't generally available, but that may change in the future. Google TV doesn't support the NDK.

Non-Obfuscation Strategies Conclusion

The fact that the Java class file and now the DEX file contain so much information makes it exceptionally difficult to protect the underlying source. And yet most software developers continue to ignore the consequences, leaving their intellectual property at risk. A good obfuscation process should take polynomial time to produce and exponential time to reverse. I hope this section's fairly exhaustive list of obfuscation transformations helps you approach something nearing that goal. At the very least, Collberg et al's paper contains enough information for any developer who wants to get started in this area.

Table 4-3 summarizes the approaches discussed in this chapter. It's worth noting that many of the original obfuscation tools didn't survive the dot-com implosion, and the companies have either folded or moved into other areas of specialization.

Table 4-3. *Protection Strategies Overview*

Strategy	Potency	Resilience	Cost	Notes
Writing two versions of the applet or application	High	High	Medium	
Obfuscation	Medium	Medium	Medium	May break DVM
Web services and server-side execution	High	High	High	
Fingerprinting your code	Low	Low	Low	Useful for legal protection
Native methods	High	High	Low	Breaks code portability

One final word: be very careful about relying on obfuscation as your only method of protection. Remember that disassemblers can also be used to rip apart your `classes.dex` file and allow someone to edit the bytecode directly. Don't forget that interactive demonstrations over the Web or limited-functionality demonstration versions of your software can be very effective.

Obfuscators

Based on your newfound understanding of obfuscation techniques, let's take a quick tour of the available Android obfuscators.

Crema

Although it won't work for Android APKs, it's worth mentioning Crema for historical reasons. Like many of the Java obfuscators of its day, it's no longer around. As mentioned earlier in the chapter, Crema was the original obfuscator and was a complementary program to the oft-mentioned Mocha, written by the late Hanpeter Van Vliet. Mocha was given away free, but Crema cost somewhere around $30. To safeguard against Mocha, you had to buy Crema.

Crema performs some rudimentary obfuscation and has one interesting side effect: it flags class files so that Mocha refuses to decompile any applets or applications that were previously run through Crema. But other decompilers soon came onto the market that were not so Crema friendly.

ProGuard

ProGuard is an open source obfuscator that ships with the Android SDK. In order to enable it in your build process, add the following to your `project.properties` file before building a release build. Everyone should do this to get basic obfuscation into their Android projects:

```
proguard.config=proguard.cfg
```

ProGuard provides mostly layout obfuscation protection, as you can see from Figure 4-8. It doesn't hide usernames and passwords but renames the methods and strings so that they no longer provide any contextual information to the hacker.

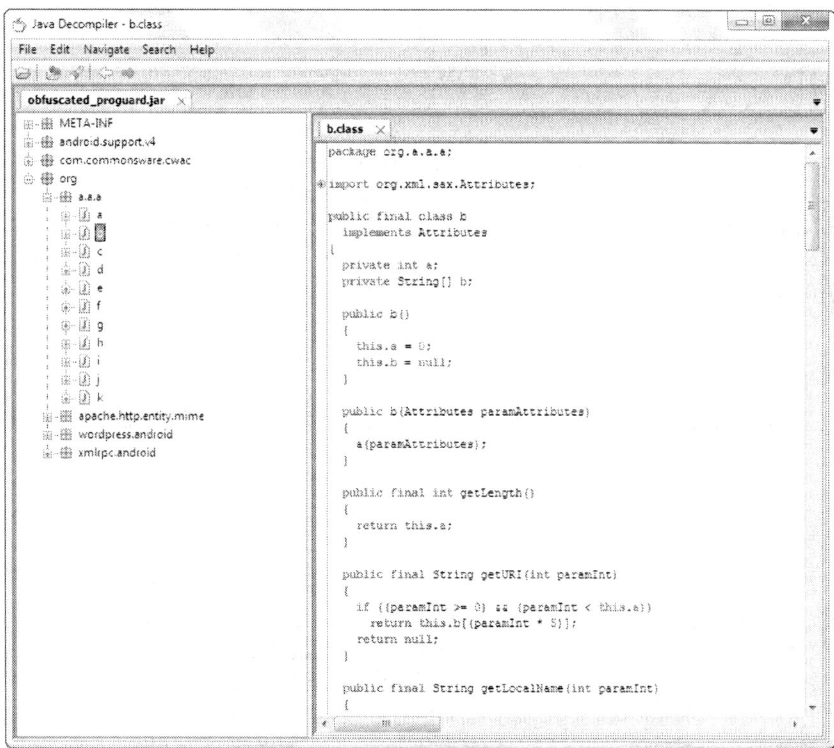

Figure 4-8. *ProGuard-protected code*

If you're using ProGuard, be careful how many public classes you use, because by default they won't be obfuscated. Practicing good object-oriented design pays off when using ProGuard. A good rule of thumb is to always decompile you APK after obfuscation to make sure it's doing exactly what you think it's doing.

DashO

DashO is a commercial obfuscator from PreEmptive software that has been around since the early Java days. It performs layout, control, and data obfuscations. Use the wizard to get DashO to obfuscate an Android app. Figure 4-9 shows the DashO GUI; in the left menu you can see the Control Flow, Renaming, and String Encryption options.

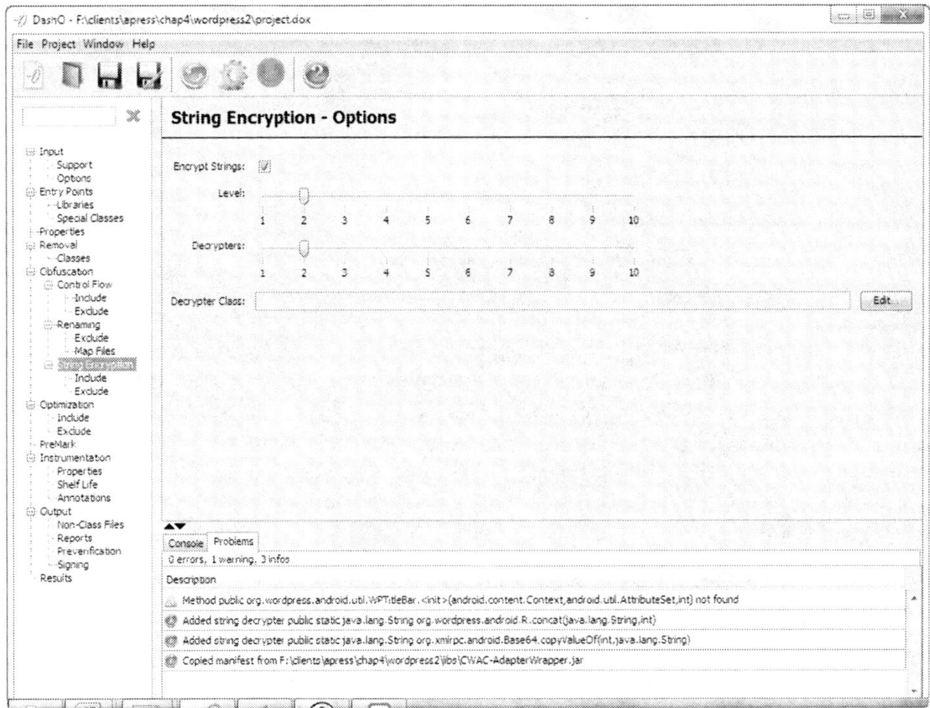

Figure 4-9. *DashO GUI*

Figure 4-10 uses the same app as in Figure 4-8, but this time it's been obfuscated using DashO instead of ProGuard. Note the string encryption.

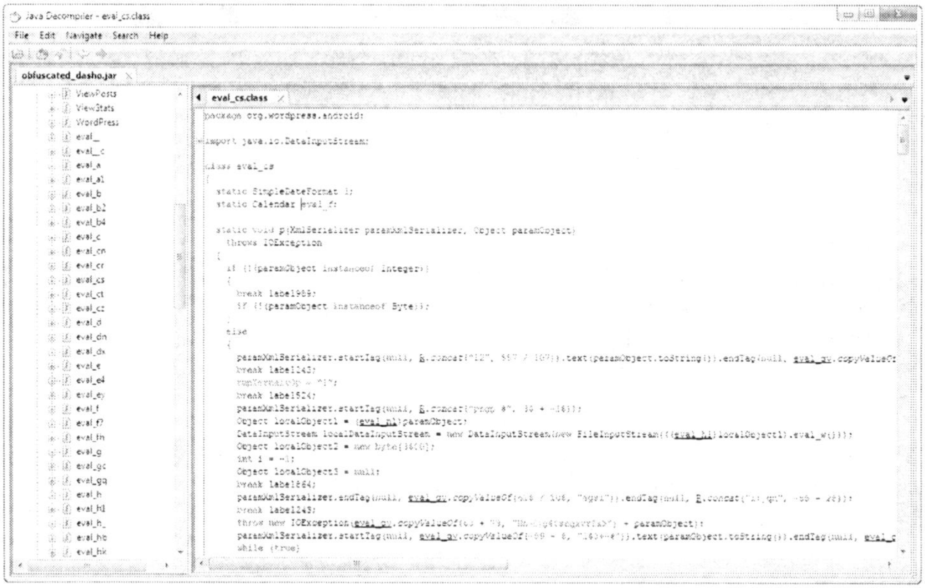

Figure 4-10. *DashO-protected code*

JavaScript Obfuscators

Just like Java obfuscators, there are a wide variety of JavaScript obfuscators. If you're using a HTML5/CSS approach to coding your Android app, then it would benefit you to use a JavaScript obfuscator or compressor to at least remove the comments from your code. Comments are simply too useful to someone who is trying to hack your app. Hackers also don't need to decompile a HTML5/CSS app—all they need to do is unzip it. This makes it very easy to create a fake version of your app.

Here are two JavaScript obfuscators are worth investigating:

- YUI Compressor, available from `https://github.com/yui/yuicompressor`
- JSMin, available from `www.crockford.com/javascript/jsmin.html`

I didn't include any web-based products because you want to be able to run an obfuscator from the command line to include it in your build process. That way, you can make sure your JavaScript is always obfuscated.

YUI Compressor is called as follows, where the minimized versions of the JavaScript files are named `decompilingandroid-min.js` instead of `decompilingandroid.js`:

```
java -jar yuicompressor.jar -o '.js$:-min.js' *.js
```

Listing 4-31 shows the code before YUI Compressor, and Listing 4-32 shows the code after YUI Compressor.

Listing 4-31. *Before YUI Compressor*

```
window.$ = $telerik.$;
$(document).ready(function() {
movePageElements();

var text = $('textarea').val();

if (text != "")
$('textarea').attr("style", "display: block;");
else
$('textarea').attr("style", "display: none;");

//cleanup
text = null;
});

function movePageElements() {
var num = null;
var pagenum = $(".pagecontrolscontainer");
if (pagenum.length > 0) {
var num = pagenum.attr("pagenumber");
if ((num > 5) && (num < 28)) {
var x = $('div#commentbutton');
$("div.buttonContainer").prepend(x);
}
else {
$('div#commentbutton').attr("style", "display: none;");
}
}

//Add in dropshadowing
if ((num > 5) && (num < 28)) {
var top = $('.dropshadow-top');
var middle = $('#dropshadow');
var bottom = $('.dropshadow-bottom');
$('#page').prepend(top);
$('#topcontainer').after(middle);
middle.append($('#topcontainer'));
middle.after(bottom);
}
```

```
//cleanup
num = null;
pagenum = null;
top = null;
middle = null;
bottom=null;
}

function expandCollapseDiv(id) {
$telerik.$(id).slideToggle("slow");
}

function expandCollapseHelp() {
$('.helpitems').slideToggle("slow");

//Add in dropshadowing
if ($('#helpcontainer').length) {
$('#help-dropshadow-bot').insertAfter('#helpcontainer');
$('#help-dropshadow-bot').removeAttr("style");
}
}

function expandCollapseComments() {
var style = $('textarea').attr("style");
if (style == "display: none;")
$('textarea').fadeIn().focus();
else
$('textarea').fadeOut();

//cleanup
style = null;
}
```

Listing 4-32. *After YUI Compressor*

```
window.$=$telerik.$;$(document).ready(function(){movePageElements();var
a=$("textarea").val();if(a!=""){$("textarea").attr("style","display:
block;")}else{$("textarea").attr("style","display: none;")}a=null});function
movePageElements(){var e=null;var
b=$(".pagecontrolscontainer");if(b.length>0){var
e=b.attr("pagenumber");if((e>5)&&(e<28)){var
a=$("div#commentbutton");$("div.buttonContainer").prepend(a)}else{$("div#comment
button").attr("style","display: none;")}}if((e>5)&&(e<28)){var f=$(".dropshadow-
top");var d=$("#dropshadow");var c=$(".dropshadow-
bottom");$("#page").prepend(f);$("#topcontainer").after(d);d.append($("#topconta
iner"));d.after(c)}e=null;b=null;f=null;d=null;c=null}function
expandCollapseDiv(a){$telerik.$(a).slideToggle("slow")}function
expandCollapseHelp(){$(".helpitems").slideToggle("slow");if($("#helpcontainer").
length){$("#help-dropshadow-bot").insertAfter("#helpcontainer");$("#help-
```

```
dropshadow-bot").removeAttr("style")}}function expandCollapseComments(){var
a=$("textarea").attr("style");if(a=="display:
none;"){$("textarea").fadeIn().focus()}else{$("textarea").fadeOut()}a=null};
```

Whereas YUI Compressor obfuscates as well as minimizes, JSMin just minimizes the JavaScript. Be warned that there are also JavaScript beautifiers that can reverse the process; see `http://jsbeautifier.org`.

Summary

In this chapter, you've learned how to root a phone, download and decompile an APK, and obfuscate the APK using a couple of tools. That's a lot to digest. In the next two chapters, you build your own Android obfuscator and decompiler. In Chapter 5, you work on the design, and in Chapter 6 you complete the decompiler implementation. In the final chapter of the book, you return to the many of the tools you first used in this chapter to see how effective they are against a series of real-world Android apps. Each of them will act as a case study in which you have the original source code to test your source protection against the decompilers and disassemblers.

Chapter 5

Decompiler Design

The next two chapters focus on how to create the decompiler, which is in fact a cross-compiler that translates bytecode to source code. I cover the theory behind the relevant design decisions as they arise, but the intention is to provide enough background information to get you going rather than give you a full-blown chapter on compiler theory.

Don't expect your decompiler, DexToSource to be more comprehensive or better than anything currently on the market; to be honest, it's probably closer to Mocha than Jad or JD-GUI. As with most things, the first 80–90% is the easiest, and the last 10–20% takes much longer to complete. But DexToSource shows you in basic steps how to write a simple Android decompiler that can reverse-engineer the majority of code you'll come across. And it's also the first pure `classes.dex` decompiler—everything else requires that you translate the `classes.dex` to Java class files before you can decompile it.

I cover the general design of the DexToSource decompiler in this chapter and delve into its implementation in the next. I'll round off the book by showing you how to decompile some open source APKs and looking at what the future may have in store for Android decompilers, obfuscators, and bytecode rearrangers.

The tone of the next two chapters is as practical as possible; I try not to burden you with too much theory. It's not that it isn't tempting to pad the book with endless pages of compiler theory; it's just that there are too many other good books on the subject. *Compilers: Principles, Techniques, and Tools* by Alfred Aho, Ravi Sethi, and Jeffrey Ullman (Prentice Hall, 2006), also known as the Dragon book because of its cover design, is just one of the better examples that quickly springs to mind. Andrew Appel's *Modern Compiler Implementation in Java* (Cambridge University Press, 2002) is another highly recommended tome. I'm going more for the style of *Crafting a Compiler With C* by Charles Fischer and Richard LeBlanc (Addison Wesley, 1991). Having said that, when there are theoretical considerations that you need to know about, I discuss them as necessary.

Theory Behind the Design

As mentioned earlier, writing a decompiler is pretty similar to writing a compiler or cross-compiler because both translate data from one format to another. The essential difference between a decompiler and a compiler is that they go in opposite directions. In a standard compiler, source code is converted to tokens and then parsed and analyzed to finally produce a binary executable.

As it happens, decompiling is a very similar process to compilation, but in this case the back end of the compiler is changing the intermediary symbols back into source code rather than into assembler. Because of the binary format of an Android `classes.dex` file, you can quickly transform the binary into bytecode; then you can treat the bytecode as just another language, and the decompiler becomes a cross-compiler or source code translator that transforms bytecode to Java.

An abundance of other source code translators translate between different languages: for example, from COBOL to C, or even from Java to Ada or C, which gives you plenty of places to look for ideas.

In case you're confused about the difference between opcodes and bytecodes, an *opcode* is a single instruction such as `sget-object` that may or may not be followed by a data value or operand. Opcodes and operands together are generally referred to as bytecodes. [max 255]

Defining the Problem

At its simplest, the problem you're trying to solve is how to convert `classes.dex` into a series of files of corresponding Java source code. Listing 5-1 shows the bytecode from a disassembled version of the `classes.dex` file of the `Casting.java` source code from the previous chapter's Listing 4-15. These are your before (bytecode) and after (`Casting.java`) pictures.

Listing 5-1. *Casting Bytecode*

```
const/4 v0,0
const/16        v1,128
if-ge           v0,v1,28
sget-object     v1, field[2]
new-instance    v2, type[6]
invoke-direct   method[4], {v2}
```

```
const-string             v3, string[20]
invoke-virtual           method[7], {v2, v3}
move-result-object       v2
invoke-virtual           method[6], {v2, v0}
move-result-object       v2
const-string             v3, string[0]
invoke-virtual           method[7], {v2, v3}
move-result-object       v2
invoke-virtual           method[5], {v2, v0}
move-result-object       v2
invoke-virtual           method[8], {v2}
move-result-object       v2
invoke-virtual           method[2], {v1,v2}
add-int/lit8             v0, v0, 1
int-to-char              v0, v0
goto                     d7
return-void
```

Filling in the overall structure of the file, field, and the method names looks straightforward enough; you can get that information from DexToXML. But the real meat of the problem is converting the opcodes and operands into Java. You need a parser that can match these opcodes and convert the data back into Java source. You also need to be able to mirror the control flow and any explicit transfers (note the `goto` statements) as well as handle any corresponding labels.

Opcodes can be broken down into the following types:

- Load and save instructions
- Arithmetic instructions
- Type-conversion instructions
- Object creation and manipulation
- Operand stack-management instructions
- Control-transfer instructions
- Method-invocation and return instructions
- Handling exceptions
- Implementing `finally`
- Synchronization

Every opcode has a defined behavior that you use in the parser to re-create the original Java. Google's "Bytecode for the Dalvik VM" at `www.netmite.com/android/mydroid/dalvik/docs/dalvik-bytecode.html` does a good job of describing Dalvik opcodes in what can only be termed Technicolor detail. You'll use this information in the decompiler's grammar to create a parser that will convert the opcodes and operands in Listing 5-1 back into the original source.

The goal of this chapter is to show you how to achieve this. The structure of your parser at its most basic will be similar to Figure 5-1.

Figure 5-1. *DexToSource parser*

The incoming character stream of bytecode needs to be split into a token stream (what is known as the lexer) for the parser to analyze. The parser consumes this token stream and outputs Java source based on a series of rules defined in the parser.

This chapter explains how to create the lexer and parser and discusses whether this approach makes the most sense and how you can tweak it to create something more robust. To begin, the next section talks about the compiler tools available to help you create the lexer and parser pieces of Figure 5-1, rather than building them by hand.

(De)Compiler Tools

You need to make a number of choices before writing your decompiler. You could code the entire decompiler by hand, as has been done for several Java decompilers; or you can look at tools that help make the job a lot easier to code. These tools are called *compiler-compilers*, and they're defined as any tools that help create a parser, interpreter, or compiler. This is the approach I outline here, focusing on the following tools:

- Lex
- Yacc
- JLex
- CUP
- ANTLR

The most common of these tools are Lex and Yacc (Yet Another Compiler-Compiler). Such compiler-compiler tools can be used to scan and parse the bytecode and have been used by many developers for more complex tasks. Lex and Yacc operate on textual input files. The Lex input file defines how the input character stream is to be tokenized using pattern matching. The Yacc input file consists of a series of production rules for the tokens. These define the grammar, and the corresponding actions generate a user-defined output.

The tokenizing rules and the pattern matching rules defined in Lex and Yacc are used to generate typically C files that are then compiled and used to transform the input files into the desired target output. For your purposes, the compiler-compiler tools will generate Java files, not C files, which will become the source for your decompiler engine.

There are two principal reasons for using compiler-compiler tools. First, these tools dramatically reduce the number of lines of code, which makes it a lot easier for readers to understand concepts. Second, using such tools cuts development time in half.

On the negative side, the generated code, once compiled, can be much slower than what can be achieved by handcrafting a compiler front end. But making the code easy to follow is a prerequisite of this book—nobody wants to read reams of code to understand what is happening. So, the book uses a version or derivative of Lex and Yacc.

Myriad alternatives are based on Lex and Yacc. If you take Java as the target output language, then your choices are JLex or JFlex and CUP (Construction of Useful Parsers) or BYACC/J as classic Lex and Yacc variants. Then there is Another Tool for Language Recognition (ANTLR, `www.antlr.org`), the compiler-compiler tool formerly known as PCCTS, and JavaCC (`http://javacc.java.net`), which combine the lexer and parser steps into one file.

Lex and Yacc

Lex and Yacc work together. Lex parses the incoming stream into tokens, and Yacc parses these tokens and generates output. Lex and Yacc are Unix command-line tools that come with most variations of Unix and Linux, although they're oddly absent on Mac OSs.

Lex uses regular expressions to break up the incoming stream into tokens, and Yacc tries to take these tokens and match them to a number of production rules using a shift/reduce mechanism. Most production rules are associated with an action, and it's these context-sensitive actions that output, in this case, Java source code.

Tokens are also known as *terminals*. Production rules are identified by a single *non-terminal*. Each non-terminal is made up of a series of terminals and other non-terminals. An analogy that most people use is to think of terminals (tokens) as leaves and non-terminals as branches on a tree.

Yacc is a bottom-up LALR(1) parser. *Bottom up* means you construct the parse tree from the leaves, whereas a *top-down* parser tries to construct the tree from the root. LALR(1) means this type of parser processes tokens supplied by the scanner Lex from left to right (**L**A**LR**(1)) using the rightmost derivation and can look ahead one token (**LA**LR(**1**)). An LR parser is also known as a *predictive* parser, and an LALR is the result of merging two LR sets whose items are identical except for the lookahead sets. It's very similar to an LR(1) parser, but LALR(1) parsers are typically much smaller because the lookahead token helps reduce the number of possible patterns.

LALR(1) parser generators are the de facto standard in the rest of the computing world. But Java parsers are more likely to fall into the LL(k) category. LL(k) parsers are top-down parsers, scanning from left to right (LL(k)) using the leftmost derivation (LL(k))—which is where the top down comes from—and looking ahead *k* tokens.

Many of the standard compiler-construction books heavily feature Lex and Yacc rather than any other LL(k) alternatives. See `http://dinosaur.compilertools.net/` for more information and links to some excellent resources.

Stephen Johnson at AT&T Bell Laboratories in New Jersey wrote the original version of Yacc. Lex and Yacc as well as Sed and Awk were have been included in every Unix implementation since the early days of Berkeley in the 1980s. Sed and Awk were typically used for simple command-line parsing tools, and Lex and Yacc were reserved for complicated parsers. Unix system administrators and developers typically use some or all of these tools from time to time in an effort to transform or translate an input file into some other format. These days Perl, Python and Ruby have largely taken over from such utilities with Lex and Yacc being reserved for only the most difficult of tasks (if they're used at all).

Lex and Yacc have been copied many times and are available on many platforms. Commercial and public-domain variants are available on Windows—for example, from MKS and GNU (Flex/Bison).

It's doubtful that are many commercial compilers are built around Lex and Yacc, because they have limited functionality and can't deal with quirky aspects of some programming languages. Fortran, for example, is a nightmare to tokenize, because (among other things) it's oblivious to whitespace.

JLex and CUP Example

Whereas Lex and Yacc generate C code, JLex and CUP are versions of Lex and Yacc that generate Java code. Elliot Berk originally developed JLex at Princeton University; JLex has also been maintained by Andrew Appel (also at Princeton), the author of *Modern Compilers in Java/ML/C* (Cambridge University Press, 2002); and C. Scott Ananian, who is a director at the One Laptop per Child.

Like all versions of Lex, JLex allows you to use regular expressions to break up the input stream and turn it into tokens. It can be used in conjunction with CUP to define grammars, but first let's use JLex on its own as a simple scanner.

Lex, whether it's running on Unix or DOS in C or in Java, is a preprocessing language that transforms the specification or rules into the target language. A C language specification becomes `lex.yy.c` and a Java specification becomes `filename.lex.java` after it's run through the Lex program. The code output then needs to be compiled like any other C or Java program. Lex is normally used in conjunction with Yacc, but it can also be used on its own for simple tasks such as removing comments from source code. If you need to attach any logic to the program, you'll almost certainly need to hook it up to some sort of parser, such as Yacc or, in this case, CUP.

Earlier, the chapter mentioned that Lex and Yacc have been used for many years by compiler developers in the Unix community. If you're used to Lex, JLex does differ in a number of ways. Let's take a closer look.

JLex

A JLex file is split into three sections:

- User code
- JLex directives
- Regular-expression rules

Although the structure (shown later, in Listing 5-3) is different from the Unix version of Lex typically compiled using C instead of Java, and the definitions and macros are quite different too, fortunately the regular-expression rules use standard regular expressions. So, if you're familiar with Lex or even vi or Perl, it won't seem as though you've strayed too far from familiar ground. If you haven't come across regular expressions before, then the JLex manual (`www.cs.princeton.edu/~appel/modern/java/JLex/current/manual.html`) is a great place to start.

Everything that precedes the first %% is user code. It's copied "as is" into the generated Java file. Typically, this is a series of `import` statements. And because you're using JLex in conjunction with CUP, your user code consists of the following:

```
import java_cup.runtime.Symbol;
```

The directives section is next, beginning after the first %% and ending with another %%. This series of directives or flags tells JLex how to behave. For example, if you use the `%notunix` operating system compatibility directive, then JLex expects a newline to be represented by `\r\n` and not `\n` as it is in the Unix world. The remaining directives, listed next, allow you to enter your own code into various parts of the generated file or change the default name of the generated lex class, function, or type (for example, from `yylex` to `scanner`):

- Internal code
- Init class code
- End of file class
- Macro definitions
- State declarations
- Character counting
- Line counting
- Java CUP compatibility
- Component titles
- Default token type
- End of file
- Operating system compatibility
- Character sets
- Format to and from file
- Exceptions code
- End-of-file return value
- Interface to implement
- Making the generated class public

This example is only interested in a few of the directives, such as the %cup (CUP compatibility) directive. For your purposes, the directives section is something as simple as Listing 5-2.

Listing 5-2. *JLex Directives*

```
%%

%cup

digit  = [0-9]
whitespace  = [\ \t\n\r]
%%
```

The regular-expressions section is where the real scanning takes place. The rules are a collection of regular expressions that break up the incoming stream into tokens for the parser to do its job. As a simple example to put this all together, Listing 5-3 adds line numbers to any file input from the command line.

Listing 5-3. *JLex Scanner that Adds Line Numbers to Files*

```
import java.io.IOException;            // include the import statement in the
generated scanner

%%                                     // start of the directives

%public                                // define the class as public
%notunix                               // example is running on Windows
%class  Num                            // rename the class to Num

%type  void                            // Yytoken return type is void
%eofval{                               // Java code for execution at end-of-
file
   return;
%eofval}

%line                                  // turn line counting on

%{                                     // internal code to add to the scanner
                                       // to make it a standalone scanner
public static void main (String args []) throws IO Exception{
   new Num(System.in).yylex();
}
%}

%%                                     // regular expressions section
^\r\n                                  { System.out.println((yyline+1)); }
\r\n                                   { ; }
\n                                     { System.out.println(); }
```

```
.*$    { System.out.println((yyline+1)+"\t"+yytext()); }
```

Install JLex by obtaining a copy of `Main.java` from `www.cs.princeton.edu/~appel/modern/java/JLex/`. Copy it into a directory called `JLex`, and compile it using your favorite Java compiler. Save the `Num.lex` file (see Listing 5s-3), removing all the comments, and compile it as follows:

```
java JLex.Main Num.lex
mv  Num.lex.java Num.java
javac Num.java
```

Now you can add line numbers to your file by typing

```
java Num < Num.java > Num_withlineno.java
```

Normally, in a scanner/parser combination, the scanner operates as parser input. In the first example, you didn't even generate a token, so there is nothing to pass to CUP, your Java parser. Lex generates a `yylex()` function that eats tokens and passes them on to `yyparse()`, which is generated by Yacc. You'll rename these functions or methods `scanner()` and `parse()`, but the idea is the same.

CUP

CUP, being a Yacc parser, is closest to an LALR(1) (lookahead left-right) parser. It's one of a number of Yacc parser generators written for the Java language; BYACC and Jell are two other examples. If you're happier with an LL parser and don't want to use an LALR grammar, then you might want to look at ANTLR or JavaCC.

As explained earlier, Yacc lets you define grammar rules to parse incoming lexical tokens and produce the desired output as defined by your grammar. CUP is a public-domain Java variant of Yacc, which because of Java's portability compiles on any machine that has a JVM and JDK.

Be warned: CUP doesn't have exactly the same functionality or format as a Yacc grammar written for any C compiler, but it does behave in a somewhat similar fashion. CUP can be compiled on any operating system that supports a JDK.

To install CUP, copy the source files from `http://www2.cs.tum.edu/projects/cup/`. Compile by typing the following in the CUP root directory:

```
javac java_cup/*java java_cup/runtime/*.java
```

CUP files are made up of the following four sections:

- Preamble or declarations
- User routines
- List of symbols or tokens
- Grammar rules

The declarations section consists of a series Java package and import statements that vary depending on what other packages or classes you want to import. Assuming the CUP classes are in your classpath, add the following line of code to include the CUP classes:

```
import java_cup.runtime*;
```

All other imports or package references are optional. A start declaration tells the parser where to look for the start rule if you want it to start with some other parser rule. The default is to use the top production rule, so in most grammars you'll come across the start rule is redundant information.

Four possible user routines are allowed in CUP: action and parser are used to insert new code and override default scanner code and variables, init is used for any parser initialization, and scan is used by the parser to call the next token. All of these user routines are optional (see Listing 5-4).

Listing 5-4. *CUP User Routines*

```
action code {:
        // allows code to be included in the parser class
        public int max_narrow = 10;
        public double narrow_eps = 0.0001;
:};

parser code {:
        // allows methods and variables to be placed
        // into the generated parser class
        public void report_error(String message, Token tok) {
             errorMsg.error(tok.left, message);
        }
:};

// Preliminaries to set up and use the scanner.
init with {: scanner.init(); :};
scan with {: return scanner.yylex(); :};
```

Both init and scan are commonly used, even if only to change the name of the scanner/lexer to something more meaningful than Yylex(). Any routines within init are executed before the first token is requested.

Most parsers have a series of actions defined in the grammar section. CUP puts all these actions in a single class file. The action user routine allows you to define variables and add extra code, such as symbol-table manipulation routines, that can be referenced in the non-public action class. Parser routines are used to add extra code to the generated parser class—don't expect to use them often, if at all, except perhaps for better error handling.

CUP, like the original Yacc, acts like a stack machine. Every time a token is read, it's converted into a symbol and placed or shifted onto the stack. These tokens are defined in the symbols section.

Unreduced symbols are called *terminal* symbols, and symbols that have been reduced into some sort of rule or expression are called *non-terminal* symbols. To put it another way, terminal symbols are the symbols/tokens used by the JLex scanner, and non-terminal symbols are what the terminals become after they satisfy one of the patterns or rules in the grammar section. Listing 5-5 shows a good example of both terminal and non-terminal tokens.

Symbols can have associated integer, float, or string values that are propagated up the grammar rules until the group of tokens either satisfies a rule and can be reduced or alternatively crashes the parser if no rule is ever satisfied.

Listing 5-5. *Parser.CUP*

```
import java_cup.runtime.*;

// Interface to scanner generated by JLex.
parser code {:
        Parser(Scanner s) { super(); scanner = s; }
        private Scanner scanner;
:};
scan with {: return scanner.yylex(); :};

terminal NUMBER, BIPUSH, NEWARRAY, INT, ASTORE_1, ICONST_1;
terminal ISTORE_2, GOTO, ALOAD_1, ILOAD_2, ISUB, IMUL;
terminal IASTORE, IINC, IF_ICMPLE, RETURN, END;

non terminal    function, functions, keyword;
non terminal    number;

functions       ::=     function
                        |       functions function
                        ;

function        ::=     number keyword number number END
                        |       number keyword number END
                        |       number keyword keyword END
                        |       number keyword END
```

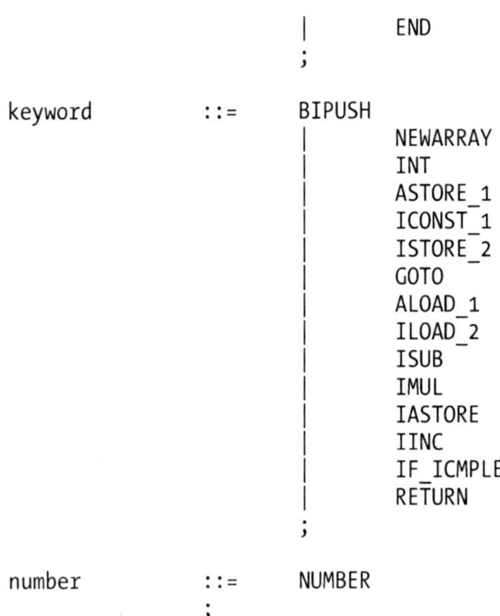

```
                                |       END
                                ;

keyword         ::=     BIPUSH
                                |       NEWARRAY
                                |       INT
                                |       ASTORE_1
                                |       ICONST_1
                                |       ISTORE_2
                                |       GOTO
                                |       ALOAD_1
                                |       ILOAD_2
                                |       ISUB
                                |       IMUL
                                |       IASTORE
                                |       IINC
                                |       IF_ICMPLE
                                |       RETURN
                                ;

number          ::=     NUMBER
                        ;
```

A parser's functionality depends on its ability to interpret a stream of input tokens and turn these tokens into the desired output as defined by the language's grammar. In order for the parser to have any chance of success, it needs to know every symbol along with its type before any shift/reduce cycles can take place. This symbol table is generated from the symbol list in the previous section.

The list of terminals in the symbol table is used by CUP to generate its own Java symbol table (`Sym.java`), which needs to be imported into the JLex scanner for JLex and CUP to work together.

As mentioned earlier, CUP is an LALR(1) machine, meaning it can look ahead one token or symbol to try to satisfy a grammar rule. If a production rule is satisfied, then the symbols are popped off the stack and reduced with the production rule. The aim of every parser is to convert these input symbols into a series of reduced symbols, right back to the start symbol or token.

In layman's terms, given a string of tokens and a number of rules, the goal is to trace the rightmost derivation in reverse by starting with the input string and working backward to the start symbol. You reduce the series of non-terminals to a terminal using bottom-up parsing. All input tokens are terminal symbols that are subsequently combined into non-terminals or other intermediate terminals using this shift/reduce principle. As each group of symbols is matched to a production rule, it ultimately kicks off an action that generates some sort of output defined in the production-rule action.

The parser in Listing 5-5 parses the input from the main method bytecode shown in Listing 5-6. The corresponding scanner is shown in Listing 5-7. It doesn't produce any output, to keep it as simple as possible.

Listing 5-6. *Main Method Bytecode*

```
0 getstatic #7 <Field java.io.PrintStream out>
3 ldc #1 <String "Hello World">
5 invokevirtual #8 <Method void println(java.lang.String)>
8 return
```

Listing 5-7. *Decompiler.lex*

```
package Decompiler;                          // create a package for the
Decompiler
import java_cup.runtime.Symbol;              // import the CUP classes

%%
%cup                                         // CUP declaration
%%

"getstatic"          { return new Symbol(sym.GETSTATIC, yytext()); }
"ldc"                { return new Symbol(sym.LDC, yytext()); }
"invokevirtual"      { return new Symbol(sym.INVOKEVIRTUAL, yytext()); }
"Method"             { return new Symbol(sym.METHOD, yytext()); }
"return"             { return new Symbol(sym.RETURN, yytext()); }
\"[a-zA-Z ]+\"       { return new Symbol(sym.BRSTRING, yytext()); }
[a-zA-Z\.]+          { return new Symbol(sym.BRSTRING, yytext()); }
\<                   { return new Symbol(sym.LABR, yytext()); }
\>                   { return new Symbol(sym.RABR, yytext()); }
\(                   { return new Symbol(sym.LBR, yytext()); }
\)                   { return new Symbol(sym.RBR, yytext()); }
\#[0-9]+|[0-9]+      { return new Symbol(sym.NUMBER, yytext());}
[ \t\r\n\f]          { /* ignore white space. */ }
.                    { System.err.println("Illegal character: "+yytext()); }
```

Under certain circumstances, it's possible that input tokens or intermediate symbols can satisfy multiple production rules: this is known as an *ambiguous grammar*. The precedence keyword in the symbol section allows the parser to decide which symbol takes higher precedence—for example, giving the symbols for multiplication and division precedence over the addition and subtraction symbols.

It's worth mentioning that CUP lets you dump the shift/reduction table for debugging purposes. The command to produce a human-readable dump of the symbols and grammar, the parse-state machine, and the parse tables and show the complete transitions is as follows (some of the output is shown in Listing 5-8):

```
java java_cup.Main -dump < Parser.CUP
```

Listing 5-8. *Partial CUP Debug Output*

```
-------- ACTION_TABLE --------
From state #0
 [term 2:SHIFT(to state 2)] [term 18:SHIFT(to state 5)]
From state #1
 [term 0:REDUCE(with prod 0)] [term 2:REDUCE(with prod 0)]
 [term 18:REDUCE(with prod 0)]
From state #2
 [term 2:REDUCE(with prod 23)] [term 3:REDUCE(with prod 23)]
 [term 4:REDUCE(with prod 23)] [term 5:REDUCE(with prod 23)]
 [term 6:REDUCE(with prod 23)] [term 7:REDUCE(with prod 23)]
 [term 8:REDUCE(with prod 23)] [term 9:REDUCE(with prod 23)]
 [term 10:REDUCE(with prod 23)] [term 11:REDUCE(with prod 23)]
 [term 12:REDUCE(with prod 23)] [term 13:REDUCE(with prod 23)]
 [term 14:REDUCE(with prod 23)] [term 15:REDUCE(with prod 23)]
 [term 16:REDUCE(with prod 23)] [term 17:REDUCE(with prod 23)]
 [term 18:REDUCE(with prod 23)]
From state #3
 [term 3:SHIFT(to state 13)] [term 4:SHIFT(to state 14)]
 [term 5:SHIFT(to state 8)] [term 6:SHIFT(to state 18)]
 [term 7:SHIFT(to state 11)] [term 8:SHIFT(to state 10)]
 [term 9:SHIFT(to state 23)] [term 10:SHIFT(to state 12)]
 [term 11:SHIFT(to state 17)] [term 12:SHIFT(to state 15)]
 [term 13:SHIFT(to state 20)] [term 14:SHIFT(to state 9)]
 [term 15:SHIFT(to state 19)] [term 16:SHIFT(to state 22)]
 [term 17:SHIFT(to state 21)]
From state #4
 [term 0:SHIFT(to state 7)] [term 2:SHIFT(to state 2)]
 [term 18:SHIFT(to state 5)]
From state #5
 [term 0:REDUCE(with prod 7)] [term 2:REDUCE(with prod 7)]
 [term 18:REDUCE(with prod 7)]
From state #6
 [term 0:REDUCE(with prod 2)] [term 2:REDUCE(with prod 2)]
 [term 18:REDUCE(with prod 2)]
From state #7
 [term 0:REDUCE(with prod 1)]
```

ANTLR

ANTLR stands for ANother Tool for Language Recognition. It's available for download at `www.antlr.org`. ANTLR is a recursive descent, LL(k), or top-down parser, whereas Yacc is an LR or bottom-up parser. ANTLR starts at the uppermost rule and tries to recognize the tokens, working outward to the leaves; Yacc starts with the leaves and works up to the highest rule.

ANTLR also differs fundamentally from JLex and CUP in that the lexer and parser are in the same file. Lexical rules that create tokens are all uppercase (for example, `IDENT`), and the token-parsing rules are all lowercase (for example, `program`).

The next example uses ANTLR v3, which was a complete rewrite of ANTLR v2. v3 also includes some very useful additional functionality, such as `StringTemplates` that pull your output statements out of the parser.

Figure 5-2 shows ANTLR integration with the Eclipse IDE. Scott Stanchfield has some excellent videos of setting up ANTLR in Eclipse and creating a parser at `http://vimeo.com/groups/29150`. This is one of best ANTLR resources to hit the ground running regardless of whether you're using Eclipse as your IDE. If you don't want to use Eclipse, ANTLRWorks is an excellent alternative.

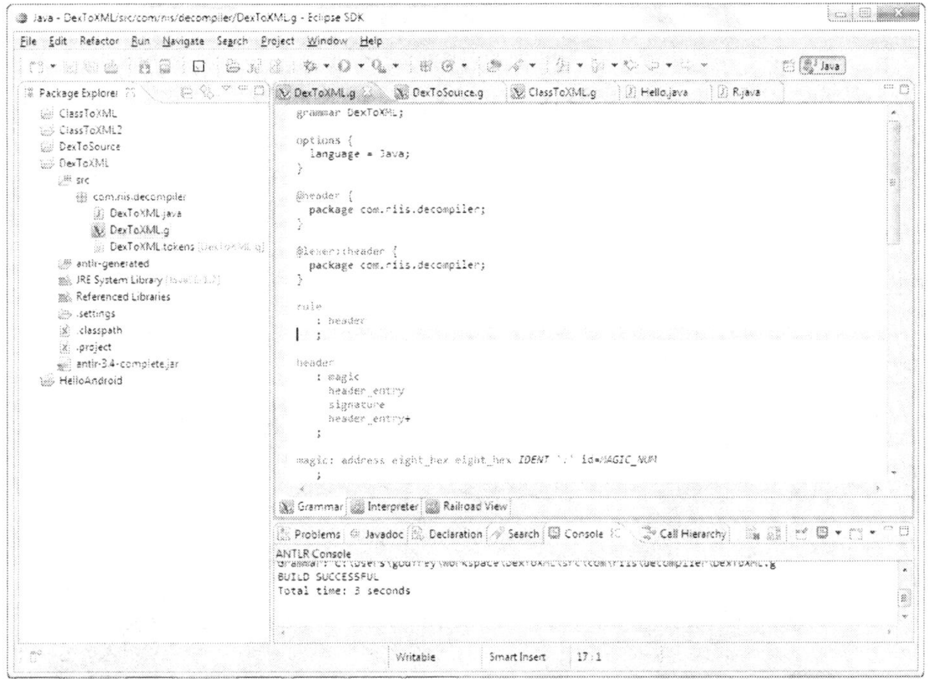

Figure 5-2. *ANTLR plug-in for Eclipse*

Terence Parr, the main force behind ANTLR, has also published two books on ANTLR: *The Definitive ANTLR Reference* (Pragmatic Bookshelf, 2007) and *Language Implementation Patterns* (Pragmatic Bookshelf, 2010).

ANTLR Example

DexToXML is the `classes.dex` parser from Chapter 3. DexToXML is completely written in ANTLR v3; here it parses dedexer output and converts the text into XML.

The way DexToXML parses hexadecimal digits serves as a simple example of how you can put together an ANTLR grammar file. The first line of the dedexer output shows the magic number header line from the `classes.dex` file:

```
00000000 :  64 65 78 0A     30 33 35 00     magic: dex\n035\0
```

ANTLR, like most other parsers, uses regular expressions (regex) in its lexer. The lexer breaks the input stream into tokens that are then consumed by rules in the parser. You can use the following regex to recognize the hex digit pairs in your ANTLR grammar:

```
HEX_DIGIT : ('0'..'9'|'a'..'f'|'A'..'F')('0'..'9'|'a'..'f'|'A'..'F') ;
```

Unlike Lex and Yacc, in ANTLR the lexer and parser are in the same file (see Listing 5-9). The lexer uses the uppercase rules, and the parser works with the lowercase rules.

Listing 5-9. *DexToXML.g*

```
grammar DexToXML;
options {
  language = Java;
}
@header {
  package com.riis.decompiler;
}
@lexer::header {
  package com.riis.decompiler;
}
rule: HEX_PAIR+;

HEX_PAIR : ('0'..'9'|'a'..'f'|'A'..'F')('0'..'9'|'a'..'f'|'A'..'F') ;
WS : ' '+ {$channel = HIDDEN;};
```

Each ANTLR parser has a number of sections. At its most basic, the `grammar` section defines the name of the parser. The output language of the generated ANTLR parser is set to Java in the `options` section, and the package name for the parser and lexer are set in the `@header` and `@lexer::header` sections. These are followed by the parser and lexer rules. The lexer recognizes groups of two hexadecimal digits, and the rule recognizes multiple groups of these hexadecimal pairs. Any whitespace is ignored by the `WS` rule and placed on a hidden channel.

For example, suppose you pass `64 65 78 0A`. Figure 5-3 illustrates what the parser sees.

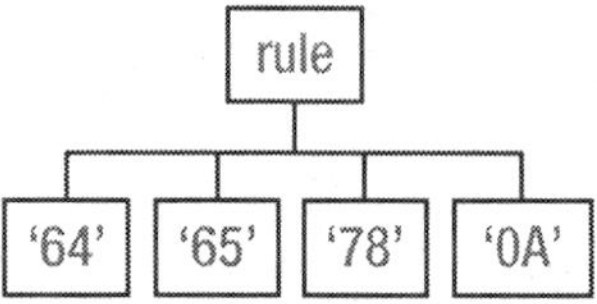

Figure 5-3. *Parsed pairs of hexadecimal numbers*

Strategy: Deciding on your Parser Design

ANTLR has been completely rewritten and continues to be developed; it also has many extras such as the ANTLRWorks tool and Eclipse plug-ins that make debugging parsers a treat. As you've seen, debugging Yacc output isn't for the faint hearted.

So, you'll build the parser using ANTLR v3. Doing so offers a number of benefits:

- Lexer and parser are in the same file
- `StringTemplates` functionality pulls the output functionality from the parser
- ANTLRWorks tool allows you to debug your parser
- Plenty of parser patterns to use
- Simple AST integration
- Eclipse integration

Adding `StringTemplates` and AST to the original design in Figure 5-1 yields a new parser design, shown in Figure 5-4.

Figure 5-4. *Final decompiler design*

`StringTemplates` means there is no longer any need for endless `System.out.println` statements in the parser to output the Java code. From a programmer's point of view, those `printlns` always troubled me when I designed parsers in the past. They have a bad code smell. `StringTemplates` allow you to separate the output from the logic that produces it. That alone is a good enough reason to choose ANTLR over JLex and CUP because it dramatically increases your ability to understand how the parser grammar works. It's also another reason why the parser is called DexToSource and not DexToJava: you could potentially write your own templates that would output C# or C++ by retargeting the templates to write the output in a different language.

For simplicity's sake, you can use one of the disassamblers such as DexToXML, baksmali, dedexer, or dx from the Android toolkit to provide the bytecode as a character stream rather than making your decompiler parse binary files. Then your ANTLR parser will convert the bytecode files into Java source.

A significant part of the problem with building a decompiler is making it general enough to deal with arbitrary cases. When Mocha comes across an unexpected language idiom, it either aborts or shoots out illegal `goto`s. Ideally, you should be able to code a general-solution decompiler rather than one that is little more than a series of standard routines and an awful lot of exception cases. You don't want DexToSource to fail on any construct, so a general solution is very attractive.

Before you take that approach, though, you need to know whether it has any disadvantages and whether you'll gain a better solution at the expense of outputting illegible code that looks nothing like the original source. Or, worse still, will it take an inordinate amount of time to get there? You could replace all the control structures in a program with a program counter and a single `while` loop, but that would destroy the mapping—and losing structural or syntactical equivalence is definitely not your goal, even if it's a general solution.

From my discussion, you know that unlike in other languages, you don't have the headache of separating data and instructions because all the data is in the `data` section. The remainder of this chapter and the next also show that recovering source-level expressions is relatively easy. So it seems that your main problem and any corresponding strategy you use mainly involve handling the bytecode's control flow.

The focus here is on the simpler approach where high-level structures are hard-coded, because it fits well with the parser methodology I've discussed. But this chapter also looks at some advanced strategies where the decompiler infers all complicated high-level structures from the series of `goto` statements in the bytecode.

This section looks at a couple of different strategies you can use to overcome this problem of synthesizing high-level control constructs from `goto`-like primitives. As I said, an ideal general solution would let you decompile every possible `if-then-else` or `for` loop combination without requiring any exception cases, while keeping the source as close as possible to the original. The alternative is to attempt to anticipate all high-level control idioms.

You may wonder why you need to have a strategy—why can't you just build a grammar in ANTLR and see what comes out the other side? Unfortunately, the parser can recognize only sequential instruction sequences. So, you might not be able to parse all Dalvik instructions in a single pass, because bytecodes have an awful habit of branching. Registers are used as temporary storage areas, and you need to be able to control what happens to that partial sequence when the code branches. ANTLR on its own doesn't offer that level of functionality, so you need to figure out what approach you need to take to store these partially recognized sequences.

Choice One

The first choice is to use the techniques based on Cristina Cifuentes' and K. John Gough's work described in the paper "A Methodology for Decompilation," available from `www.itee.uq.edu.au/~cristina/clei1.ps`. The paper describes `dcc`, Cifuentes' decompiler for C programs on Intel boxes. Although `dcc` recovers C and not Java code, a great deal of the discussion and design of this universal decompiler is directly applicable to the task at hand.

Choice Two

The second choice is more general— you transform `goto` statements into equivalent forms. It would be much simpler if you could fire off an ANTLR scanner and parser at the `classes.dex` file and decompile the code in a single pass or at the very least dispense with any control-flow analysis. Well, that's what Todd Proebsting and Scott Watterson attempt to do in their paper "Krakatoa: Decompilation in Java," available at `www.usenix.org/publications/library/proceedings/coots97/full_papers/proebsting2/proebsting2.pdf`.

Krakatoa, an early decompiler and now part of the Sumatra/Toba project, uses Ramshaw's algorithm to transform `goto`s into loops and multilevel breaks. It claims to offer a neat one-pass solution while still keeping the original structure. The Krakatoa approach is tempting, because it's less likely to fail due to control-flow analysis problems.

Choice Three

The third choice comes from Daniel Ford of IBM Research and was part of possibly the very first decompiler, Jive—which I believe never made it out of IBM Research. In his paper "Jive: A Java Decompiler," Ford puts forward a truly multipass decompiler that "integrates its parse state information with the sequence of machine instructions it is parsing." Jive decompiles by reducing tokens as more and more information becomes available with each successive pass.

Choice Four

A final choice is to use the concept of abstract syntax trees (AST) to help you generalize your decompiler. Rather than having a single-pass parser, you can abstract out the meaning of the tokens into an AST; then a second parser writes out the tokens in Java source code. Figure 5-5 shows an AST of (2+3). You can output this in a number of different ways, as shown in Listing 5-10.

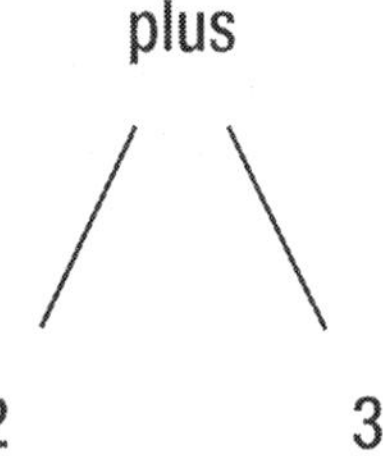

Figure 5-5. *AST of (2+3)*

Listing 5-10. *Possible Outputs for the AST in Figure 5-3*

```
2 + 3
(2 3 +)
bipush 2
bipush 3
iadd
```

The example in Listing 5-10 expresses the AST in standard mathematical notation, in reverse Polish or postfix notation, and finally in Java bytecode. All the outputs are representations of the same AST, but they aren't cluttered with any output language implementation. Like `StringTemplates`, but at a higher level, the output is divorced from the parsing, giving you a more concise or abstract representation of what you're trying to model in your parser.

Parser Design

The main difference between understanding a conversation and a compiler generating machine code is that the compiler requires many fewer keywords and rules to produce output the computer can understand—what is called its *native format*. If compiling a computer program is a smaller subset of understanding a human language, then decompiling Dalvik bytecode is a still smaller subset.

The number of keywords and the limited number of grammar rules allow you to easily tokenize the input and subsequently parse the tokens into Java phrases. Turning that back into code requires some further analysis, but I get to that a little later. You need to turn the input data stream into tokens. Listing 5-10 shows some Dalvik bytecode from the `Casting.java` file.

Listing 5-10. *`Casting.smali` Method*

```
sget-object     v1, field[2]
new-instance    v2, type[6]
invoke-direct   method[4], {v2}
const-string    v3, string[20]
invoke-virtual  method[7], {v2, v3}
```

Looking at the bytecode, you see that tokens can be split into the following types:

- *Identifiers:* Typically, references that take the form `{v1}` or `{v2}`.
- *Integers:* Usually the data or numbers that follow the opcode to make up a complete bytecode statement. Good examples are numbers that are placed on the stack or labels for a `goto` statement, such as `goto_1`.
- *Keywords:* The 200 or so opcodes that make up the bytecode language. You look at these and their constructs in Chapter 6.
- *Whitespace:* Includes tabs, blank spaces, newlines, and carriage returns if you're using DOS or Windows. Most decompilers don't encounter a lot of whitespace in a real `classes.dex`, but you need to deal with it in Dalvik bytecode

All these tokens are crucial for the parser to be able to do its job and try to match them with the predefined grammatical rules.

The design of the decompiler is shown in Figure 5-4. Everything starts with the `bytecode` file or character stream. ANTLR parses this into a token stream, which is converted into an AST. The AST is parsed by a second parser that converts the abstract representation into Java; and the templates written using the `StringTemplate` library output the tokens into Java text.

Summary

So far, I've talked about the tools that are available to help you create a working decompiler. You've seen the different strategies you may choose to employ. I've included alternatives to our design in case you want to take one of the other options and run with it yourself. If you're more comfortable with Lex and Yacc then you're likely to want to use JLex and CUP and not ANTLR. Personally I think that JLex and CUP have not changed much in recent years which is why I'm recommending ANTLR now. And now you have a decompiler design to implement. By the end of the next chapter, you'll have a working decompiler that can handle the simple `classes.dex` files. Chapter 6 looks at the various internal structures and gradually walks through creating a more effective decompiler that can handle more than the `Casting.java` example.

Chapter 6

Decompiler Implementation

You're now at the point where you learn to deal with the individual bytecodes and decompile the opcodes into partial statements and expressions and, ultimately (that's the plan, anyway), back into complete blocks of source code.

If I'm gauging my audience correctly, this chapter, and possibly the Chapter 5, will appeal to a significant cross section of readers. This is the nub of the problem of how to implement a decompiler using a parser built using ANTLR.

To keep this chapter as practical as possible, you use a test suite of simple programs, each with a different language construct. For each program, you reconstruct the original source gradually, building the decompiler as you go. Each program is first compiled and then disassembled. You then look at the Java source code and the corresponding method bytecode and create a parser specification for each example to convert the bytecode back into source.

Because the `classes.dex` file is more than method bytecode, you also need to be able to incorporate the remaining information in the class file to recover import statements, package names, and variable names from the non-data section of the file.

You start by getting more comfortable with ANTLR by completing the implementation of DexToXML from Chapter 3. DexToXML is a basic ANTLR parser with no bells and whistles. After that you look at DexToSource (the decompiler) to decompile the bytecode instructions back into Java source.

DexToXML

DexToXML functions as an easy introduction to ANTLR parsing. It uses ANTLR as its parser technology. The earlier version of this book used JLex and CUP, which were difficult to get working and even more difficult to debug—you could spend hours trying to figure out why adding a simple change to a rule broke the entire parser. A lot has changed since 2004, and ANTLR now offers excellent integration with Eclipse as well as ANTLRWorks, a standalone ANTLR tool that turns the art of creating a parser back into a simpler coding task.

ANTLR is also an excellent technology to create your own parsers for all sorts of domain-specific language (DSL) tools. These are typically one-off mini-programming languages, rules engines, graphing tools, and so on that are created to solve a particular problem; they're often used when scripting tools such as grep, sed, and awk aren't up to the job.

Let's first look at parsing `dex.log`, which is one of the outputs from the dedexer tool. Dedexer is a dex file disassembler that is typically used to generate smali-like disassembler output in a DDX file but can also give you complete output of `classes.dex` in the `dex.log` file. You could also use the output from the dexdump file that is part of the Android SDK, but personally I prefer the simpler output of the `dex.log` file.

Parsing the dex.log Output

`dex.log` is the log file created when you run the following dedexer command on the compiled version of your `Casting.java` file:

```
c:\temp>java -jar ddx1.18.jar -o -d c:\temp casting\classes.dex
```

`dex.log` is raw output of a `classes.dex` file that allows you to decompile without the overhead of parsing the bytes, which is just what you want. Listing 6-1 shows the output of the header of the `classes.dex` file.

Listing 6-1. *Header of the Class*

```
00000000 :  64 65 78 0A
       30 33 35 00
       magic: dex\n035\0
00000008 :  62 8B 44 18
       checksum
0000000C :  DA A9 21 CA
       9C 4F B4 C5
       21 D7 77 BC
       2A 18 4A 38
```

```
        0D A2 AA FE
        signature
00000020 :  50 04 00 00
        file size: 0x00000450
00000024 :  70 00 00 00
        header size: 0x00000070
00000028 :  78 56 34 12
        00 00 00 00
        link size: 0x00000000
00000030 :  00 00 00 00
        link offset: 0x00000000
00000034 :  A4 03 00 00
        map offset: 0x000003A4
00000038 :  1A 00 00 00
        string ids size: 0x0000001A
0000003C :  70 00 00 00
        string ids offset: 0x00000070
00000040 :  0A 00 00 00
        type ids size: 0x0000000A
00000044 :  D8 00 00 00
        type ids offset: 0x000000D8
00000048 :  07 00 00 00
        proto ids size: 0x00000007
0000004C :  00 01 00 00
        proto ids offset: 0x00000100
00000050 :  03 00 00 00
        field ids size: 0x00000003
00000054 :  54 01 00 00
        field ids offset: 0x00000154
00000058 :  09 00 00 00
        method ids size: 0x00000009
0000005C :  6C 01 00 00
        method ids offset: 0x0000016C
00000060 :  01 00 00 00
        class defs size: 0x00000001
00000064 :  B4 01 00 00
        class defs offset: 0x000001B4
00000068 :  7C 02 00 00
        data size: 0x0000027C
0000006C :  D4 01 00 00
        data offset: 0x000001D4
```

Let's begin by taking a look at the magic number section, which is at the start of the file; see Listing 6-2.

Listing 6-2. *Magic Number*

```
00000000 :  64 65 78 0A
        30 33 35 00
        magic: dex\n035\0
```

The format is the same for all `classes.dex` files. The goal is to parse the magic number and output

`<root><header><magic>dex\n035\0</magic></header></root>`

using this information:

- Eight hexadecimal digits, the address in the file
- A colon
- Two series of eight hexadecimal digits
- The `magic` keyword
- Another colon
- The `classes.dex` magic number

ANTLR at Work

ANTLR works by first tokenizing the input and then, through a series of parsing rules, producing the desired output. The first step is to break the information into tokens. An obvious token is a hexadecimal digit (`HEX_DIGIT`) along with the `WS` or whitespace that you want the parser to ignore. The ANTLR parser for tokenizing the magic-number header information is shown in Listing 6-3. The grammar, the options, and `@header` and `@lexer` tell the parser the name of the grammar, the language in which the parser will be generated, and the package names for the parser and lexer, respectively.

Listing 6.3. *ANTLR Magic-Number Parser*

```
grammar DexToXML;
options {language = Java;}
@header {package com.riis.decompiler;}
@lexer::header {package com.riis.decompiler;}

rule : header
  ;

header : magic
  ;

magic: address eight_hex eight_hex IDENT ':' MAGIC_NUM
  ;

hex_address: '0x' eight_hex
  ;
```

```
address
  : eight_hex ':'
  ;

eight_hex
  : DIGIT DIGIT DIGIT DIGIT DIGIT DIGIT DIGIT DIGIT
  ;

IDENT: ('a'..'z')+;
MAGIC_NUM: 'dex\\n035\\0';
DIGIT : ('0'..'9'|'A'..'F');
WS: (' ' | '\t' | '\n' | '\r' | '\f' | ',')+ {$channel = HIDDEN;};
```

Working from the bottom up in Listing 6-3, `WS` defines what you mean by whitespace that is sent to a hidden channel and is ignored. `DIGIT` defines a hexadecimal digit as being 0–F. `MAGIC_NUM` is the escaped version of `dex\n035\0`; and finally, `IDENT` is any string of characters. The parser rules take these tokens and arrange them into an expected pattern. For example, you know from Listing 6-2 that the hexadecimal digits are grouped in eights for the addresses and the magic number. And an address has a colon after it. Listing 6-2 looks something like Listing 6-4 when it's tokenized.

Listing 6-4. *Tokenized Magic Number*

```
address  eight_hex
            eight_hex
            IDENT MAGIC_NUM
```

Rules

In ANTLR, as in all parsers, you need a `rule` to tell the parser where to start parsing. The `rule` says that the incoming file consists of a `header`; and that `header`, for the moment only, has a magic number. The `magic` rule expects the incoming file to be formatted as in Listing 6-4. See `http://vimeo.com/8001326` for directions on how to set up an ANTLR project in Eclipse. Using Eclipse, the incoming tokens from Listing 6-2 are parsed as shown in Figure 6-1.

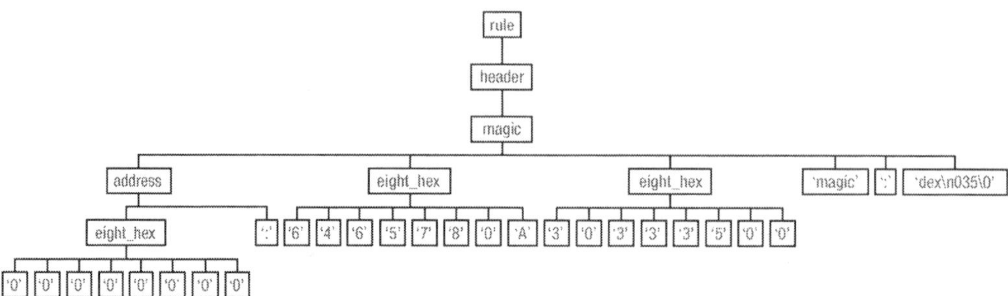

Figure 6-1. *Magic-number parsing rules*

Now that the magic number has been successfully parsed, the next step is to output it in the correct format.

Outputting the Magic Number

Listing 6-5 is updated with the `System.out.println` statements. Use the `@init` and `@after` ANTLR statements to print the `<root>` and `<header>` statements in the correct order. You can also use ANTLR `StringTemplates` to remove all the `println` statements if you don't like all the extra Java code in your parser.

Listing 6-5. *DexToXML Magic-Number Parser*

```
grammar DexToXML;
options {language = Java;}
@header {package com.riis.decompiler;}
@lexer::header {package com.riis.decompiler;}

rule
  @init {System.out.println("<root>");}
  @after {System.out.println("</root>");}
  : header
  ;

header
  @init {System.out.println("<header>");}
  @after {System.out.println("</header>");}
  : magic
  ;

magic: address eight_hex eight_hex IDENT ':' id=MAGIC_NUM
  {System.out.println("<magic>" + id.getText() + "</magic>");}
  ;
```

```
hex_address: '0x' eight_hex
  ;

address
  : eight_hex ':'
  ;

eight_hex
  : DIGIT DIGIT DIGIT DIGIT DIGIT DIGIT DIGIT DIGIT
  ;

IDENT: ('a'..'z')+;
MAGIC_NUM: 'dex\\n035\\0';
DIGIT : ('0'..'9'|'A'..'F');
WS: (' ' | '\t' | '\n' | '\r' | '\f' | ',')+ {$channel = HIDDEN;};
```

Listing 6-6 has the Java code necessary to call the ANTLR code from the command line outside of Eclipse. This takes the input from `c:\temp\input.log`.

Listing 6-6. *DexToXML.java*

```
package com.riis.decompiler;

import java.io.*;

import org.antlr.runtime.ANTLRInputStream;
import org.antlr.runtime.CommonTokenStream;
import org.antlr.runtime.RecognitionException;
import org.antlr.runtime.TokenStream;


public class DexToXML {

  public static void main(String[] args) throws RecognitionException, IOException {
     DexToXMLLexer lexer = new DexToXMLLexer(new ANTLRInputStream(System.in));
     TokenStream tokenStream = new CommonTokenStream(lexer);
     DexToXMLParser parser = new DexToXMLParser(tokenStream);

     parser.rule();
  }

}
```

Compile the code in a `com\riis\decompiler` directory using the following commands, making sure the ANTLR v3.4 library is in your classpath. The first command generates the lexer and parser, and the second command compiles the DexToXML code:

```
java org.antlr.Tool DexToXML.g
javac DexToXMLLexer.java DexToXMLParser.java DexToXML.java
```

Save Listing 6-2 as `magic.log`, and run the following command in the top-level directory to get the DexToXML output shown in Listing 6-7:

```
java com.riis.decompiler.DexToXML < magic.log
```

Listing 6-7. *DexToXML Output*

```
<root>
<header>
<magic>dex\n035\0</magic>
</header>
</root>
```

Next create the grammar for the rest of the header. Initially you can set up the rule to break out the header as shown in Listing 6-8.

Listing 6-8. *Header Rule*

```
header
  @init {System.out.println("<header>");}
  @after {System.out.println("</header>");}
  : magic
    checksum
    signature
    file_size
    header_size
    link_size
    link_offset
    map_offset
    string_ids_size
    string_ids_offset
    type_ids_size
    type_ids_offset
    proto_ids_size
    proto_ids_offset
    fields_ids_size
    fields_ids_offset
    method_ids_size
    method_ids_offset
    class_defs_size
    class_defs_offset
    data_size
    data_offset
  ;
```

But many of the patterns are repeated—for example, the sizes and offsets are very similar, so you can refactor the parser by pulling out the name of the node. You can put these patterns together as shown in Listing 6-9, which matches the different header entries.

Listing 6-9. *Refactored* `header_entry` *Rule*

```
header_entry
    : address eight_hex IDENT
    | address eight_hex xml_id ':' hex_address
    | address eight_hex eight_hex xml_id ':' hex_address
    ;
```

Putting this code together into the modified parser, you get the complete header shown in Listing 6-10.

Listing 6-10. *Refactored DexToXML Header Grammar*

```
grammar DexToXML;
options {language = Java;}
@header {package com.riis.decompiler;}
@lexer::header {package com.riis.decompiler;}

rule
    : header
    ;

header
    : magic
      header_entry
      signature
      header_entry+
    ;

magic: address eight_hex eight_hex IDENT ':' MAGIC_NUM
    ;

header_entry
    : address eight_hex IDENT
    | address eight_hex xml_id ':' hex_address
    | address eight_hex eight_hex xml_id ':' hex_address
    ;

xml_id
    : IDENT IDENT
    | IDENT IDENT IDENT
    ;

signature: address signature_hex 'signature'
    ;
```

```
signature_hex: eight_hex eight_hex eight_hex eight_hex eight_hex
   ;

hex_address: '0x' eight_hex
   ;

address
   : eight_hex ':'
   ;

eight_hex
   : DIGIT DIGIT DIGIT DIGIT DIGIT DIGIT DIGIT DIGIT
   ;

IDENT: ('a'..'z')+;
MAGIC_NUM: 'dex\\n035\\0';
DIGIT : ('0'..'9'|'A'..'F');
WS: (' ' | '\t' | '\n' | '\r' | '\f' | ',')+ {$channel = HIDDEN;};
```

More of the file is parsed in Listing 6-11, right up to the `code_item` section. I've also included the code to output the XML so you can see how that is done.

Listing 6-11. *DexToXML ANTLR Grammar*

```
grammar DexToXML;

options {
  language = Java;
}

@header {
  package com.riis.decompiler;
}

@lexer::header {
  package com.riis.decompiler;
}

rule
        @init {System.out.println("<root>");}
        @after {System.out.println("</root>");}
        : header
          string_ids
          type_ids
          proto_ids
          field_ids
          method_ids
          class_defs
          data
        ;
```

```
header
        @init {System.out.println("<header>");}
        @after {System.out.println("</header>");}
        : magic
          header_entry
          signature
          header_entry+
        ;

magic: address eight_hex eight_hex IDENT ':' id=MAGIC_NUM
        {System.out.println("<magic>" + id.getText() + "</magic>");}
        ;

header_entry
        : address id1=eight_hex id2=IDENT
                {System.out.println("<" + $id2.text + ">" + $id1.text + "</" +
$id2.text + ">");}
        | address eight_hex id3=xml_id ':' id4=hex_address
                {System.out.println("<" + $id3.result + ">" + $id4.text + "</" +
$id3.result + ">");}
        | address eight_hex eight_hex id5=xml_id ':' id6=hex_address
                {System.out.println("<" + $id5.result + ">" + $id6.text + "</" +
$id5.result + ">");}
        ;

xml_id returns [String result]
        : id1=IDENT id2=IDENT
                {$result = id1.getText() + "_" + id2.getText();}
        | id1=IDENT id2=IDENT id3=IDENT
                {$result = id1.getText() + "_" + id2.getText() + "_" +
id3.getText();}
        ;

signature: address id=signature_hex 'signature'
        {System.out.println("<signature>" + $id.text + "</signature>");}
        ;

signature_hex: eight_hex eight_hex eight_hex eight_hex eight_hex
        ;

string_ids
        @init {System.out.println("<string_ids>");}
        @after {System.out.println("</string_ids>");}
        : string_address+
        ;

string_address
        : address eight_hex IDENT id1=array_digit  ':' 'at' id2=hex_address
                {System.out.println("<string>\n<id>" + $id1.result +
```

```
"</id>\n<address>" + $id2.text + "</address>\n</string>");}
        ;

type_ids
        @init {System.out.println("<type_ids>");}
        @after {System.out.println("</type_ids>");}
        : type_address+
        ;

type_address
        : address eight_hex IDENT id1=array_digit  'index:' id2=eight_hex '('
id3=proto_type_string ')'
                {int addr = Integer.parseInt($id2.text,16);
                 System.out.println("<type>\n<id>" + $id1.result +
"</id>\n<string_id>"
                                        + addr + "</string_id>\n<string>" +
$id3.text + "<string>\n</type>");}
        ;

proto_ids
        @init {System.out.println("<proto_ids>");}
        @after {System.out.println("</proto_ids>");}
        : proto_address+
        ;

proto_address
        : address eight_hex eight_hex eight_hex IDENT id1=array_digit ':'
                        'short signature:' id2=proto_type_string ';'
                        'return type:' id3=proto_type_string ';'
                        'parameter block offset:' eight_hex
                 {System.out.println("<proto>\n<id>" + $id1.result +
"</id>\n<string>"
                + $id3.text + "</string>\n<signature>" + $id2.text +
"<signature>\n</proto>");}
        ;

field_ids
        @init {System.out.println("<field_ids>");}
        @after {System.out.println("</field_ids>");}
        : field_address+
        ;

field_address
        : address eight_hex eight_hex IDENT id1=array_digit ':'
id2=proto_type_string id3=proto_type_string
                 {System.out.println("<field>\n<id>" + $id1.result +
"</id>\n<name>"
                        + $id2.text + "</name>\n<type>" + $id3.text +
```

```
"<type>\n</field>");}

        ;

method_ids
        @init {System.out.println("<method_ids>");}
        @after {System.out.println("</method_ids>");}
        : method_address+
        ;

method_address
        : address eight_hex eight_hex IDENT id1=array_digit ':'
id2=proto_type_string '(' id3=proto_type_string ')'
                  {System.out.println("<method>\n<id>" + $id1.result +
"</id>\n<name>"
                         + $id2.text + "</name>\n<proto>" + $id3.text +
"<proto>\n</method>");}
        ;


class_defs
        @init {System.out.println("<classes>");}
        @after {System.out.println("</classes>");}
        : class_address+
        ;

class_address
        : address id1=eight_hex id2=eight_hex id3=eight_hex id4=eight_hex
id5=eight_hex id6=eight_hex id7=eight_hex id8=eight_hex id9=IDENT id10=IDENT
                  {System.out.println("<class>\n"
                                +"<class_id>" + $id9.text + " " + $id10.text +
"</class_id>\n"
                                +"<type_id>" + $id1.text + "</type_id>\n"

                                +"<access_flags>" + $id2.text +
"</access_flags>\n"
                                +"<superclass_id>" + $id3.text +
"<superclass>\n"
                                +"<interfaces_offset>" + $id4.text +
"<interfaces_offset>\n"
                                +"<source_file_id>" + $id5.text +
"<source_file_id>\n"
                                +"<annotations_offset>" + $id6.text +
"<annotations_offset>\n"
                                +"<class_data_offset>" + $id7.text +
"<class_data_offset>\n"
                                +"<static_values_offset>" + $id8.text +
                                +"<static_values_offset>\n" + "</class>");}
        ;
```

```
data
        @init {System.out.println("<data>");}
        @after {System.out.println("</data>");}
        : class_+
        ;

class_
        @init {System.out.println("<class>");}
        @after {System.out.println("</class>");}
        : class_data_items
        ;

class_data_items
        @init {System.out.println("<class_data_items>");}
        @after {System.out.println("</class_data_items>");}
        : class_data_item
        ;

class_data_item
        @init {System.out.println("<class_data_item>");}
        @after {System.out.println("</class_data_item>");}
        : class_data_item_header static_fields //instance_methods
                direct_methods  // virtual_methods
                encoded_arrays
        ;

class_data_item_header
        :       address HEX_DOUBLE 'static fields size:' id1=DIGIT
                address HEX_DOUBLE 'instance fields size:' id2=DIGIT
                address HEX_DOUBLE 'direct methods size:' id3=DIGIT
                address HEX_DOUBLE 'virtual methods size:' id4=DIGIT
                 {System.out.println("<static_field_size>" + $id1.getText()
                        + "</static_field_size>\n"
                +"<instance_field_size>" + $id2.getText() +
                "</instance_field_size>\n"
                +"<direct_methods_size>" + $id3.getText() +
                "</direct_methods_size>\n"
                 +"<virtual_methods_size>" + $id4.getText() +
"</virtual_methods_size>");}
        ;

static_fields
        @init {System.out.println("<static_fields>");}
        @after {System.out.println("</static_fields>");}
        : static_field+
        ;

static_field
        @init {System.out.println("<static_field>");}
        @after {System.out.println("</static_field>");}
```

```
        : address id1=HEX_DOUBLE id2=HEX_DOUBLE
                {System.out.println("<field_id>" + $id1.getText() +
"</field_id>\n"
                                +"<access_flags>" + $id2.getText() +
"</access_flags>");}
        ;

direct_methods
        @init {System.out.println("<direct_methods>");}
        @after {System.out.println("</direct_methods>");}
        : direct_method+
        ;

direct_method
        @init {System.out.println("<direct_method>");}
        @after {System.out.println("</direct_method>");}
        : address id1=HEX_DOUBLE id2=HEX_DOUBLE
        id3=HEX_DOUBLE id4=HEX_DOUBLE id5=HEX_DOUBLE id6=HEX_DOUBLE
                {System.out.println("<method_id>" + $id1.getText() +
"</method_id>\n"
                +"<access_flags>" + $id2.getText()  + $id3.getText()  +
        $id4.getText()
                + "</access_flags>\n"
                +"<address>0x" + $id5.getText() + $id6.getText() +
"</address>");}
        | address id1=HEX_DOUBLE id2=HEX_DOUBLE id3=HEX_DOUBLE id4=HEX_DOUBLE
                {System.out.println("<method_id>" + $id1.getText() +
"</method_id>\n"
                                +"<access_flags>" + $id2.getText() +
"</access_flags>\n"
                        +"<address>0x" + $id3.getText() + $id4.getText() +
"</address>");}
        ;

encoded_arrays
        : address HEX_DOUBLE 'array item count:' DIGIT encoded_array+
        ;

encoded_array
        : address HEX_DOUBLE HEX_DOUBLE IDENT IDENT array_digit ':' '"' IDENT
'"'
        ;

proto_type_string
        : IDENT
        | IDENT ';'
        | IDENT '.' IDENT
        | IDENT '/' IDENT
        | IDENT '/' '<' IDENT '>'
        | '<' IDENT '>' '()' IDENT
```

```
        | IDENT '/' IDENT '/' IDENT ';'
        | '[' IDENT '/' IDENT '/' IDENT ';'
        | IDENT '()' IDENT '/' IDENT '/' IDENT ';'
        | IDENT '/' IDENT '/' IDENT '.' IDENT
        | IDENT '/' IDENT '/' IDENT '/' IDENT
        | IDENT '/' IDENT '/' IDENT '/' '<' IDENT '>'
        | IDENT '(' IDENT '/' IDENT '/' IDENT ';' ')' IDENT
        | IDENT '(' '[' IDENT '/' IDENT '/' IDENT ';' ')' IDENT
        | IDENT '(' IDENT ')' IDENT '/' IDENT '/' IDENT ';'
        | IDENT '(' IDENT '/' IDENT '/' IDENT ';' ')' IDENT '/' IDENT '/' IDENT
';'            ;

hex_address: '0x' eight_hex
        ;

address
        : eight_hex ':'
        ;

eight_hex
        : HEX_DOUBLE HEX_DOUBLE HEX_DOUBLE HEX_DOUBLE
        ;

array_digit returns [String result]
        : id=ELEMENT
                {String str = id.getText(); $result = str.substring(1,
str.length()-1);}
        ;

HEX_DOUBLE:
('0'..'9')('0'..'9')|('0'..'9')('A'..'F')|('A'..'F')('0'..'9')|('A'..'F')('A'..'
F');
MAGIC_NUM: 'dex\\n035\\0';
IDENT: ('a'..'z'|'A'..'Z')+;
DIGIT: ('0'..'9');
ELEMENT: ('[')('0'..'9')+(']');
CONST_4: 'const/4';
CONST_16: 'const/16';
CONST_HIGH_16: 'const/high16';
COMMENT:  '//' ~( '\r' | '\n' )* {$channel = HIDDEN;};
WS: (' ' | '\t' | '\n' | '\r' | '\f' | ',' | '-' | '*')+ {$channel = HIDDEN;};
```

Listing 6-12 shows the XML output from the grammar from Listing 6-11. This doesn't include all the XML nodes as we already covered that in Chapter 3 and it is lengthy.. The larger and more complete DexToXML that parses all `classes.dex` files and not just `Casting.java` is available in the source code on the Apress web site (`www.apress.com`).

Listing 6-12. *DexToXML Output*

```
<root>
<header>
<magic>dex\n035\0</magic>
<checksum>62 8B 44 18</checksum>
<signature>DA A9 21 CA  9C 4F B4 C5
 21 D7 77 BC
 2A 18 4A 38
 0D A2 AA FE</signature>
<file_size>0x00000450</file_size>
<header_size>0x00000070</header_size>
<link_size>0x00000000</link_size>
<link_offset>0x00000000</link_offset>
<map_offset>0x000003A4</map_offset>
<string_ids_size>0x0000001A</string_ids_size>
<string_ids_offset>0x00000070</string_ids_offset>
<type_ids_size>0x0000000A</type_ids_size>
<type_ids_offset>0x000000D8</type_ids_offset>
<proto_ids_size>0x00000007</proto_ids_size>
<proto_ids_offset>0x00000100</proto_ids_offset>
<field_ids_size>0x00000003</field_ids_size>
<field_ids_offset>0x00000154</field_ids_offset>
<method_ids_size>0x00000009</method_ids_size>
<method_ids_offset>0x0000016C</method_ids_offset>
<class_defs_size>0x00000001</class_defs_size>
<class_defs_offset>0x000001B4</class_defs_offset>
<data_size>0x0000027C</data_size>
<data_offset>0x000001D4</data_offset>
</header>
<string_ids>
<string>
<id>0</id>
<address>0x00000272</address>
</string>
<string>
<id>1</id>
<address>0x0000027F</address>
</string>
<string>
<id>2</id>
<address>0x00000287</address>
</string>
<string>
<id>3</id>
<address>0x0000028A</address>
</string>
<string>
<id>4</id>
<address>0x00000298</address>
```

```
</string>
<string>
<id>5</id>
<address>0x0000029B</address>
</string>
<string>
<id>6</id>
<address>0x0000029E</address>
</string>
<string>
<id>7</id>
<address>0x000002A2</address>
</string>
<string>
<id>8</id>
<address>0x000002AD</address>
</string>
<string>
<id>9</id>
<address>0x000002B1</address>
</string>
<string>
<id>10</id>
<address>0x000002B5</address>
</string>
<string>
<id>11</id>
<address>0x000002CC</address>
</string>
<string>
<id>12</id>
<address>0x000002E0</address>
</string>
<string>
<id>13</id>
<address>0x000002F4</address>
</string>
<string>
<id>14</id>
<address>0x0000030F</address>
</string>
<string>
<id>15</id>
<address>0x00000323</address>
</string>
<string>
<id>16</id>
<address>0x00000326</address>
</string>
<string>
```

```
<id>17</id>
<address>0x0000032A</address>
</string>
<string>
<id>18</id>
<address>0x0000033F</address>
</string>
<string>
<id>19</id>
<address>0x00000347</address>
</string>
<string>
<id>20</id>
<address>0x0000034F</address>
</string>
<string>
<id>21</id>
<address>0x00000357</address>
</string>
<string>
<id>22</id>
<address>0x0000035F</address>
</string>
<string>
<id>23</id>
<address>0x00000365</address>
</string>
<string>
<id>24</id>
<address>0x0000036A</address>
</string>
<string>
<id>25</id>
<address>0x00000373</address>
</string>
</string_ids>
<type_ids>
<type>
<id>0</id>
<string_id>2</string_id>
<string>C<string>
</type>
<type>
<id>1</id>
<string_id>4</string_id>
<string>I<string>
</type>
<type>
<id>2</id>
<string_id>7</string_id>
```

```
<string>LCasting;<string>
</type>
<type>
<id>3</id>
<string_id>10</string_id>
<string>Ljava/io/PrintStream;<string>
</type>
<type>
<id>4</id>
<string_id>11</string_id>
<string>Ljava/lang/Object;<string>
</type>
<type>
<id>5</id>
<string_id>12</string_id>
<string>Ljava/lang/String;<string>
</type>
<type>
<id>6</id>
<string_id>13</string_id>
<string>Ljava/lang/StringBuilder;<string>
</type>
<type>
<id>7</id>
<string_id>14</string_id>
<string>Ljava/lang/System;<string>
</type>
<type>
<id>8</id>
<string_id>15</string_id>
<string>V<string>
</type>
<type>
<id>9</id>
<string_id>17</string_id>
<string>[Ljava/lang/String;<string>
</type>
</type_ids>
<proto_ids>
<proto>
<id>0</id>
<string>Ljava/lang/String;</string>
<signature>L<signature>
</proto>
<proto>
<id>1</id>
<string>Ljava/lang/StringBuilder;</string>
<signature>LC<signature>
</proto>
<proto>
```

```
<id>2</id>
<string>Ljava/lang/StringBuilder;</string>
<signature>LI<signature>
</proto>
<proto>
<id>3</id>
<string>Ljava/lang/StringBuilder;</string>
<signature>LL<signature>
</proto>
<proto>
<id>4</id>
<string>V</string>
<signature>V<signature>
</proto>
<proto>
<id>5</id>
<string>V</string>
<signature>VL<signature>
</proto>
<proto>
<id>6</id>
<string>V</string>
<signature>VL<signature>
</proto>
</proto_ids>
<field_ids>
<field>
<id>0</id>
<name>Casting.ascStr</name>
<type>Ljava/lang/String;<type>
</field>
<field>
<id>1</id>
<name>Casting.chrStr</name>
<type>Ljava/lang/String;<type>
</field>
<field>
<id>2</id>
<name>java/lang/System.out</name>
<type>Ljava/io/PrintStream;<type>
</field>
</field_ids>
</root>
```

DexToSource

To implement DexToSource, the Android decompiler, this section looks at three examples of how the code was compiled into the `classes.dex` file; then you reverse-engineer it back into Java and code your ANTLR parser to automate the process. The three examples are the `Casting.java` code from Chapters 2 and 3; Hello World Android; and an `if` statement from the WordPress Android app (an open source Android app), which is available at `http://android.svn.wordpress.org/trunk/src/org/wordpress/android/`.

The analysis of each example starts with a raw bytecode that is then broken down and parsed into something resembling the original Java source code. Two resources are very helpful when pulling apart the bytecode: Google's bytecode for the Dalvik virtual machine (DVM), at `www.netmite.com/android/mydroid/dalvik/docs/dalvik-bytecode.html`; and Gabor Paller's excellent "Dalvik Opcodes" paper from his blog, which you can find at `http://pallergabor.uw.hu/androidblog/dalvik_opcodes.html`.

Example 1: Casting.java

Each example starts with the original Java code followed by the bytecode you want to reverse-engineer from `classes.dex`, the parser, and finally the reverse-engineered Java source. See Listing 6-13 for the `Casting.java` code.

Listing 6-13. *Casting.java*

```
public class Casting {

 static final String ascStr = "ascii ";
 static final String chrStr = " character ";

 public static void main(String args[]){

  for(char c=0; c < 128; c++) {
      System.out.println(ascStr + (int)c + chrStr + c);
  }
 }
}
```

Compiling `Casting.java` into `classes.dex` and running it through dedexer results in the bytecode shown in Listing 6-14.

Listing 6-14. *Casting.ddx*

```
.class public Casting
.super java/lang/Object
.source Casting.java

.field static final ascStr Ljava/lang/String; = "ascii "
.field static final chrStr Ljava/lang/String; = " character "

.method public <init>()V
.limit registers 1
; this: v0 (LCasting;)
.line 1
        invoke-direct   {v0},java/lang/Object/<init>    ; <init>()V
        return-void
.end method

.method public static main([Ljava/lang/String;)V
.limit registers 5
; parameter[0] : v4 ([Ljava/lang/String;)
.line 8
        const/4 v0,0
l1fe:
        const/16        v1,128
        if-ge   v0,v1,l252
.line 9
        sget-object        v1,java/lang/System.out Ljava/io/PrintStream;
        new-instance       v2,java/lang/StringBuilder
        invoke-direct      {v2},java/lang/StringBuilder/<init>  ; <init>()V
        const-string       v3,"ascii "
        invoke-virtual     {v2,v3},java/lang/StringBuilder/append       ;
append(Ljava/lang/String;)Ljava/lang/StringBuilder;
        move-result-object v2
        invoke-virtual     {v2,v0},java/lang/StringBuilder/append       ;
append(I)Ljava/lang/StringBuilder;
        move-result-object v2
        const-string       v3," character "
        invoke-virtual     {v2,v3},java/lang/StringBuilder/append       ;
append(Ljava/lang/String;)Ljava/lang/StringBuilder;
        move-result-object v2
        invoke-virtual     {v2,v0},java/lang/StringBuilder/append       ;
append(C)Ljava/lang/StringBuilder;
        move-result-object v2
        invoke-virtual     {v2},java/lang/StringBuilder/toString        ;
toString()Ljava/lang/String;
        move-result-object v2
        invoke-virtual     {v1,v2},java/io/PrintStream/println  ;
println(Ljava/lang/String;)V
.line 8
        add-int/lit8       v0,v0,1
```

```
        int-to-char       v0,v0
        goto    l1fe
l252:
.line 11
        return-void
.end method
```

Bytecode Analysis

Before you can begin coding the parser, you need to understand bytecode. Table 6-1 shows the raw bytecode along with the corresponding opcodes and operands and a running tally of the values in the Program Counter (PC), v0, v1, v2, and v3 DVM registers.

Table 6-1. *`Casting.java` Android Bytecode Analysis*

PC	RawBy	Opcode	Operand	v0	v1	v2	v3	Comments
0	1200	const/4	v0, 0	0				Put the integer 0 into register v0
1	1301 0800	const/16	v1, 128		128			Put the integer 128 into register v1
3	3510 2800	if-ge	v0, v1, 28					Jump to PC 2b (plus 28) if v0>=v1
5	6201 0200	sget-object	v1, field[2]		java.lang.System.out:Ljava/io/PrintStream			Read the object in field[2], java.lang.System.out:Ljava/io/PrintStream, and store in v1
7	2202 0600	new-instance	v2, type[6]			java/lang/StringBuilder		Create an object type[6], java/lang/StringBuilder, and store in v2
9	7010 0400 0200	invoke-direct	method[4], {v2}					Call method[4] with one argument, java/lang/Strin

PC	RawBy	Opcode	Operand	v0	v1	v2	v3	Comments
								gBuilder/<init> (<init>()V) with parameters {v2}
c	1a03 1400	const-string	v3, string[20]				"ascii"	Store string[20], "ascii " in v3
e	6e20 0700 3200	invoke-virtual	method[7], {v2, v3}					Call method[7], java/lang/StringBuilder/append (append(Ljava/lang/String;)Ljava/lang/StringBuilder;), with parameters {v2, v3}
11	0c02	move-result-object	v2			"ascii " +		Move the result of the previous method call to v2
12	6e20 0600 0200	invoke-virtual	method[6], {v2, v0}					Call method[6], java/lang/StringBuilder/append (append(I)Ljava/lang/StringBuilder;), with parameters {v2, v0}
15	0c02	move-result-object	v2			"ascii " + "0"		Move the result of the previous method call to v2
16	1a03 0000	const-string	v3, string[0]				" character"	Store string[0], " character" in v3

PC	RawBy	Opcode	Operand	v0	v1	v2	v3	Comments
18	6e20 0700 3200	invoke-virtual	method[7], {v2, v3}					Call method[7], java/lang/StringBuilder/append (append(Ljava/lang/String;)Ljava/lang/StringBuilder;), with parameters {v2, v3}
1b	0c02	move-result-object	v2			"ascii " + "0" + " character"		Move the result of the previous method call to v2
1c	6e20 0500 0200	invoke-virtual	method[5], {v2, v0}					Call method[5], java/lang/StringBuilder/append (append(C)Ljava/lang/StringBuilder;), with parameters {v2, v0}
1f	0c02	move-result-object	v2			"ascii " + "c" + " character" + "c"		Move the result of the previous method call to v2
20	6e10 0800 0200	invoke-virtual	method[8], {v2}					Call method[8], java/lang/StringBuilder/toString (toString()Ljava/lang/String;), with parameters {v2}

PC	RawBy	Opcode	Operand	v0	v1	v2	v3	Comments
23	0c02	move-result-object	v2			"ascii" + "c" + " character" + "c".toString()		Move the result of the previous method call to v2
24	6e20 0200 2100	invoke-virtual	method[2], {v1,v2}			println		Call method[2], java/io/PrintStream/println (println(Ljava/lang/String;)V), with parameters {v1, v2}
27	d800 0001	add-int/lit8	v0, v0, 1					Add int 1 to v0
29	8e00	int-to-char	v0, v0					Convert v0 to char and store in v0
2a	28d7	goto	d7					Goto PC = 1 (go back –29)
2b	0e00	return-void						Return

Parser

Much of the outside shell of the Java code, such as the name of the class and the name of the strings, methods, fields, and so on, seen in the `Casting.ddx` file. Listing in 6-14 can be transformed using the parser in Listing 6-15. The output is shown in Listing 6-16.

Listing 6-15. *`Casting.java` Without Bytecode Parser*

```
grammar DexToSource;
```

```
options {language = Java;}
@header {package com.riis.decompiler;}
@lexer::header {package com.riis.decompiler;}
@members{String flag_result = "";}

rule
        @after {System.out.println("}");}
        :       class_name super_ source fields methods+
        ;

class_name
        : CLASS f1=flags id2=IDENT
                {System.out.println($f1.text + " class " + $id2.text + " {");}
        ;

super_: SUPER package_;
source: SOURCE IDENT '.java';
fields: field+  ;

methods: method_start method_end;

field: FIELD f1=flags id2=IDENT p1=package_ ';' '=' '"' id4=IDENT '"'
        {System.out.println($f1.text + " " + $p1.result + " " + $id2.text + " =
\"" + $id4.text + "\"" );}
        ;

method_start: METHODSTRT f1=flags INIT p1=params r1=return_
        {System.out.println($f1.text + " " + $r1.result + " init " + $p1.result
+ " {");}
        | METHODSTRT f1=flags id1=IDENT p1=params r1=return_
        {System.out.println($f1.text + " " + $r1.result + " " + $id1.text + " ("
+ $p1.result + ") {");}
        ;

method_end
        @after {System.out.println("}");}
        : METHODEND
        ;

flags: flag+;

flag  returns [String flag_result]
        :       f1='public'  {flag_result += $f1.text;}
        |       f1='static'      {flag_result += $f1.text;}
        |       f1='final'       {flag_result += $f1.text;}
        ;


params returns [String result]
        : '(' ')' {$result = "()";}
```

```
        | '(' '[L' id1=package_ ';' ')' {$result = $id1.result + " args[]";}
//([Ljava/lang/String;)
        ;

package_ returns [String result]
        : IDENT '/' IDENT '/' id1=IDENT {$result = id1.getText();}
        ;

return_ returns [String result]
        : 'V' {$result = "void";}
        ;

CLASS: '.class';
PUBLIC: 'public';
STATIC: 'static';
FINAL: 'final';
SUPER: '.super';
SOURCE: '.source';
FIELD: '.field';
METHODSTRT: '.method';
METHODEND: '.end method';
INIT: '<init>';
IDENT: ('a'..'z'|'A'..'Z')+;
COMMENT:  '//' ~( '\r' | '\n' )* {$channel = HIDDEN;};
WS: (' ' | '\t' | '\n' | '\r' | '\f' | ',')+ {$channel = HIDDEN;};
```

The structure of the file, before parsing any bytecode, is now shown in Listing 6-16.

Listing 6-16. `Casting.java` ***Without Pytecode***

```
public class Casting {
static final String ascStr = "ascii"
static final String chrStr = "character"
public void init () {
}
public static void main (String args[]) {
}
}
```

But the core logic of the Java code is in the opcodes at the end of the DDX file. Looking at Table 6-1, it should be clearer how the opcodes map to the target Java code `Casting.java`; see Listing 6-13, which you've been using throughout the book.

The method code has two parts: the `for` loop and the `System.out.println` statement within the `for` loop. From the parser's perspective, you can create the `for` loop as follows in Listing 6-17. Note that reserved keywords such as `return` have an added underscore so the generated ANTLR code compiles without any errors.

Listing 6-17. *for Loop Parser*

```
rule: class_name super_ source fields methods+ ;

class_name : CLASS flags IDENT  ;

super_: SUPER package_;

source: SOURCE IDENT '.java';

fields: field+  ;

field: FIELD flags IDENT package_ ';' '=' '"' IDENT '"';

methods: method_start scrap* method_end
        |       method_start scrap* for_start for_body scrap* for_end method_end
        ;

method_start: METHODSTRT flags INIT params return_
        | METHODSTRT flags IDENT params return_
        ;

method_end: METHODEND;

for_start : put_in_reg label put_in_reg if_ge scrap*;

const_string: CONST_STRING reg ddx_string;

ddx_string: '"' IDENT '"';

for_end : add_int int_to_char goto_ label scrap*;

new_instance: NEW_INSTANCE reg package_ scrap*;

add_int: ADD_INT reg reg DIGIT;

int_to_char: INT_TO_CHAR reg reg;

goto_: GOTO label;

if_ge: IF_GE reg reg label;

put_in_reg: const_ reg DIGIT;

reg_args: '{' reg+ '}';

label: LABEL
```

```
        | LABEL ':'
        ;

invoke_direct: INVOKE_DIRECT regs package_ ;

flags: flag+;

flag    :       f1='public'
        |       f1='static'
        |       f1='final'
        ;

params  : '(' ')'
        | '(' '[L' package_ ';' ')'
        | '(' IDENT ';' ')'
        | IDENT '(' package_ ';' ')'
        | IDENT '(' IDENT ')'
        | IDENT '(' ')'
        ;

package_
        : IDENT '/' IDENT '/' IDENT
        | IDENT '/' IDENT '/' IDENT '/' IDENT
        | IDENT '/' IDENT '/' IDENT '.' IDENT
        | IDENT '/' IDENT '/' IDENT '/' '<init>'
        |  'L' IDENT '/' IDENT '/' IDENT
        ;

return_ : 'V';

regs: '{' reg+ '}';

reg : 'v' DIGIT;

const_ : CONST_4
        | CONST_16
        | CONST_HIGH_16
        ;

scrap: LIMIT REGISTERS DIGIT
        | ';' 'this:' reg params
        | LINE DIGIT+
        | invoke_direct ';' '<init>' params return_
        | RETURN_VOID
        | ';' 'parameter[' DIGIT ']' ':' reg params
        ;

CLASS: '.class';
PUBLIC: 'public';
STATIC: 'static';
```

```
FINAL: 'final';
SUPER: '.super';
SOURCE: '.source';
FIELD: '.field';
METHODSTRT: '.method';
METHODEND: '.end method';
INIT: '<init>';
LIMIT: '.limit';
REGISTERS: 'registers';
LINE: '.line';
INVOKE_DIRECT: 'invoke-direct';
RETURN_VOID: 'return-void';
IF_GE: 'if-ge';
ADD_INT: 'add-int/lit8';
INT_TO_CHAR: 'int-to-char';
GOTO: 'goto';
CONST_STRING: 'const-string';
CONST_4: 'const/4';
CONST_16: 'const/16';
CONST_HIGH_16: 'const/high16';
DIGIT: ('0'..'9')+;
IDENT: ('a'..'z'|'A'..'Z')+;
LABEL: 'l' ('0'..'9'|'a'..'f')('0'..'9'|'a'..'f')('0'..'9'|'a'..'f');
COMMENT:  '//' ~( '\r' | '\n' )* {$channel = HIDDEN;};
WS: (' ' | '\t' | '\n' | '\r' | '\f' | ',')+ {$channel = HIDDEN;};
```

The lexer tokens are in uppercase, and the parser rules are in lowercase. `for_start` is a greater-than-or-equal-to condition followed by a label to jump to if the condition is true. The `for_end` rule, as you saw in the table breakdown, adds 1 to the variable c and then jumps back to the `for_start` condition. Note this isn't generic: it won't work for any other for loop. I'm showing it to give you an idea of how to put the parser together.

Next you need to add the parser code for the `System.out.println` or `for_body` statement, which you place between the `for_start` and `for_end` parts of the `for_loop` rule; see Listing 6-18.

Listing 6-18. *`Casting.java` Parser*

```
for_body: sget stmt_builder invoke_virtual;

stmt_builder returns : new_instance invoke_move+;

invoke_move
        : invoke_virtual move_result
        | const_string invoke_virtual move_result
        ;
```

```
move_result: MOVE_RESULT_OBJECT reg;

const_string: CONST_STRING reg ddx_string;

ddx_string: '"' IDENT '"';

new_instance: NEW_INSTANCE reg package_ scrap*;

sget : SGET_OBJECT reg package_ package_ ';';

invoke_virtual
        : INVOKE_VIRTUAL reg_args package_ ';' params 'V'
        | INVOKE_VIRTUAL reg_args package_ ';' params package_ ';'
        ;
```

Now that the opcodes can be parsed, you can add your own println statements to output the Java code; see Listing 6-19. Although this listing is long, it is one of the most complete parsers provided and thus important to review in its entirety.

Listing 6-19. *Casting.ddx Parser*

```
grammar DexToSource;

options {language = Java;}
@header {package com.riis.decompiler;}
@lexer::header {package com.riis.decompiler;}
@members{String flag_result = "";}

rule
        @after {System.out.println("}");}
        :       class_name super_ source fields methods+
        ;

class_name
        : CLASS f1=flags id2=IDENT
                {System.out.println($f1.text + " class " + $id2.text + " {");}
        ;

super_: SUPER package_;
source: SOURCE IDENT '.java';
fields: field+  ;

field: FIELD f1=flags id2=IDENT p1=package_ ';' '=' '"' id4=IDENT '"'
        {System.out.println($f1.text + " " + $p1.result + " " + $id2.text + " =
\"" + $id4.text + "\"" );}
        ;
```

```
methods: method_start scrap* method_end
        |       method_start scrap* for_start for_body scrap* for_end method_end
        ;


method_start: METHODSTRT f1=flags INIT p1=params r1=return_
        {System.out.println($f1.text + " " + $r1.result + " init " + $p1.result
+ " {");}
        | METHODSTRT f1=flags id1=IDENT p1=params r1=return_
        {System.out.println($f1.text + " " + $r1.result + " " + $id1.text + " ("
+ $p1.result + ") {");}
        ;

method_end
        @after {System.out.println("}");}
        : METHODEND
        ;

for_start : id1=put_in_reg label id2=put_in_reg if_ge scrap*
                {System.out.println("for(a=" + $id1.result + "; a < " +
$id2.result + "; a++){");}
        ;


for_body: id1=sget id3=stmt_builder id2=invoke_virtual
                {System.out.println($id1.result + "." + $id2.result + "(" +
$id3.result);}
        ;

stmt_builder returns [String result]
        : new_instance id1=invoke_move id2=invoke_move id3=invoke_move
                id4=invoke_move id5=invoke_move
{$result = "\"" + $id1.result + "\" + " + $id2.result + " + \"" + $id3.result +
"\" +" + $id4.result + ")";}
        ;

invoke_move returns [String result]
        : id1=invoke_virtual move_result
                {$result = $id1.result;}
        | id1=const_string invoke_virtual move_result
                {$result = $id1.result;}
        ;

move_result: MOVE_RESULT_OBJECT reg
        ;

const_string returns [String result]
        : CONST_STRING reg id1=ddx_string {$result = $id1.result;}
        ;
```

```
ddx_string returns [String result]
        : '"' id1=IDENT '"' {$result = $id1.getText();}
        ;

for_end : add_int int_to_char goto_ label scrap*
                {System.out.println("}");}
        ;

new_instance: NEW_INSTANCE reg package_ scrap*;

sget returns [String result]
        : SGET_OBJECT reg id1=package_ id2=package_ ';' {$result = $id1.result;}
        ;

invoke_virtual returns [String result]
        : INVOKE_VIRTUAL reg_args id1=package_ ';' params 'V' {$result =
$id1.result;}
        | INVOKE_VIRTUAL reg_args package_ ';' id1=params package_ ';' {if
($id1.result.compareTo("I") == 0) { $result = "(int)a"; } else {$result =
"(char)a";}}
        ;

add_int: ADD_INT reg reg DIGIT
        ;

int_to_char: INT_TO_CHAR reg reg
        ;

goto_: GOTO label
        ;

if_ge: IF_GE reg reg label
        ;

put_in_reg returns [String result]
        : const_ reg id1=DIGIT {$result = $id1.getText();}
        ;

reg_args: '{' reg+ '}'
        ;

label: LABEL
        | LABEL ':'
        ;

invoke_direct: INVOKE_DIRECT regs package_
        ;

flags: flag+;
```

```
flag  returns [String flag_result]
        :       f1='public'  {flag_result += $f1.text;}
        |       f1='static'     {flag_result += $f1.text;}
        |       f1='final'      {flag_result += $f1.text;}
        ;


params returns [String result]
        : '(' ')' {$result = "()";}
        | '(' '[L' id1=package_ ';' ')' {$result = $id1.result + " args[]";}
        | '(' id2=IDENT ';' ')' {$result = $id2.getText();}
        | IDENT '(' id3=package_ ';' ')' {$result=$id3.result;}
        | IDENT '(' id4=IDENT ')' {$result = $id4.getText();}
        | IDENT '(' ')' {$result = "()";}
        ;

package_ returns [String result]
        : IDENT '/' IDENT '/' id1=IDENT         {$result = id1.getText();}
        | IDENT '/' IDENT '/' IDENT '/' id1=IDENT       {$result =
id1.getText();}
        | IDENT '/' IDENT '/' id1=IDENT '.' id2=IDENT{$result = id1.getText() +
"." + id2.getText();}
        | IDENT '/' IDENT '/' IDENT '/' '<init>'        {$result = "init";}
        |  'L' IDENT '/' IDENT '/' id1=IDENT            {$result =
$id1.getText();}
        ;


return_ returns [String result]
        : 'V' {$result = "void";}
        ;


regs: '{' reg+ '}';

reg : 'v' DIGIT;

const_ : CONST_4
        | CONST_16
        | CONST_HIGH_16
        ;

scrap: LIMIT REGISTERS DIGIT
        | ';' 'this:' reg params
        | LINE DIGIT+
        | invoke_direct ';' '<init>' params return_
        | RETURN_VOID
        | ';' 'parameter[' DIGIT ']' ':' reg params
        ;
```

```
CLASS: '.class';
PUBLIC: 'public';
STATIC: 'static';
FINAL: 'final';
SUPER: '.super';
SOURCE: '.source';
FIELD: '.field';
METHODSTRT: '.method';
METHODEND: '.end method';
INIT: '<init>';
LIMIT: '.limit';
REGISTERS: 'registers';
LINE: '.line';
INVOKE_DIRECT: 'invoke-direct';
INVOKE_VIRTUAL: 'invoke-virtual';
MOVE_RESULT_OBJECT: 'move-result-object';
NEW_INSTANCE: 'new-instance';
RETURN_VOID: 'return-void';
IF_GE: 'if-ge';
SGET_OBJECT: 'sget-object';
ADD_INT: 'add-int/lit8';
INT_TO_CHAR: 'int-to-char';
GOTO: 'goto';
CONST_STRING: 'const-string';
CONST_4: 'const/4';
CONST_16: 'const/16';
CONST_HIGH_16: 'const/high16';
DIGIT: ('0'..'9')+;
IDENT: ('a'..'z'|'A'..'Z')+;
LABEL: 'l' ('0'..'9'|'a'..'f')('0'..'9'|'a'..'f')('0'..'9'|'a'..'f');
COMMENT:  '//' ~( '\r' | '\n' )* {$channel = HIDDEN;};
WS: (' ' | '\t' | '\n' | '\r' | '\f' | ',')+ {$channel = HIDDEN;};
```

Java

The generated Java code is shown in Listing 6-20. Note that dedexer made some subtle changes to the opcodes, so you lost the variables in the `print` statement. The Java code also needs some tabs to make it more readable, but you should see that `classes.dex` has been transformed back into Java.

Listing 6-20. *Generated `Casting.java`*

```
public class Casting {
static final String ascStr = "ascii"
static final String chrStr = "character"
public void init () {
}
public static void main (String args[]) {
```

```
for(a=0; a < 128; a++){
System.out.println("ascii" + (int)a + "character" +(char)a)
}
}
}
```

Example 2: Hello World

The Android SDK comes with a simple Hello World application, shown in Figure 6-2. The next example takes the code and reverse-engineers it.

Figure 6-2. *Hello Android screen*

The original Java code is shown in Listing 6-21.

Listing 6-21. `Hello.java`

```
package org.example.Hello;

import android.app.Activity;
import android.os.Bundle;

public class Hello extends Activity {
    /** Called when the activity is first created. */
    @Override
```

```
    public void onCreate(Bundle savedInstanceState) {
        super.onCreate(savedInstanceState);
        setContentView(R.layout.main);
    }
}
```

The corresponding DDX file is shown in Listing 6-22.

Listing 6-22. *HelloWorld.ddx*

```
.class public org/example/Hello/Hello
.super android/app/Activity
.source Hello.java

.method public <init>()V
.limit registers 1
; this: v0 (Lorg/example/Hello/Hello;)
.line 6
        invoke-direct   {v0},android/app/Activity/<init>        ; <init>()V
        return-void
.end method

.method public onCreate(Landroid/os/Bundle;)V
.limit registers 3
; this: v1 (Lorg/example/Hello/Hello;)
; parameter[0] : v2 (Landroid/os/Bundle;)
.line 10
        invoke-super    {v1,v2},android/app/Activity/onCreate   ;
onCreate(Landroid/os/Bundle;)V
.line 11
        const/high16    v0,32515
        invoke-virtual  {v1,v0},org/example/Hello/Hello/setContentView  ;
setContentView(I)V
.line 12
        return-void
.end method
```

Bytecode Analysis

Table 6-2 explains what each bytecode segment from Listing 6-22 means and presents a running tally of the values in the v0, v1, and v2 DVM registers.

Table 6-2. *HelloWorld.java Android Bytecode Analysis*

PC	Raw Bytecode	Operand	Opcode	v0	v1	v2	Comments
0	6f20 0100 2100	invoke-super	{v1, v2}		this	savedInstanceSt ate	Invoke the virtual method of the parent (v1) with method[1] Landroid/app/Ac tivity;.onCreat e:(Landroid/os/ Bundle;)V with argument v2
3	1500 037f	const/high16	v0, 32515	32515			Put constant #7f03 or 32515 in v0
5	6e20 0500 0100	invoke-virtual	{v1, v0}	32515			Invoke virtual method[5] Lorg/example/He llo/Hello;.setC ontentView:(I)V with argument v0
8	0e00	return-void					Return

Parser

To parse HelloWorld, you need to add support for the invoke-super and new const16/high keywords as well as the contentView structure. The parser is shown in Listing 6-23.

Listing 6-23. *Hello World and Casting Parser*

```
rule : for_loop return_
   | super_stmt return_
   ;

super_stmt : invoke_super invoke_virtual_content
  ;
```

```
for_loop : put_in_reg+ for_start println for_end
       ;

for_start: 'if-ge' reg reg HEX_DIGIT+
  ;

for_end: add_int int_to_char goto_
  ;

put_in_reg : const_ reg HEX_DIGIT+
       ;

reg : 'v' HEX_DIGIT
  ;

const_ : CONST_4
    | CONST_16
    | CONST_HIGH_16
    ;

add_int : ADD_INT reg reg HEX_DIGIT
  ;

int_to_char: 'int-to-char' reg reg
  ;

goto_: 'goto' HEX_DIGIT+
  ;

return_: 'return-void'
  ;

println: sget new_instance invoke_direct const_string invoke_virtual_move+
  ;

sget: SGET reg obj
  ;

new_instance: NEW_INSTANCE reg obj
  ;

invoke_direct: INVOKE_DIRECT obj param
  ;

invoke_super: INVOKE_SUPER param
  ;

invoke_virtual_move: invoke_virtual
  | invoke_virtual move_result_object
```

```
    | invoke_virtual move_result_object const_string
    ;

invoke_virtual_content: content_view invoke_virtual
    ;

content_view: const_ reg HEX_DIGIT+
    ;

invoke_virtual: INVOKE_VIRTUAL obj param
    | INVOKE_VIRTUAL param
    ;

move_result_object: MOVE_RESULT_OBJECT reg
    ;

const_string: CONST_STRING reg obj
    ;

obj : IDENT '[' HEX_DIGIT+ ']'
    ;

param : '{' reg '}'
    | '{' reg reg '}'
    ;

INVOKE_DIRECT: 'invoke-direct';
INVOKE_SUPER: 'invoke-super';
INVOKE_VIRTUAL: 'invoke-virtual';
NEW_INSTANCE: 'new-instance';
MOVE_RESULT_OBJECT: 'move-result-object';
SGET: 'sget-object';
CONST_STRING: 'const-string';
HEX_DIGIT: ('0'..'9'|'A'..'F'|'a'..'f');
IDENT: ('a'..'z')+;
ADD_INT: 'add-int/lit8';
CONST_4: 'const/4';
CONST_16: 'const/16';
CONST_HIGH_16: 'const/high16';
```

Java

The generated Java code is shown in Listing 6-24. `classes.dex` tells you that `savedInstanceState` is in v2 when the method is first invoked and `setContentView` is calling the numeric value of `R.layout.Main`.

Listing 6-24. *Generated* `HelloWorld.java`

```
super.onCreate(savedInstanceState);
setContentView(32515);
```

Example 3: if Statement

To complete these examples, you need an `if` statement. The open source Android app from WordPress is a great resource because it's a professional app that gives you access to the source code. `escapeHTML.java` in Listing 6-25 has a simple `if` conditions.

Listing 6-25. `escapeHTML` *Method*

```
public static void escapeHtml(Writer writer, String string) throws IOException {
    if (writer == null ) {
        throw new IllegalArgumentException ("The Writer must not be null.");
    }
    if (string == null) {
        return;
    }
    Entities.HTML40_escape.escape(writer, string);
}
```

The bytecode from the dex file is shown in Listing 6-26.

Listing 6-26. `escapeHTML.ddx`

```
.method public static escapeHtml(Ljava/io/Writer;Ljava/lang/String;)V
.throws Ljava/io/IOException;
.limit registers 4
; parameter[0] : v2 (Ljava/io/Writer;)
; parameter[1] : v3 (Ljava/lang/String;)
.line 27
        if-nez  v2,l7ba4c
.line 28
        new-instance    v0,java/lang/IllegalArgumentException
        const-string    v1,"The Writer must not be null."
        invoke-direct   {v0,v1},java/lang/IllegalArgumentException/<init>
        ; <init>(Ljava/lang/String;)V
        throw   v0
l7ba4c:
.line 30
        if-nez  v3,l7ba52
l7ba50:
.line 34
        return-void
l7ba52:
```

```
.line 33
        sget-object     v0,org/wordpress/android/util/Entities.HTML40_escape
Lorg/wordpress/android/util/Entities;
        invoke-virtual  {v0,v2,v3},org/wordpress/android/util/Entities/escape
        ; escape(Ljava/io/Writer;Ljava/lang/String;)V
        goto    17ba50
.end method
```

Bytecode Analysis

Table 6-3 explains what each bytecode segment from Listing 6-23 means along with a running tally of the values in the v0, v1, v2, and v3 DVM registers. The only real puzzle in reverse-engineering the bytecode is the last instruction: `28fa`. The `28` opcode translates to `goto` with an operand of `fa`. The operand is stored in two's complement format (see `http://en.wikipedia.org/wiki/Twos_complement` for more information). To get the address, you need to convert each of the hexadecimal digits to binary, flip the bits, and add 1. In this example, `fa` = 11111010, which when the bits are flipped becomes 00000101. If you add 1, the number is 00000110 or decimal 6. Go back six words, and you have your address: 000c.

Table 6-3. *`escapeHTML` Android Bytecode Analysis*

PC	Bytecode	Opcode	Operand	v0	v1	v2	v3	Comments
0	`3902 0a00`	`if-nez`	`v2, 000a`	`0`		`writer Ljava/io/Writer;`	`string Ljava/lang/String;`	Jump to PC=a if v2 is null
2	`2200 0202`	`new-instance`	`v0, type[514]`	`Ljava/lang/IllegalArgumentException;`				Put `type[514]` (`0x202`) into v0
4	`1a01 bf0d`	`const-string`	`v1, string[3519]`		`"The Writer must not be null"`			Put `string[3519]` (`0x0dbf`) into v1

PC	Bytecode	Opcode	Operand	v0	v1	v2	v3	Comments
6	7020 fe0b 1000	invoke-direct	{v0, v1}					Call method[3070] 0x0bfe with 2 arg, Ljava/lang/IllegalArgumentException;.<init>:(Ljava/lang/String;)V with parameters {v0, v1}
9	2700	throw	v0					Throw exception object v0
a	3903 0300	if-nez	v3, 000d					Jump to PC=d if v3 is null
c	0e00	return-void						Return
d	6200 260a	sget-object	v0, field[2598]	org/wordpress/android/util/Entities.HTML40_escape Lorg/wordpress/android/util/Entities;				Read the object in field[2598] (0xa26), org/wordpress/android/util/Entities.HTML40_escape Lorg/wordpress/android/util/Entities;, and store in v0
f	6e30 4115 2003	invoke-virtual	{v0, v2, v3} method[5441]					Call method[5441] (0x1541), org/wordpress/android/util/Entities/escape (escape(Ljava/io/Writer;Ljava/lang/String;)V), with parameters {v0, v2, v3}

PC	Bytecode	Opcode	Operand	v0	v1	v2	v3	Comments
12	28fa	goto	000c					Go to address c; fa is stored as two's complement

Parser

To parse the `if not equal then` branch as well as the `goto` statements, you need to add them to the parser. You also need to add more parameter options to the `invoke-virtual` statements; see Listing 6-27.

Listing 6-27. *Hello World, Casting, and If Parser*

```
rule : for_loop return_
    | super_stmt return_
    | if_stmt+
    ;

if_stmt: if_ new_instance const_string invoke_direct throw_
   | if_ return_ goto_stmt
   ;

goto_stmt: sget invoke_virtual goto_
   ;

if_ : IF_NEZ reg HEX_DIGIT+
   ;

throw_ : THROW reg
   ;
```

```
super_stmt : invoke_super invoke_virtual_content
  ;

for_loop : put_in_reg+ for_start println for_end
       ;

for_start: 'if-ge' reg reg HEX_DIGIT+
  ;

for_end: add_int int_to_char goto_
  ;

put_in_reg : const_ reg HEX_DIGIT+
      ;

reg : 'v' HEX_DIGIT
  ;

const_ : CONST_4
    | CONST_16
    | CONST_HIGH_16
    ;

add_int : ADD_INT reg reg HEX_DIGIT
  ;

int_to_char: 'int-to-char' reg reg
  ;

goto_: 'goto' HEX_DIGIT+
  ;

return_: 'return-void'
  ;

println: sget new_instance invoke_direct const_string invoke_virtual_move+
  ;

sget: SGET reg obj
  ;

new_instance: NEW_INSTANCE reg obj
  ;

invoke_direct: INVOKE_DIRECT obj param
  | INVOKE_DIRECT param
  ;

invoke_super: INVOKE_SUPER param
  ;
```

```
invoke_virtual_move: invoke_virtual
  | invoke_virtual move_result_object
  | invoke_virtual move_result_object const_string
  ;

invoke_virtual_content: content_view invoke_virtual
  ;

content_view: const_ reg HEX_DIGIT+
  ;

invoke_virtual: INVOKE_VIRTUAL obj param
  | INVOKE_VIRTUAL param
  | INVOKE_VIRTUAL param obj
  ;

move_result_object: MOVE_RESULT_OBJECT reg
  ;

const_string: CONST_STRING reg obj
  ;

obj : IDENT '[' HEX_DIGIT+ ']'
  ;

param : '{' reg '}'
  | '{' reg reg '}'
  | '{' reg reg reg '}'
  ;


CONST_STRING: 'const-string';
IF_NEZ: 'if-nez';
INVOKE_DIRECT: 'invoke-direct';
INVOKE_SUPER: 'invoke-super';
INVOKE_VIRTUAL: 'invoke-virtual';
NEW_INSTANCE: 'new-instance';
MOVE_RESULT_OBJECT: 'move-result-object';
SGET: 'sget-object';
THROW: 'throw';
HEX_DIGIT: ('0'..'9'|'A'..'F'|'a'..'f');
IDENT: ('a'..'z')+;
ADD_INT: 'add-int/lit8';
CONST_4: 'const/4';
CONST_16: 'const/16';
CONST_HIGH_16: 'const/high16';
WS: (' ' | '\t' | '\n' | '\r' | '\f' | ',')+ {$channel = HIDDEN;};
```

Java

The generated Java code is shown in Listing 6-28.

Listing 6-28. *Generated* `escapeHTML.java`

```
if (writer == null ) {
    throw new IllegalArgumentException ("The Writer must not be null.");
}
if (string == null) {
    return;
}
Entities.HTML40_escape.escape(writer, string);
```

Refactoring

As you build the parser, it quickly becomes clear that you need to put the instructions into different families. Otherwise, the parser may end up being unmanageable, and you'll also end up hard-coding the structures to match the input files. Without some refactoring, you'll never have a generic solution to reverse-engineering the Android APKs. Gabor Paller has split the instructions as shown in Table 6-4.

Table 6-4. *Opcode Classifications*

Classification	Opcodes
Moving between registers	`move`, `move/from16`, `move-wide`, `move-wide/from16`, `move-object`, `move-object/from16`
Obtaining and setting the result value	`move-result`, `move-result-wide`, `move-result-object`, `return-void`, `return`, `return-wide`, `return-object`
Exception handling	`throw`, `move-exception`
Constants to registers	`const/4`, `const/16`, `const`, `const/high16`, `const-wide/16`, `const-wide/32`, `const-wide`, `const-wide/high16`, `const-string`, `const-class`
Synchronization	`monitor-enter`, `monitor-exit`
Type checking	`check-cast`, `instance-of`

Classification	Opcodes
Array manipulation	new-array, array-length, filled-new-array, filled-new-array/range, fill-array-data
Instance creation	new-instance
Execution control	goto, goto/16, packed-switch, sparse-switch, if-eq, if-ne,if-lt, if-ge, if-gt, if-le, if-eqz, if-nez, if-ltz, if-gez, if-gtz, if-lez
Comparisons	cmpl-float, cmpg-float, cmpl-double, cmpg-double, cmp-long
Read/write member fields	iget, iget-wide, iget-object, iget-boolean, iget-byte, iget-char, iget-short, iput, iput-wide, iput-object, iput-boolean, iput-byte, iput-char, iput-short
Read/write array elements	aget, aget-wide, aget-object, aget-boolean, aget-byte, aget-char, aget-short, aput, aput-wide, aput-object, aput-boolean, aput-byte, aput-char, aput-short
Read/write static fields	sget, sget-wide, sget-object, sget-boolean, sget-byte, sget-char, sget-short, sput, sput-wide, sput-object, sput-boolean, sput-byte, sput-char, sput-short
Method invocation	invoke-virtual, invoke-super, invoke-direct, invoke-static, invoke-interface, invoke-virtual/range, invoke-super/range, invoke-direct/range, invoke-static/range, invoke-interface/range
Operations on int, long, float, double	add, sub, mul, div, rem, and, or, xor, shl, shr, ushr, neg-(int, long, float, double), not-(int, long)

The refactored parser is shown in Listing 6-29. Now that you have a small test suite of code from the examples, you can use it to test whether any changes have broken the parser.

Listing 6-29. *Refactored Parser*

```
rule : for_loop return_
   | stmt return_
   | stmt+
   ;
```

```
for_loop : put_in_reg+ for_start stmt for_end
       ;

stmt : if_stmt
   | super_stmt
   | println
   ;

if_stmt: if_ new_instance const_string invoke throw_
   | if_ return_ goto_stmt
   ;

println: sget new_instance invoke const_string invoke_move+
   ;

super_stmt : invoke invoke_content
   ;

goto_stmt: sget invoke goto_
   ;

for_start: 'if-ge' reg reg HEX_DIGIT+
   ;

for_end: add_int int_to_char goto_
   ;

put_in_reg : const_ reg HEX_DIGIT+
       ;

add_int : ADD_INT reg reg HEX_DIGIT
   ;

int_to_char: 'int-to-char' reg reg
   ;

invoke_move: invoke
   | invoke move_result_object
   | invoke move_result_object const_string
   ;

invoke_content: content_view invoke
   ;

invoke : invoke_virtual
   | invoke_direct
   | invoke_super
   ;
```

```
invoke_virtual: INVOKE_VIRTUAL obj param
  | INVOKE_VIRTUAL param
  | INVOKE_VIRTUAL param obj
  ;

invoke_direct: INVOKE_DIRECT obj param
  | INVOKE_DIRECT param
  ;

invoke_super: INVOKE_SUPER param
  ;

content_view: const_ reg HEX_DIGIT+
  ;

sget: SGET reg obj
  ;

new_instance: NEW_INSTANCE reg obj
  ;

if_ : IF_NEZ reg HEX_DIGIT+
  ;

reg : 'v' HEX_DIGIT
  ;

const_ : CONST_4
    | CONST_16
    | CONST_HIGH_16
    ;

move_result_object: MOVE_RESULT_OBJECT reg
  ;

const_string: CONST_STRING reg obj
  ;

obj : IDENT '[' HEX_DIGIT+ ']'
  ;

//helper functions
param : '{' reg+ '}'
  ;

goto_: 'goto' HEX_DIGIT+
  ;

throw_ : THROW reg
  ;
```

```
return_: 'return-void'
  ;

CONST_STRING: 'const-string';
IF_NEZ: 'if-nez';
INVOKE_DIRECT: 'invoke-direct';
INVOKE_SUPER: 'invoke-super';
INVOKE_VIRTUAL: 'invoke-virtual';
NEW_INSTANCE: 'new-instance';
MOVE_RESULT_OBJECT: 'move-result-object';
SGET: 'sget-object';
THROW: 'throw';
HEX_DIGIT: ('0'..'9'|'A'..'F'|'a'..'f');
IDENT: ('a'..'z')+;
ADD_INT: 'add-int/lit8';
CONST_4: 'const/4';
CONST_16: 'const/16';
CONST_HIGH_16: 'const/high16';
WS: (' ' | '\t' | '\n' | '\r' | '\f' | ',')+ {$channel = HIDDEN;};
```

At the moment the parser only handles 3 simple program structures and is missing complete coverage of all Dalvik bytecodes. If included it would make this chapter longer than the rest of the book. But for those inclined to learn more the completed decompiler is available on the Apress web site (www.apress.com), along with a larger test suite and instructions on how to run it.

Summary

In this chapter, you've created DexToXML and DexToSource using the dedexer outputs, both of that are available on the Apress web site. These can be used to break down the `classes.dex` file into XML and Java source, respectively. The DexToSource code on the web site uses an AST and `StringTemplates` for the more complicated test-suite examples.

The next chapter finishes this book with a case study of the arguments for and against obfuscation as well as best practices to obfuscate your code using open source or a commercial obfuscator.

Chapter 7

Hear No Evil, See No Evil: A Case Study

You're now almost at the end of your journey. By now you should have a sound understanding of the overall principles of how to decompile and how to make some attempts at protecting your code. Having said that, I've found from working with clients and colleagues that even if you understand what decompilation and obfuscation really mean, it doesn't help you figure out what practical measures you can take to protect your code. A little knowledge can often create more questions than answers.

As the Competency Centre for Java (JCC) says on its deCaf website FAQ:

> *Is it true that no one will ever be able to decompile my deCaf protected application? NO. deCaf does not make decompilation impossible. It make Is it true that no one will ever be able to decompile my deCaf protected application s it difficult. Making decompilation impossible is impossible.*

The goal of this book is to help raise the bar and make it more difficult for anyone to decompile your code. Currently in the Android world there seems to be a "hear no evil, see no evil" approach to decompilation, but sooner or later that will change. After reading this book you should be forewarned and, more important, forearmed about the best practical approach to safeguard your code, given your specific circumstances.

This chapter examines a case study to help overcome this conundrum. Almost everyone who tries to protect their code does so using some sort of obfuscation tool. The case study looks at this approach in more detail to help you come to a conclusion about how to best protect your code. It has the following format:

- Problem description
- Myths
- Proposed solutions: ProGuard and DashO

Obfuscation Case Study

For many people, the fear of someone decompiling their Android application is nowhere near the top of the list of things they're worrying about. It ranks way below installing the latest version of Maven or Ant. Sure, they'd like to protect against decompilation, but nobody has the time—and doesn't ProGuard take care of that anyway?

There are two simple options in this scenario: use obfuscation to protect the application, or ignore decompilation as if it's not a problem. The latter, of course, isn't a recommended choice for obvious reasons.

Myths

Over the years, I've heard many different arguments about whether it makes sense to protect your code. The most common one today is that if you create a good Android application and continue to improve it, that will safeguard you against anyone decompiling your code. It's a common belief that if you write good applications, the source will protect itself—that upgrades and good support are much better ways of protecting your code than using obfuscation or any of the other techniques discussed in this book.

Other arguments are that software development is about how you apply your knowledge, not getting access to someone else's applications. The original code these days may come from a well-described design pattern, so nobody cares if it's hacked. And all developers (the good ones, anyway) can always think of a better way of doing something after it's completed, so why worry? Chances are that if someone is so unimaginative that they have to resort to stealing your code, they won't be capable of building on the code and turning it into something useful. And it's impossible for you to read your own code six months after it's developed, so how would anyone else make sense of it?

Obfuscated code can also be very difficult to debug. Error reports from the field need to be traced back to the correct method so the developer can debug and fix the code. If not handled correctly, this can become a maintenance nightmare and make support challenging.

But surely the problem is someone cracking the program—and that can happen on iOS as well as Android. It's not like the newspapers are full of reports of people decompiling a product and rebadging it as their own; and we're forever hearing about the latest Microsoft exploit, so it can't be a problem. For me, this argument is valid for code running on web servers but not for code running on Android devices. In Chapter 4, you saw how easy it is to gain access to the code and resources in an APK. If it contains any clues to gaining access to backend systems, such as API keys or database logins, or if your application has any customer information that needs to be secure, then you owe it to your customers to take basic steps to protect your code.

If used correctly, obfuscation significantly raises the bar and stops the majority of people from recovering your source code. This chapter's case study uses the open source WordPress Android application from the last chapter as a good sample app to obfuscate. Because it's open source, you have the original source code, which you can compare against the obfuscated code to see if obfuscation is effective. The case study examines how ProGuard (which ships with the Android SDK) and DashO (a commercial obfuscator) munge the class files.

Download the WordPress source code from `http://android.svn.wordpress.org/`. The case study uses the build from March 17, 2012.

Use `android update project` to update the project for your environment:

```
android update project -t android-15 -p ./
```

Solution 1: ProGuard

By default, ProGuard isn't turned on. To enable ProGuard for obfuscation, edit the `project.properties` file and add the following line:

```
proguard.config=proguard.cfg
```

We'll cover the settings in `proguard.cfg` in more detail later in this chapter. Only production or release APKs are ever obfuscated, so make sure the `android:debuggable` flag is set to `false` in the `AndroidManifest.xml` file. Compile the application using the `ant release` command, assuming Ant is your build tool.

SDK Output

ProGuard obfuscates the Java jar file before it's converted to a `classes.dex` file. The original and obfuscated files can be found in the `bin\proguard` folder if you're using Ant or `\proguard` under the `project` folder if you're using Eclipse.

ProGuard also outputs the following files:

- `dump.txt`
- `seeds.txt`
- `usage.txt`
- `mapping.txt`

What would be useful is an obfuscation-coverage tool similar to a code-coverage tool, to show you how much code has been obfuscated. But such a tool doesn't exist yet, so these files are the closest to a coverage tool that you have.

`dump.txt` contains the output of all the information in the class files, not unlike a Java class-file disassembler; it isn't much help for your purposes. `seeds.txt` lists the classes and methods that weren't obfuscated. It's vitally important to understand why some code is obfuscated and other code isn't; more on that later in the "Double-Checking Your Work" section. But you need to check, for example, that the methods with your API keys aren't in `seeds.txt`, because as otherwise they won't be protected in any way.

ProGuard not only obfuscates but also shrinks jar files by removing any log files, classes, or code that were in the original code but never called, and so on. `usage.txt` lists all the unnecessary information that was stripped from the original jar. Because storage is at a premium on Android devices, this alone is a good reason to use an obfuscator on your code. But be careful that it doesn't remove code you might want to keep.

`mapping.txt` is probably the most useful file in this directory because it maps the original method name to the obfuscated method name. ProGuard, like most obfuscators, heavily renames methods; and if you need to do any debugging in the fields, `mapping.txt` is necessary to trace back to the original method. You use this in the next section to see how effective the obfuscation can be for the WordPress application.

Listing 7-1, using ProGuard 4.4, shows the Ant output during a build; this can also be useful for seeing how much or how little work ProGuard is doing. If the `obfuscate` section is blank, you can be sure that ProGuard isn't being called correctly. If you try this yourself, don't worry if the numbers are slightly different:

you're probably using a more recent version of ProGuard and/or the WordPress code.

Listing 7-1. *Ant Output*

```
-obfuscate:
    [mkdir] Created dir: G:\clients\apress\chap7\wordpress\bin\proguard
    [jar] Building jar:
G:\clients\apress\chap7\wordpress\bin\proguard\original.jar
 [proguard] ProGuard, version 4.4
 [proguard] ProGuard is released under the GNU General Public License. The
authors of all
 [proguard] programs or plugins that link to it (com.android.ant, ...) therefore
 [proguard] must ensure that these programs carry the GNU General Public License
as well.
 [proguard] Reading input...
 [proguard] Reading program jar
[G:\clients\apress\chap7\wordpress\bin\proguard\original.jar]
 [proguard] Reading program jar [G:\clients\apress\chap7\wordpress\libs\CWAC-
AdapterWrapper.jar]
 [proguard] Reading program jar [G:\clients\apress\chap7\wordpress\libs\CWAC-
Bus.jar]
 [proguard] Reading program jar [G:\clients\apress\chap7\wordpress\libs\CWAC-
Task.jar]
 [proguard] Reading program jar [G:\clients\apress\chap7\wordpress\libs\android-
support-v4.jar]
 [proguard] Reading program jar
[G:\clients\apress\chap7\wordpress\libs\httpmime-4.1.2.jar]
 [proguard] Reading program jar [G:\clients\apress\chap7\wordpress\libs\tagsoup-
1.2.1.jar]
 [proguard] Reading library jar [C:\Program Files (x86)\Android\android-
sdk\platforms\android-14\android.jar]
 [proguard] Initializing...
 [proguard] Note: the configuration refers to the unknown class
'com.android.vending.licensing.ILicensingService'
 [proguard] Note: there were 1 references to unknown classes.
 [proguard]       You should check your configuration for typos.
 [proguard] Ignoring unused library classes...
 [proguard]   Original number of library classes: 3133
 [proguard]   Final number of library classes:    888
 [proguard] Printing kept classes, fields, and methods...
 [proguard] Shrinking...
 [proguard] Printing usage to
[G:\clients\apress\chap7\wordpress\bin\proguard\usage.txt]...
 [proguard] Removing unused program classes and class elements...
 [proguard]   Original number of program classes: 644
 [proguard]   Final number of program classes:    469
 [proguard] Optimizing...
 [proguard]   Number of finalized classes:                 331
 [proguard]   Number of vertically merged classes:         0     (disabled)
```

```
[proguard]   Number of horizontally merged classes:      0     (disabled)
[proguard]   Number of removed write-only fields:        0     (disabled)
[proguard]   Number of privatized fields:                520   (disabled)
[proguard]   Number of inlined constant fields:          1196  (disabled)
[proguard]   Number of privatized methods:               163
[proguard]   Number of staticized methods:               61
[proguard]   Number of finalized methods:                1062
[proguard]   Number of removed method parameters:        98
[proguard]   Number of inlined constant parameters:      61
[proguard]   Number of inlined constant return values:   15
[proguard]   Number of inlined short method calls:       9
[proguard]   Number of inlined unique method calls:      169
[proguard]   Number of inlined tail recursion calls:     2
[proguard]   Number of merged code blocks:               6
[proguard]   Number of variable peephole optimizations:  1434
[proguard]   Number of arithmetic peephole optimizations: 0    (disabled)
[proguard]   Number of cast peephole optimizations:      31
[proguard]   Number of field peephole optimizations:     3
[proguard]   Number of branch peephole optimizations:    416
[proguard]   Number of simplified instructions:          196
[proguard]   Number of removed instructions:             1074
[proguard]   Number of removed local variables:          184
[proguard]   Number of removed exception blocks:         8
[proguard]   Number of optimized local variable frames:  493
[proguard] Shrinking...
[proguard] Removing unused program classes and class elements...
[proguard]   Original number of program classes: 469
[proguard]   Final number of program classes:    455
```

Double-Checking Your Work

To see how effective ProGuard can be, let's look at what it did against the `EscapeUtils.java` method that you used in Chapter 6. Listing 7-2 shows the original WordPress source.

Listing 7-2. ***Original*** `EscapeUtils.java` ***Code***

```
package org.wordpress.android.util;

import java.io.IOException;
import java.io.StringWriter;
import java.io.Writer;

public class EscapeUtils
{
        public static String escapeHtml(String str) {
             if (str == null) {
```

```
                return null;
            }
            try {
                StringWriter writer = new StringWriter ((int)(str.length() *
1.5));
                escapeHtml(writer, str);
                return writer.toString();
            } catch (IOException e) {
                //assert false;
                //should be impossible
                e.printStackTrace();
                return null;
            }
        }


        public static void escapeHtml(Writer writer, String string) throws
IOException {
            if (writer == null ) {
                throw new IllegalArgumentException ("The Writer must not be
null.");
            }
            if (string == null) {
                return;
            }
            Entities.HTML40_escape.escape(writer, string);
        }

    public static String unescapeHtml(String str) {
        if (str == null) {
            return null;
        }
        try {
            StringWriter writer = new StringWriter ((int)(str.length() * 1.5));
            unescapeHtml(writer, str);
            return writer.toString();
        } catch (IOException e) {
            //assert false;
            //should be impossible
            e.printStackTrace();
            return null;
        }
    }

    public static void unescapeHtml(Writer writer, String string) throws
IOException {
        if (writer == null ) {
            throw new IllegalArgumentException ("The Writer must not be null.");
        }
```

```
        if (string == null) {
            return;
        }
        Entities.HTML40.unescape(writer, string);
    }

}
```

Listing 7-3 shows the unobfuscated code decompiled by JD-GUI. The best way to see how well your obfuscation works is to first look at the decompiled code from the jar file before it has been transformed into a `classes.dex` file. This removes any unintended obfuscation that the dx process introduces. You can see that it's identical to the original code; the only difference is that there are no comments in the decompiled version.

Listing 7-3. *Unobfuscated `EscapeUtils.java`*

```
package org.wordpress.android.util;

import java.io.IOException;
import java.io.StringWriter;
import java.io.Writer;

public class EscapeUtils
{
  public static String escapeHtml(String str)
  {
    if (str == null)
      return null;
    try
    {
      StringWriter writer = new StringWriter((int)(str.length() * 1.5D));
      escapeHtml(writer, str);
      return writer.toString();
    }
    catch (IOException e)
    {
      e.printStackTrace();
    }return null;
  }

  public static void escapeHtml(Writer writer, String string)
    throws IOException
  {
    if (writer == null) {
      throw new IllegalArgumentException("The Writer must not be null.");
    }
    if (string == null) {
      return;
```

```
    }
    Entities.HTML40_escape.escape(writer, string);
  }

  public static String unescapeHtml(String str) {
    if (str == null)
      return null;
    try
    {
      StringWriter writer = new StringWriter((int)(str.length() * 1.5D));
      unescapeHtml(writer, str);
      return writer.toString();
    }
    catch (IOException e)
    {
      e.printStackTrace();
    }return null;
  }

  public static void unescapeHtml(Writer writer, String string) throws
IOException
  {
    if (writer == null) {
      throw new IllegalArgumentException("The Writer must not be null.");
    }
    if (string == null) {
      return;
    }
    Entities.HTML40.unescape(writer, string);
  }
}
```

Listing 7-4 shows the code obfuscated by ProGuard. I used the `mapping.txt` file to get the name of the obfuscated file, which is `t.java`. There is a certain randomness to the choice of filename, and it probably won't be `t.java` if you obfuscate the WordPress code yourself.

Listing 7-4. *Obfuscated `t.java` (`EscapeUtils.java`)*

```
package org.wordpress.android.util;

import java.io.IOException;
import java.io.StringWriter;

public final class t
{
  public static String a(String paramString)
  {
    if (paramString == null)
      return null;
```

```
    try
    {
      StringWriter localStringWriter;
      String str = paramString;
      paramString = localStringWriter = new
StringWriter((int)(paramString.length() * 1.5D));
      if (str != null)
        r.b.a(paramString, str);
      return localStringWriter.toString();
    }
    catch (IOException localIOException)
    {
      localIOException.printStackTrace();
    }
    return null;
  }

  public static String b(String paramString)
  {
    if (paramString == null)
      return null;
    try
    {
      StringWriter localStringWriter;
      String str = paramString;
      paramString = localStringWriter = new
StringWriter((int)(paramString.length() * 1.5D));
      if (str != null)
        r.a.b(paramString, str);
      return localStringWriter.toString();
    }
    catch (IOException localIOException)
    {
      localIOException.printStackTrace();
    }
    return null;
  }
}
```

The `public static String escapeHtml(String str)` and `public static String unescapeHtml(String str)` methods look very similar to the originals. But the `public static void escapeHtml(Writer writer, String string)` and `public static void unescapeHtml(Writer writer, String string)` methods have been pushed to a separate file `r.java`, which is unintelligible (see Listing 7-5).

Listing 7-5. *r.java Class*

```
package org.wordpress.android.util;

import java.io.Writer;

final class r
{
  private static final String[][] c = { { "quot", "34" }, { "amp", "38" }, {
"lt", "60" }, { "gt", "62" } };
  private static final String[][] d = { { "apos", "39" } };
  private static String[][] e = { { "nbsp", "160" }, { "iexcl", "161" }, {
"cent", "162" }, { "pound", "163" }, { "curren", "164" }, { "yen", "165" }, {
"brvbar", "166" }, { "sect", "167" }, { "uml", "168" }, { "copy", "169" }, {
"ordf", "170" }, { "laquo", "171" }, { "not", "172" }, { "shy", "173" }, {
"reg", "174" }, { "macr", "175" }, { "deg", "176" }, { "plusmn", "177" }, {
"sup2", "178" }, { "sup3", "179" }, { "acute", "180" }, { "micro", "181" }, {
"para", "182" }, { "middot", "183" }, { "cedil", "184" }, { "sup1", "185" }, {
"ordm", "186" }, { "raquo", "187" }, { "frac14", "188" }, { "frac12", "189" }, {
"frac34", "190" }, { "iquest", "191" }, { "Agrave", "192" }, { "Aacute", "193"
}, { "Acirc", "194" }, { "Atilde", "195" }, { "Auml", "196" }, { "Aring", "197"
}, { "AElig", "198" }, { "Ccedil", "199" }, { "Egrave", "200" }, { "Eacute",
"201" }, { "Ecirc", "202" }, { "Euml", "203" }, { "Igrave", "204" }, { "Iacute",
"205" }, { "Icirc", "206" }, { "Iuml", "207" }, { "ETH", "208" }, { "Ntilde",
"209" }, { "Ograve", "210" }, { "Oacute", "211" }, { "Ocirc", "212" }, {
"Otilde", "213" }, { "Ouml", "214" }, { "times", "215" }, { "Oslash", "216" }, {
"Ugrave", "217" }, { "Uacute", "218" }, { "Ucirc", "219" }, { "Uuml", "220" }, {
"Yacute", "221" }, { "THORN", "222" }, { "szlig", "223" }, { "agrave", "224" },
{ "aacute", "225" }, { "acirc", "226" }, { "atilde", "227" }, { "auml", "228" },
{ "aring", "229" }, { "aelig", "230" }, { "ccedil", "231" }, { "egrave", "232"
}, { "eacute", "233" }, { "ecirc", "234" }, { "euml", "235" }, { "igrave", "236"
}, { "iacute", "237" }, { "icirc", "238" }, { "iuml", "239" }, { "eth", "240" },
{ "ntilde", "241" }, { "ograve", "242" }, { "oacute", "243" }, { "ocirc", "244"
}, { "otilde", "245" }, { "ouml", "246" }, { "divide", "247" }, { "oslash",
"248" }, { "ugrave", "249" }, { "uacute", "250" }, { "ucirc", "251" }, { "uuml",
"252" }, { "yacute", "253" }, { "thorn", "254" }, { "yuml", "255" } };
  private static String[][] f = { { "fnof", "402" }, { "Alpha", "913" }, {
"Beta", "914" }, { "Gamma", "915" }, { "Delta", "916" }, { "Epsilon", "917" }, {
"Zeta", "918" }, { "Eta", "919" }, { "Theta", "920" }, { "Iota", "921" }, {
"Kappa", "922" }, { "Lambda", "923" }, { "Mu", "924" }, { "Nu", "925" }, { "Xi",
"926" }, { "Omicron", "927" }, { "Pi", "928" }, { "Rho", "929" }, { "Sigma",
"931" }, { "Tau", "932" }, { "Upsilon", "933" }, { "Phi", "934" }, { "Chi",
"935" }, { "Psi", "936" }, { "Omega", "937" }, { "alpha", "945" }, { "beta",
"946" }, { "gamma", "947" }, { "delta", "948" }, { "epsilon", "949" }, { "zeta",
"950" }, { "eta", "951" }, { "theta", "952" }, { "iota", "953" }, { "kappa",
"954" }, { "lambda", "955" }, { "mu", "956" }, { "nu", "957" }, { "xi", "958" },
{ "omicron", "959" }, { "pi", "960" }, { "rho", "961" }, { "sigmaf", "962" }, {
"sigma", "963" }, { "tau", "964" }, { "upsilon", "965" }, { "phi", "966" }, {
"chi", "967" }, { "psi", "968" }, { "omega", "969" }, { "thetasym", "977" }, {
"upsih", "978" }, { "piv", "982" }, { "bull", "8226" }, { "hellip", "8230" }, {
```

```
"prime", "8242" }, { "Prime", "8243" }, { "oline", "8254" }, { "frasl", "8260"
}, { "weierp", "8472" }, { "image", "8465" }, { "real", "8476" }, { "trade",
"8482" }, { "alefsym", "8501" }, { "larr", "8592" }, { "uarr", "8593" }, {
"rarr", "8594" }, { "darr", "8595" }, { "harr", "8596" }, { "crarr", "8629" }, {
"lArr", "8656" }, { "uArr", "8657" }, { "rArr", "8658" }, { "dArr", "8659" }, {
"hArr", "8660" }, { "forall", "8704" }, { "part", "8706" }, { "exist", "8707" },
{ "empty", "8709" }, { "nabla", "8711" }, { "isin", "8712" }, { "notin", "8713"
}, { "ni", "8715" }, { "prod", "8719" }, { "sum", "8721" }, { "minus", "8722" },
{ "lowast", "8727" }, { "radic", "8730" }, { "prop", "8733" }, { "infin", "8734"
}, { "ang", "8736" }, { "and", "8743" }, { "or", "8744" }, { "cap", "8745" }, {
"cup", "8746" }, { "int", "8747" }, { "there4", "8756" }, { "sim", "8764" }, {
"cong", "8773" }, { "asymp", "8776" }, { "ne", "8800" }, { "equiv", "8801" }, {
"le", "8804" }, { "ge", "8805" }, { "sub", "8834" }, { "sup", "8835" }, {
"sube", "8838" }, { "supe", "8839" }, { "oplus", "8853" }, { "otimes", "8855" },
{ "perp", "8869" }, { "sdot", "8901" }, { "lceil", "8968" }, { "rceil", "8969"
}, { "lfloor", "8970" }, { "rfloor", "8971" }, { "lang", "9001" }, { "rang",
"9002" }, { "loz", "9674" }, { "spades", "9824" }, { "clubs", "9827" }, {
"hearts", "9829" }, { "diams", "9830" }, { "OElig", "338" }, { "oelig", "339" },
{ "Scaron", "352" }, { "scaron", "353" }, { "Yuml", "376" }, { "circ", "710" },
{ "tilde", "732" }, { "ensp", "8194" }, { "emsp", "8195" }, { "thinsp", "8201"
}, { "zwnj", "8204" }, { "zwj", "8205" }, { "lrm", "8206" }, { "rlm", "8207" },
{ "ndash", "8211" }, { "mdash", "8212" }, { "lsquo", "8216" }, { "rsquo", "8217"
}, { "sbquo", "8218" }, { "ldquo", "8220" }, { "rdquo", "8221" }, { "bdquo",
"8222" }, { "dagger", "8224" }, { "Dagger", "8225" }, { "permil", "8240" }, {
"lsaquo", "8249" }, { "rsaquo", "8250" }, { "euro", "8364" } };
  private static r g;
  private static r h;
  public static final r a;
  public static final r b;
  private s i = new ag();

  private void a(String[][] paramArrayOfString)
  {
    for (int j = 0; j < paramArrayOfString.length; j++)
    {
      int k = Integer.parseInt(paramArrayOfString[j][1]);
      String str = paramArrayOfString[j][0];
      this.i.a(str, k);
    }
  }

  public final void a(Writer paramWriter, String paramString)
  {
    int j = paramString.length();
    for (int k = 0; k < j; k++)
    {
      int m = paramString.charAt(k);
      int n = m;
      String str;
      if ((str = this.i.a(n)) == null)
```

```
      {
        if (m > 127)
        {
          paramWriter.write("&#");
          paramWriter.write(Integer.toString(m, 10));
          paramWriter.write(59);
        }
        else
        {
          paramWriter.write(m);
        }
      }
      else
      {
        paramWriter.write(38);
        paramWriter.write(str);
        paramWriter.write(59);
      }
    }
  }

  public final void b(Writer paramWriter, String paramString)
  {
    int j;
    if ((j = paramString.indexOf('&')) < 0)
    {
      paramWriter.write(paramString);
      return;
    }
    int k = j;
    String str1 = paramString;
    paramString = paramWriter;
    paramWriter = this;
    paramString.write(str1, 0, k);
    int m = str1.length();
    while (k < m)
    {
      int n;
      String str2;
      if ((n = str1.charAt(k)) == '&')
      {
        int i1 = k + 1;
        String str4;
        if ((str4 = str1.indexOf(';', i1)) == -1)
        {
          paramString.write(n);
        }
        else
        {
          int i2;
```

```
if (((i2 = str1.indexOf('&', k + 1)) != -1) && (i2 < str4))
{
  paramString.write(n);
}
else
{
  str2 = str1.substring(i1, str4);
  n = -1;
  if ((i1 = str2.length()) > 0)
    if (str2.charAt(0) == '#')
    {
      if (i1 > 1)
      {
        n = str2.charAt(1);
        try
        {
          switch (n)
          {
          case 88:
          case 120:
            n = Integer.parseInt(str2.substring(2), 16);
            break;
          default:
            n = Integer.parseInt(str2.substring(1), 10);
          }
          if (n > 65535)
            n = -1;
        }
        catch (NumberFormatException localNumberFormatException)
        {
          n = -1;
        }
      }
    }
    else
    {
      String str3 = str2;
      n = paramWriter.i.a(str3);
    }
  if (n == -1)
  {
    paramString.write(38);
    paramString.write(str2);
    paramString.write(59);
  }
  else
  {
    paramString.write(n);
  }
  str2 = str4;
```

```
          }
        }
      }
      else
      {
        paramString.write(n);
      }
      str2++;
    }
  }

  static
  {
    (r.g = new r()).a(c);
    g.a(d);
    (r.h = new r()).a(c);
    h.a(e);
    r localr;
    (localr = r.a = new r()).a(c);
    localr.a(e);
    localr.a(f);
    b = new r();
    (localr = a).a(e);
    localr.a(f);
  }
}
```

From Chapter 4, you can see that ProGuard is using layout obfuscation by renaming the variables, which is only mildly effective. But it also employs some impressive data obfuscation by splitting variables and converting static data to procedural data. Round 1 to ProGuard.

Look at the left menu in Figure 7-1, which shows the obfuscated jar file opened in JD-GUI. A significant number of the class names haven't been obfuscated. The methods have some layout obfuscation, but the class names contain information that makes it easy to understand what the methods are doing. By default, all `Activity`, `Application`, `Service`, `BroadcastReceiver`, and `ContentProvider` classes listed in the `manifest.xml` file aren't obfuscated by ProGuard. The best solution is to minimize these type of classes.

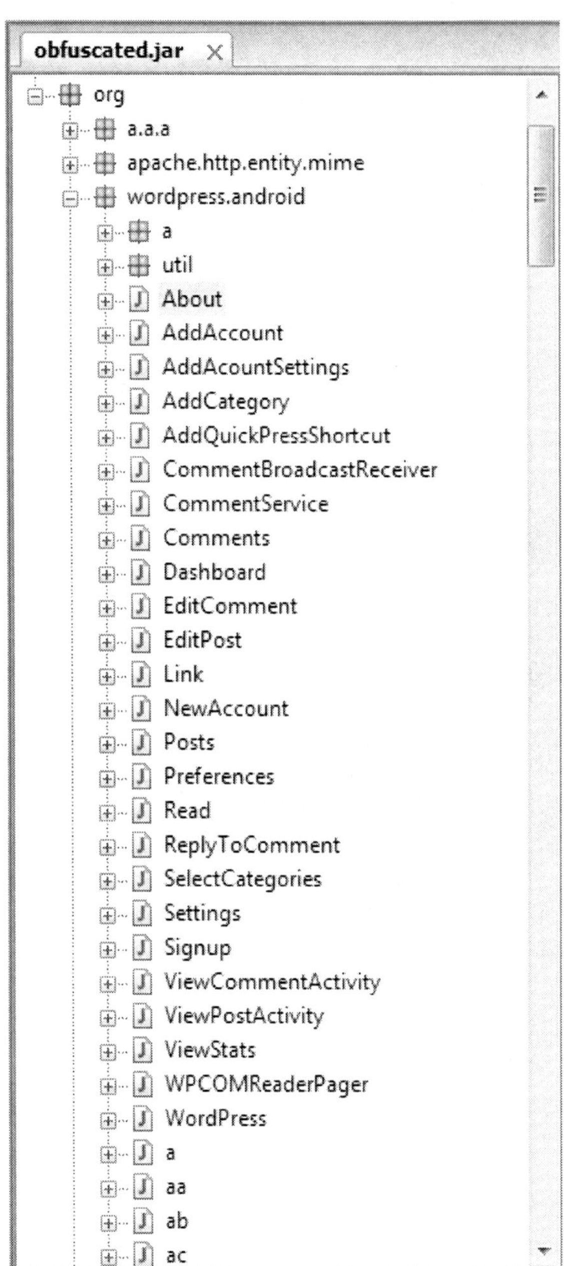

Figure 7-1. *Obfuscated WordPress jar file in JD-GUI*

Configuration

ProGuard is configured in the proguard.cfg file. The default configuration file is shown in Listing 7-6. At its simplest, the file tells ProGuard not to use mixed-case class names (which can cause problems on Windows when the jar file is unzipped); not to perform the preverify step; to keep the class names for Activity, Application, Service, BroadcastReceiver, and ContentProvider classes; not to remove any native classes; and much more.

Listing 7-6. *proguard.cfg File for the WordPress App*

```
-optimizationpasses 5
-dontusemixedcaseclassnames
-dontskipnonpubliclibraryclasses
-dontpreverify
-verbose
-optimizations !code/simplification/arithmetic,!field/*,!class/merging/*

-keep public class * extends android.app.Activity
-keep public class * extends android.app.Application
-keep public class * extends android.app.Service
-keep public class * extends android.content.BroadcastReceiver
-keep public class * extends android.content.ContentProvider
-keep public class * extends android.app.backup.BackupAgentHelper
-keep public class * extends android.preference.Preference
-keep public class com.android.vending.licensing.ILicensingService

-keepclasseswithmembernames class * {
    native <methods>;
}

-keepclasseswithmembers class * {
    public <init>(android.content.Context, android.util.AttributeSet);
}

-keepclasseswithmembers class * {
    public <init>(android.content.Context, android.util.AttributeSet, int);
}

-keepclassmembers class * extends android.app.Activity {
   public void *(android.view.View);
}

-keepclassmembers enum * {
    public static **[] values();
    public static ** valueOf(java.lang.String);
}

-keep class * implements android.os.Parcelable {
```

```
  public static final android.os.Parcelable$Creator *;
}
```

A good configuration settings resource for Android APKs that echoes many of these settings can be found at `http://proguard.sourceforge.net/manual/examples.html#androidapplication`. It's useful especially if your APK fails on your device after using ProGuard.

An easier option is to use the ProGuard GUI, which walks you through the configuration settings with much more explanation. For example, the optimization settings in `proguard.cfg` are arcane, but they're much easier to understand and set in the GUI (see Figure 7-2).

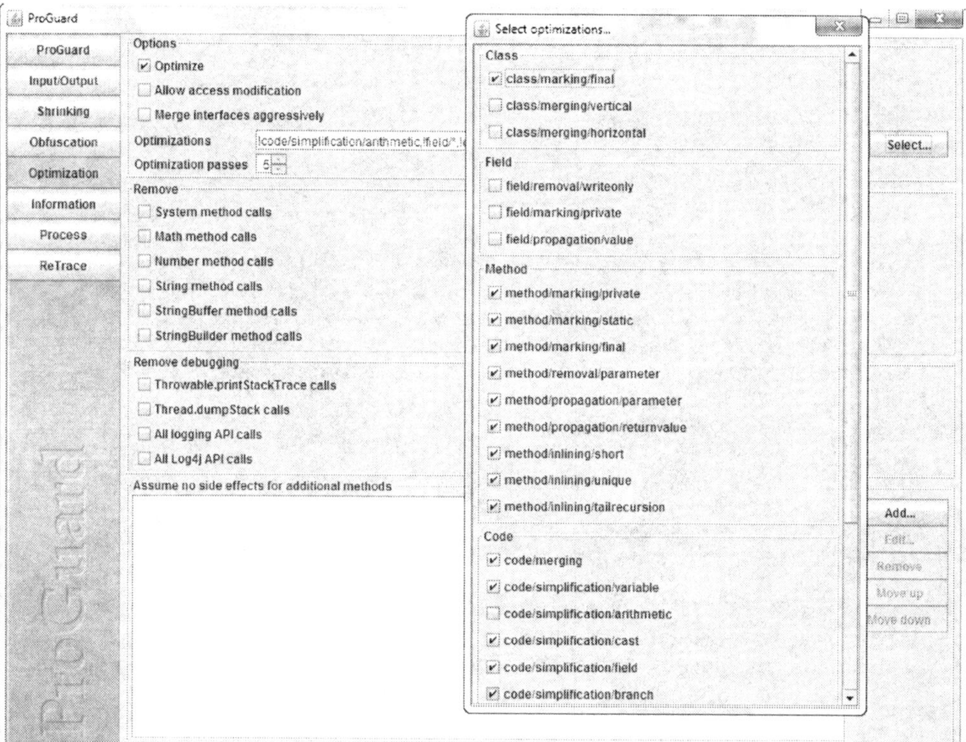

Figure 7-2. *ProGuard GUI*

To launch the GUI, first make sure you've downloaded from SourceForge at `http://proguard.sourceforge.net`. Unzip it and execute the following command in the `lib` folder, assuming you've copied your target `proguard.cfg` file into the `proguard\lib` folder. You should see that many of the optimization options are straight out of the obfuscation transformations from Chapter 4:

```
java -jar proguardgui.jar proguard.cfg
```

Debugging

You may find that your APK fails in the field after it's been obfuscated. Debugging the code is difficult because many of the method names are changed by ProGuard. Fortunately, ProGuard has a `retrace` option that allows you to get back to the original names. The command is as follows:

```
java -jar retrace.jar mapping.txt stackfile.trace
```

`mapping.txt` is in the `bin\proguard` folder, and `stackfile.trace` is the stack trace saved when the application crashed.

Solution 2: DashO

ProGuard isn't your only obfuscation option. Commercial obfuscators such as PreEmptive's DashO, available at `www.preemptive.com`, are worthy alternatives that do much more control-flow and string-encryption obfuscation than ProGuard. Figure 7-3 shows the DashO interface, which includes Control Flow, Renaming, and String Encryption obfuscation options.

Figure 7-3. *DashO GUI*

The Control Flow option reorders the bytecode and aims to make it impossible to decompile. The String Encryption option encrypts many of the strings, which can be very useful as another defense against someone stealing API keys or passwords. Overload Induction (one of the Renaming options) is a more intense form of class renaming: more than one class can be named `a()` or `b()` because doing so is legal Java, as long as the classes have different method parameters.

The simplest way to obfuscate an Android project in DashO is to use the DashO wizard (see Figure 7-4). Later, you can use the GUI to tweak any options you may want to set.

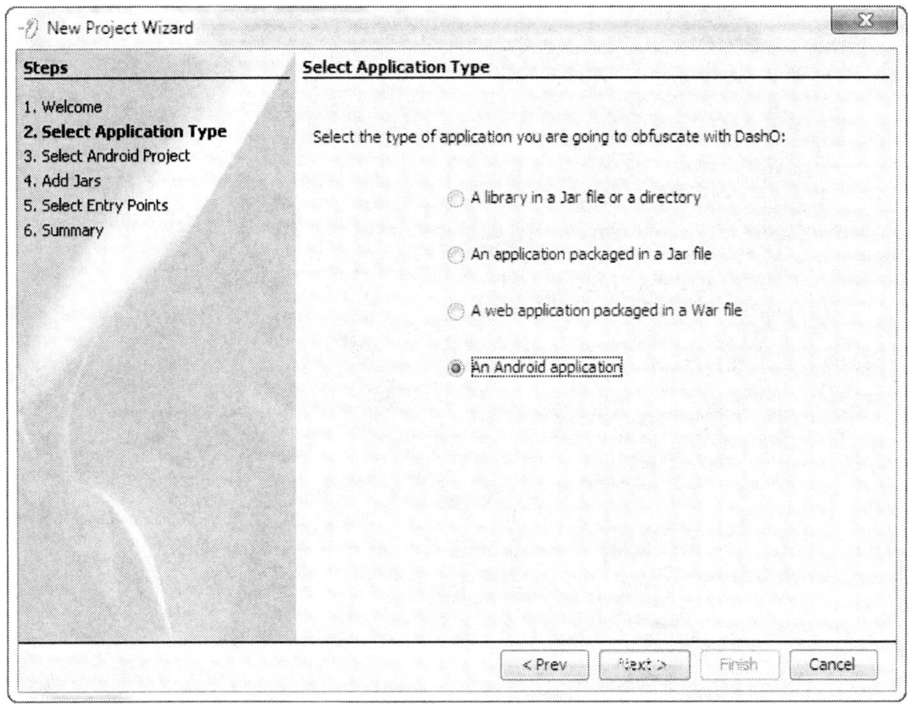

Figure 7-4. *DashO wizard*

Output

DashO outputs a project report file and a `mapreport` or mapping file into the `ant-bin\dasho-results` folder. For example, the `mapreport` file tells me that the `EscapeUtils.class` has been renamed to `i_`:

```
org.wordpress.android.i_          public org.wordpress.android.util.EscapeUtils
```

Listing 7-7 shows the JD-GUI output after decompilation.

Listing 7-7. *`EscapeUtils`, Obfuscated by DashO*

```
package org.wordpress.android;

import java.io.IOException;
import java.io.StringWriter;
import java.io.Writer;
```

```
public class i_
{
  public static String e(String paramString)
  {
    if (paramString != null);
    try
    {
      StringWriter localStringWriter = new
StringWriter((int)(paramString.length() * 1.5D));
      o(localStringWriter, paramString);
      return localStringWriter.toString();
      return null;
    }
    catch (IOException localIOException)
    {
      localIOException.printStackTrace();
    }
    return null;
  }

  public static void o(Writer paramWriter, String paramString)
    throws IOException
  {
    if (paramWriter == null)
      break label24;
    do
      return;
    while (paramString == null);
    xd.v.v(paramWriter, paramString);
    return;
    label24: throw new
IllegalArgumentException(R.endsWith("Rom)]yeyk}0|g``5xxl9x~<sksl/", 554 / 91));
  }

  // ERROR //
  public static String f(String paramString)
  {
    // Byte code:
    //   0: aload_0
    //   1: ifnonnull +16 -> 17
    //   4: goto +10 -> 14
    //   7: astore_1
    //   8: aload_1
    //   9: invokevirtual 33 java/io/IOException:printStackTrace    ()V
    //   12: aconst_null
    //   13: areturn
    //   14: aconst_null
    //   15: areturn
    //   16: areturn
    //   17: new 7 java/io/StringWriter
```

```
    //    20: dup
    //    21: aload_0
    //    22: invokevirtual 29   java/lang/String:length ()I
    //    25: i2d
    //    26: ldc2_w 3
    //    29: dmul
    //    30: d2i
    //    31: invokespecial 30  java/io/StringWriter:<init>   (I)V
    //    34: astore_1
    //    35: aload_1
    //    36: aload_0
    //    37: invokestatic 37   org/wordpress/android/i_:d
(Ljava/io/Writer;Ljava/lang/String;)V
    //    40: aload_1
    //    41: invokevirtual 32
java/io/StringWriter:toString()Ljava/lang/String;
    //    44: goto -28 -> 16
    //
    // Exception table:
    //    from  to target  type
    //    17 477  java/io/IOException
  }

  public static void d(Writer paramWriter, String paramString)
    throws IOException
  {
    if (paramWriter != null)
    {
      if (paramString != null)
      {
        xd.t.h(paramWriter, paramString);
        return;
      }
    }
    else
      throw new IllegalArgumentException(d9.insert(49 * 25, "\035\".1\032<&$4 s9
%#x75/|?;•.4./j"));
  }
}
```

The most obvious thing in the code is that either the escapeHTML or unescapeHTML method failed to decompile. There is also some interesting use of Java, such as variable names labels and string encryption. The following code snippet is a good example of the confusing code when decompiled using JD-GUI:

```
    label24: throw new
IllegalArgumentException(R.endsWith("Rom)]yeyk}0|g``5xxl9x~<sksl/", 554 / 91));
```

It would take some effort to recompile this code. Round 2 to DashO.

Reviewing the Case Study

I hope this case study has shown you how much code JD-GUI can recover from unprotected code and how close that code is to the original source. In this chapter's random sample, the only difference between the two source files was the missing comments. ProGuard and DashO make any decompiled code much more difficult to understand. At the very least, you should add `proguard.config=proguard.cfg` to your `project.properties` file; and commercial obfuscators can offer additional protection.

Always double check that any sensitive information has been protected by downloading the production APK and decompiling it. If you have any API keys or usernames to backend systems, and they aren't hidden to your satisfaction by ProGuard or DashO, you might want to consider hiding the code in C++ using the Android Native Development Kit (NDK; see Chapter 4 for more information).

Summary

When the idea for this book was conceived, it seemed that Java decompilation was going to be a significant issue. But that never happened. Sure, there were some desktop applications; but most of the code was written for web servers, and jar files were firmly locked away behind firewalls.

It's fair to say that with Android, Java has outgrown its early roots. Android APKs are readily accessible on a user's device, and the decompilation techniques first developed for Java now make it very easy to recover any unprotected APKs. These APKs are typically small enough that a programmer or hacker can quickly understand how they work. If you're trying to hide anything in an APK, you need to protect it.

Will this situation change in the near future? Not if there is still the link between the DVM, the JVM, and Java code. I predict that the tools will move to the DVM, and, if anything, the situation will probably get worse. The arms race between obfuscation and decompilation will be played out in fast motion, replicating many of the same steps that took place in the last 10 years—but this time on the DVM.

The premise of this book is to show individual users how to decompile code from `classes.dex` files, what protection schemes are available, and what they mean. In general, people are much more curious than fraudulent, and it's highly unlikely that anyone will use a decompiler to steal a software company's crown jewels. Instead, they just want to take a peek and see how it all fits together—

Java decompilers enable the average programmer to look much further into what are normally black boxes. This book helps you peek over that edge.

Things to try from here include using ANTLR and extending the code if it doesn't decompile your particular `classes.dex` file. There are also several open source decompilers available on the Web—such as JODE, available at `http://jode.sourceforge.net`—that provide a wealth of information. Smali and baksmali, available at `http://code.google.com/p/smali/`, are also excellent places to begin your research.

I've tried my best to make this book easy to read. I consciously decided to make it more practical than theoretical while trying to avoid it becoming *Android Decompilers for Dummies*. I hope it was worth the effort on my part and yours. Just remember, things change quickly around here, so keep on eye on the Apress website for updates.

Appendix

Opcode Tables

In Chapter 2, you saw that Java bytecode is found in the code attribute part of the Java class file. Table A-1 lists all the possible Java bytecodes. The hex value for each opcode is shown along with the assembler-like opcode mnemonic.

Table A-1. *Java Bytecode-to-Opcode Mapping*

Opcode	Hex Value	Opcode Mnemonic
0	(0x00)	Nop
1	(0x01)	aconst_null
2	(0x02)	iconst_m1
3	(0x03)	iconst_0
4	(0x04)	iconst_1
5	(0x05)	iconst_2
6	(0x06)	iconst_3
7	(0x07)	iconst_4
8	(0x08)	iconst_5
9	(0x09)	lconst_0

Opcode	Hex Value	Opcode Mnemonic
10	(0x0a)	lconst_1
11	(0x0b)	fconst_0
12	(0x0c)	fconst_1
13	(0x0d)	fconst_2
14	(0x0e)	dconst_0
15	(0x0f)	dconst_1
16	(0x10)	bipush
17	(0x11)	sipush
18	(0x12)	ldc
19	(0x13)	ldc_w
20	(0x14)	ldc2_w
21	(0x15)	iload
22	(0x16)	lload
23	(0x17)	fload
24	(0x18)	dload
25	(0x19)	aload
26	(0x1a)	iload_0
27	(0x1b)	iload_1
28	(0x1c)	iload_2
29	(0x1d)	iload_3
30	(0x1e)	lload_0

31	(0x1f)	lload_1
32	(0x20)	lload_2
33	(0x21)	lload_3
34	(0x22)	fload_0
35	(0x23)	fload_1
36	(0x24)	fload_2
37	(0x25)	fload_3
38	(0x26)	dload_0
39	(0x27)	dload_1
40	(0x28)	dload_2
41	(0x29)	dload_3
42	(0x2a)	aload_0
43	(0x2b)	aload_1
44	(0x2c)	aload_2
45	(0x2d)	aload_3
46	(0x2e)	iaload
47	(0x2f)	laload
48	(0x30)	faload
49	(0x31)	daload
50	(0x32)	aaload
51	(0x33)	baload
52	(0x34)	caload

Opcode	Hex Value	Opcode Mnemonic
53	(0x35)	saload
54	(0x36)	istore
55	(0x37)	lstore
56	(0x38)	fstore
57	(0x39)	dstore
58	(0x3a)	astore
59	(0x3b)	istore_0
60	(0x3c)	istore_1
61	(0x3d)	istore_2
62	(0x3e)	istore_3
63	(0x3f)	lstore_0
64	(0x40)	lstore_1
65	(0x41)	lstore_2
66	(0x42)	lstore_3
67	(0x43)	fstore_0
68	(0x44)	fstore_1
69	(0x45)	fstore_2
70	(0x46)	fstore_3
71	(0x47)	dstore_0
72	(0x48)	dstore_1
73	(0x49)	dstore_2

74	(0x4a)	dstore_3
75	(0x4b)	astore_0
76	(0x4c)	astore_1
77	(0x4d)	astore_2
78	(0x4e)	astore_3
79	(0x4f)	iastore
80	(0x50)	lastore
81	(0x51)	fastore
82	(0x52)	dastore
83	(0x53)	aastore
84	(0x54)	bastore
85	(0x55)	castore
86	(0x56)	sastore
87	(0x57)	pop
88	(0x58)	pop2
89	(0x59)	dup
90	(0x5a)	dup_x1
91	(0x5b)	dup_x2
92	(0x5c)	dup2
93	(0x5d)	dup2_x1
94	(0x5e)	dup2_x2
95	(0x5f)	swap

Opcode	Hex Value	Opcode Mnemonic
96	(0x60)	iadd
97	(0x61)	ladd
98	(0x62)	fadd
99	(0x63)	dadd
100	(0x64)	isub
101	(0x65)	lsub
102	(0x66)	fsub
103	(0x67)	dsub
104	(0x68)	imul
105	(0x69)	lmul
106	(0x6a)	fmul
107	(0x6b)	dmul
108	(0x6c)	idiv
109	(0x6d)	ldiv
110	(0x6e)	fdiv
111	(0x6f)	ddiv
112	(0x70)	irem
113	(0x71)	lrem
114	(0x72)	frem
115	(0x73)	drem
116	(0x74)	ineg

117	(0x75)	lneg
118	(0x76)	fneg
119	(0x77)	dneg
120	(0x78)	ishl
121	(0x79)	lshl
122	(0x7a)	ishr
123	(0x7b)	lshr
124	(0x7c)	iushr
125	(0x7d)	lushr
126	(0x7e)	iand
127	(0x7f)	land
128	(0x80)	ior
129	(0x81)	lor
130	(0x82)	ixor
131	(0x83)	lxor
132	(0x84)	iinc
133	(0x85)	i2l
134	(0x86)	i2f
135	(0x87)	i2d
136	(0x88)	l2i
137	(0x89)	l2f
138	(0x8a)	l2d

Opcode	Hex Value	Opcode Mnemonic
139	(0x8b)	f2i
140	(0x8c)	f2l
141	(0x8d)	f2d
142	(0x8e)	d2i
143	(0x8f)	d2l
144	(0x90)	d2f
145	(0x91)	i2b
146	(0x92)	i2c
147	(0x93)	i2s
148	(0x94)	lcmp
149	(0x95)	fcmpl
150	(0x96)	fcmpg
151	(0x97)	dcmpl
152	(0x98)	dcmpg
153	(0x99)	ifeq
154	(0x9a)	ifne
155	(0x9b)	iflt
156	(0x9c)	ifge
157	(0x9d)	ifgt
158	(0x9e)	ifle
159	(0x9f)	if_icmpeq

160	(0xa0)	if_icmpne
161	(0xa1)	if_icmplt
162	(0xa2)	if_icmpge
163	(0xa3)	if_icmpgt
164	(0xa4)	if_icmple
165	(0xa5)	if_acmpeq
166	(0xa6)	if_acmpne
167	(0xa7)	goto
168	(0xa8)	jsr
169	(0xa9)	ret
170	(0xaa)	tableswitch
171	(0xab)	lookupswitch
172	(0xac)	ireturn
173	(0xad)	lreturn
174	(0xae)	freturn
175	(0xaf)	dreturn
176	(0xb0)	areturn
177	(0xb1)	return
178	(0xb2)	getstatic
179	(0xb3)	putstatic
180	(0xb4)	getfield
181	(0xb5)	putfield

Opcode	Hex Value	Opcode Mnemonic
182	(0xb6)	invokevirtual
183	(0xb7)	invokespecial
184	(0xb8)	invokestatic
185	(0xb9)	invokeinterface
186	(0xba)	invokedynamic
187	(0xbb)	new
188	(0xbc)	newarray
189	(0xbd)	anewarray
190	(0xbe)	arraylength
191	(0xbf)	athrow
192	(0xc0)	checkcast
193	(0xc1)	instanceof
194	(0xc2)	monitorenter
195	(0xc3)	monitorexit
196	(0xc4)	wide
197	(0xc5)	multianewarray
198	(0xc6)	ifnull
199	(0xc7)	ifnonnull
200	(0xc8)	goto_w
201	(0xc9)	jsr_w

Table A-2 lists all the possible Dalvik bytecodes encountered first in Chapter 3 and then throughput the book. The hex value for each opcode is shown along with the assembler-like opcode mnemonic.

Table A-2. *Dalvik Bytecode-to-Opcode Mapping*

Opcode	Hex Value	Opcode Mnemonic
1	(0x00)	Nop
2	(0x01)	move vx, vy
3	(0x02)	move/from16 vx, vy
4	(0x03)	move/16
5	(0x04)	move-wide
6	(0x05)	move-wide/from16 vx, vy
7	(0x06)	move-wide/16
8	(0x07)	move-object vx, vy
9	(0x08)	move-object/from16 vx, vy
10	(0x09)	move-object/16
11	(0x0A)	move-result vx
12	(0x0B)	move-result-wide vx
13	(0x0C)	move-result-object vx
14	(0x0D)	move-exception vx
15	(0x0E)	return-void
16	(0x0F)	return vx
17	(0x10)	return-wide vx
18	(0x11)	return-object vx
19	(0x12)	const/4 vx, lit4

Opcode	Hex Value	Opcode Mnemonic
20	(0x13)	const/16 vx, lit16
21	(0x14)	const vx, lit32
22	(0x15)	const/high16 v0, lit16
23	(0x16)	const-wide/16 vx, lit16
24	(0x17)	const-wide/32 vx, lit32
25	(0x18)	const-wide vx, lit64
26	(0x19)	const-wide/high16 vx, lit16
27	(0x1A)	const-string vx, string_id
28	(0x1B)	const-string-jumbo
29	(0x1C)	const-class vx, type_id
30	(0x1D)	monitor-enter vx
31	(0x1E)	monitor-exit
32	(0x1F)	check-cast vx, type_id
33	(0x20)	instance-of vx, vy, type_id
34	(0x21)	array-length vx, vy
35	(0x22)	new-instance vx, type
36	(0x23)	new-array vx, vy, type_id
37	(0x24)	filled-new-array {parameters}, type_id
38	(0x25)	filled-new-array-range {vx..vy}, type_id
39	(0x26)	fill-array-data vx, array_data_offset
40	(0x27)	throw vx

41	(0x28)	goto target
42	(0x29)	goto/16 target
43	(0x2A)	goto/32 target
44	(0x2B)	packed-switch vx, table
45	(0x2C)	sparse-switch vx, table
46	(0x2D)	cmpl-float
47	(0x2E)	cmpg-float vx, vy, vz
48	(0x2F)	cmpl-double vx, vy, vz
49	(0x30)	cmpg-double vx, vy, vz
50	(0x31)	cmp-long vx, vy, vz
51	(0x32)	if-eq vx, vy, target
52	(0x33)	if-ne vx, vy, target
53	(0x34)	if-lt vx, vy, target
54	(0x35)	if-ge vx, vy, target
55	(0x36)	if-gt vx, vy, target
56	(0x37)	if-le vx, vy, target
57	(0x38)	if-eqz vx, target
58	(0x39)	if-nez vx, target
59	(0x3A)	if-ltz vx, target
60	(0x3B)	if-gez vx, target
61	(0x3C)	if-gtz vx, target
62	(0x3D)	if-lez vx, target

Opcode	Hex Value	Opcode Mnemonic
63	(0x3E)	unused_3E
64	(0x3F)	unused_3F
65	(0x40)	unused_40
66	(0x41)	unused_41
67	(0x42)	unused_42
68	(0x43)	unused_43
69	(0x44)	aget vx, vy, vz
70	(0x45)	aget-wide vx, vy, vz
71	(0x46)	aget-object vx, vy, vz
72	(0x47)	aget-boolean vx, vy, vz
73	(0x48)	aget-byte vx, vy, vz
74	(0x49)	aget-char vx, vy, vz
75	(0x4A)	aget-short vx, vy, vz
76	(0x4B)	aput vx, vy, vz
77	(0x4C)	aput-wide vx, vy, vz
78	(0x4D)	aput-object vx, vy, vz
79	(0x4E)	aput-boolean vx, vy, vz
80	(0x4F)	aput-byte vx, vy, vz
81	(0x50)	aput-char vx, vy, vz
82	(0x51)	aput-short vx, vy, vz
83	(0x52)	iget vx, vy, field_id

84	(0x53)	iget-wide vx, vy, field_id
85	(0x54)	iget-object vx, vy, field_id
86	(0x55)	iget-boolean vx, vy, field_id
87	(0x56)	iget-byte vx, vy, field_id
88	(0x57)	iget-char vx, vy, field_id
89	(0x58)	iget-short vx, vy, field_id
90	(0x59)	iput vx, vy, field_id
91	(0x5A)	iput-wide vx, vy, field_id
92	(0x5B)	iput-object vx, vy,field_id
93	(0x5C)	iput-boolean vx, vy, field_id
94	(0x5D)	iput-byte vx, vy, field_id
95	(0x5E)	iput-char vx, vy, field_id
96	(0x5F)	iput-short vx, vy, field_id
97	(0x60)	sget vx, field_id
98	(0x61)	sget-wide vx, field_id
99	(0x62)	sget-object vx, field_id
100	(0x63)	sget-boolean vx, field_id
101	(0x64)	sget-byte vx, field_id
102	(0x65)	sget-char vx, field_id
103	(0x66)	sget-short vx, field_id
104	(0x67)	sput vx, field_id
105	(0x68)	sput-wide vx, field_id

Opcode	Hex Value	Opcode Mnemonic
106	(0x69)	sput-object vx, field_id
107	(0x6A)	sput-boolean vx, field_id
108	(0x6B)	sput-byte vx, field_id
109	(0x6C)	sput-char vx, field_id
110	(0x6D)	sput-short vx, field_id
111	(0x6E)	invoke-virtual { parameters }, methodtocall
112	(0x6F)	invoke-super {parameter}, methodtocall
113	(0x70)	invoke-direct { parameters }, methodtocall
114	(0x71)	invoke-static {parameters}, methodtocall
115	(0x72)	invoke-interface {parameters}, methodtocall
116	(0x73)	unused_73
117	(0x74)	invoke-virtual/range {vx..vy}, methodtocall
118	(0x75)	invoke-super/range
119	(0x76)	invoke-direct/range {vx..vy}, methodtocall
120	(0x77)	invoke-static/range {vx..vy}, methodtocall
121	(0x78)	invoke-interface-range
122	(0x79)	unused_79
123	(0x7A)	unused_7A
124	(0x7B)	neg-int vx, vy
125	(0x7C)	not-int vx, vy
126	(0x7D)	neg-long vx, vy

127	(0x7E)	not-long vx, vy
128	(0x7F)	neg-float vx, vy
129	(0x80)	neg-double vx, vy
130	(0x81)	int-to-long vx, vy
131	(0x82)	int-to-float vx, vy
132	(0x83)	int-to-double vx, vy
133	(0x84)	long-to-int vx, vy
134	(0x85)	long-to-float vx, vy
135	(0x86)	long-to-double vx, vy
136	(0x87)	float-to-int vx, vy
137	(0x88)	float-to-long vx, vy
138	(0x89)	float-to-double vx, vy
139	(0x8A)	double-to-int vx, vy
140	(0x8B)	double-to-long vx, vy
141	(0x8C)	double-to-float vx, vy
142	(0x8D)	int-to-byte vx, vy
143	(0x8E)	int-to-char vx, vy
144	(0x8F)	int-to-short vx, vy
145	(0x90)	add-int vx, vy, vz
146	(0x91)	sub-int vx, vy, vz
147	(0x92)	mul-int vx, vy, vz
148	(0x93)	div-int vx, vy, vz

Opcode	Hex Value	Opcode Mnemonic
149	(0x94)	rem-int vx, vy, vz
150	(0x95)	and-int vx, vy, vz
151	(0x96)	or-int vx, vy, vz
152	(0x97)	xor-int vx, vy, vz
153	(0x98)	shl-int vx, vy, vz
154	(0x99)	shr-int vx, vy, vz
155	(0x9A)	ushr-int vx, vy, vz
156	(0x9B)	add-long vx, vy, vz
157	(0x9C)	sub-long vx, vy, vz
158	(0x9D)	mul-long vx, vy, vz
159	(0x9E)	div-long vx, vy, vz
160	(0x9F)	rem-long vx, vy, vz
161	(0xA0)	and-long vx, vy, vz
162	(0xA1)	or-long vx, vy, vz
163	(0xA2)	xor-long vx, vy, vz
164	(0xA3)	shl-long vx, vy, vz
165	(0xA4)	shr-long vx, vy, vz
166	(0xA5)	ushr-long vx, vy, vz
167	(0xA6)	add-float vx, vy, vz
168	(0xA7)	sub-float vx, vy,vz
169	(0xA8)	mul-float vx, vy, vz

170	(0xA9)	div-float vx, vy, vz
171	(0xAA)	rem-float vx,vy,vz
172	(0xAB)	add-double vx, vy, vz
173	(0xAC)	sub-double vx, vy, vz
174	(0xAD)	mul-double vx, vy, vz
175	(0xAE)	div-double vx, vy, vz
176	(0xAF)	rem-double vx, vy, vz
177	(0xB0)	add-int/2addr vx, vy
178	(0xB1)	sub-int/2addr vx, vy
179	(0xB2)	mul-int/2addr vx, vy
180	(0xB3)	div-int/2addr vx, vy
181	(0xB4)	rem-int/2addr vx, vy
182	(0xB5)	and-int/2addr vx, vy
183	(0xB6)	or-int/2addr vx, vy
184	(0xB7)	xor-int/2addr vx, vy
185	(0xB8)	shl-int/2addr vx, vy
186	(0xB9)	shr-int/2addr vx, vy
187	(0xBA)	ushr-int/2addr vx, vy
188	(0xBB)	add-long/2addr vx, vy
189	(0xBC)	sub-long/2addr vx, vy
190	(0xBD)	mul-long/2addr vx, vy
191	(0xBE)	div-long/2addr vx, vy

Opcode	Hex Value	Opcode Mnemonic
192	(0xBF)	rem-long/2addr vx, vy
193	(0xC0)	and-long/2addr vx, vy
194	(0xC1)	or-long/2addr vx, vy
195	(0xC2)	xor-long/2addr vx, vy
196	(0xC3)	shl-long/2addr vx, vy
197	(0xC4)	shr-long/2addr vx, vy
198	(0xC5)	ushr-long/2addr vx, vy
199	(0xC6)	add-float/2addr vx, vy
200	(0xC7)	sub-float/2addr vx, vy
201	(0xC8)	mul-float/2addr vx, vy
202	(0xC9)	div-float/2addr vx, vy
203	(0xCA)	rem-float/2addr vx, vy
204	(0xCB)	add-double/2addr vx, vy
205	(0xCC)	sub-double/2addr vx, vy
206	(0xCD)	mul-double/2addr vx, vy
207	(0xCE)	div-double/2addr vx, vy
208	(0xCF)	rem-double/2addr vx, vy
209	(0xD0)	add-int/lit16 vx, vy, lit16
210	(0xD1)	sub-int/lit16 vx, vy, lit16
211	(0xD2)	mul-int/lit16 vx, vy, lit16
212	(0xD3)	div-int/lit16 vx, vy, lit16

213	(0xD4)	rem-int/lit16 vx, vy, lit16
214	(0xD5)	and-int/lit16 vx, vy, lit16
215	(0xD6)	or-int/lit16 vx, vy, lit16
216	(0xD7)	xor-int/lit16 vx, vy, lit16
217	(0xD8)	add-int/lit8 vx, vy, lit8
218	(0xD9)	sub-int/lit8 vx, vy, lit8
219	(0xDA)	mul-int/lit8 vx, vy, lit8
220	(0xDB)	div-int/lit8 vx, vy, lit8
221	(0xDC)	rem-int/lit8 vx, vy, lit8
222	(0xDD)	and-int/lit8 vx, vy, lit8
223	(0xDE)	or-int/lit8 vx, vy, lit8
224	(0xDF)	xor-int/lit8 vx, vy, lit8
225	(0xE0)	shl-int/lit8 vx, vy, lit8
226	(0xE1)	shr-int/lit8 vx, vy, lit8
227	(0xE2)	ushr-int/lit8 vx, vy, lit8
228	(0xE3)	unused_E3
229	(0xE4)	unused_E4
230	(0xE5)	unused_E5
231	(0xE6)	unused_E6
232	(0xE7)	unused_E7
233	(0xE8)	unused_E8
234	(0xE9)	unused_E9

Opcode	Hex Value	Opcode Mnemonic
235	(0xEA)	unused_EA
236	(0xEB)	unused_EB
237	(0xEC)	unused_EC
238	(0xED)	unused_ED
239	(0xEE)	execute-inline {parameters}, inline ID
240	(0xEF)	unused_EF
241	(0xF0)	invoke-direct-empty
242	(0xF1)	unused_F1
243	(0xF2)	iget-quick vx, vy, offset
244	(0xF3)	iget-wide-quick vx, vy, offset
245	(0xF4)	iget-object-quick vx, vy, offset
246	(0xF5)	iput-quick vx, vy, offset
247	(0xF6)	iput-wide-quick vx, vy, offset
248	(0xF7)	iput-object-quick vx, vy, offset
249	(0xF8)	invoke-virtual-quick {parameters}, vtable offset
250	(0xF9)	invoke-virtual-quick/range {parameter range}, vtable offset
251	(0xFA)	invoke-super-quick {parameters}, vtable offset
252	(0xFB)	invoke-super-quick/range {register range}, vtable offset
253	(0xFC)	unused_FC
254	(0xFD)	unused_FD

255	(0xFE)	unused_FE
256	(0xFF)	unused_FF

Index

B

C

D, E

R

S

T

U

V

W, X

Y

Z